WITHDRAWN

Milton's Good God

"Sculpture" for book III of *Paradise Lost,* 1688 folio edition. Artist, John Baptist Medina. (Courtesy of the British Library.)

Milton's Good God

A Study in Literary Theodicy

Dennis Richard Danielson
University of Ottawa

Cambridge University Press

Cambridge
London   New York   New Rochelle
Melbourne   Sydney

Published by the Press Syndicate of the University of Cambridge
The Pitt Building, Trumpington Street, Cambridge CB2 1RP
32 East 57th Street, New York, NY 10022, USA
296 Beaconsfield Parade, Middle Park, Melbourne 3206, Australia

First published 1982

Printed in the United States of America

Library of Congress Cataloging in Publication Data
Danielson, Dennis Richard, 1949–
Milton's good God.
Based upon the author's thesis (doctoral)
Bibliography: p.
Includes index.
1. Milton, John, 1608–1674.   Paradise lost.
2. Milton, John, 1608–1674 – Religion and ethics.
3. God in literature.   4. Good and evil in
literature.   I. Title.
PR3562.D28   821'.4   81-15535
ISBN 0 521 23744 0   AACR2

PR
3562
D28
1982

Contents

vii

Preface

Does Milton worship, and present, a good God? Is his epic, *Paradise Lost*, any good? These two questions must be connected, given the fact that in *Paradise Lost* Milton openly sets out to justify the ways of God. If Milton presents a God who is wicked, or untruthful, or manipulative, or feeble, or unwise, then his epic poem must suffer accordingly. But if that poem recognizes the case that is brought against the Christian God and counters it (even if not conclusively) with a high degree of philosophical and literary credibility, then the poem and the poet must be praised accordingly. There have been enough critics who have affirmed that Milton and his epic are indeed undermined by the case against God. The purpose of this book is to argue systematically the second, contrary hypothesis, that Milton's theology informs and enhances his literary achievement, and that in fact his justification of God is all the more impressive for its being literary.

My study of Milton and of the problem of evil has its roots in concerns and interests I have had for what now seems a long time, and I take great pleasure in recording here my thanks to a number of people without whose spirit, wisdom, and encouragement my project could not have been the adventure it has been. My most long-standing scholarly debt of gratitude is to Patrick Grant, who first taught me Milton ten years ago in Victoria, who has been a valued friend and adviser since even before that, and who has often done his best to steer me away from a desiccated rigor. I extend my appreciation, too, to Laurence Lerner, Anthony Nuttall, and Stephen Medcalf, who in

ix

Sussex in 1973 encouraged my first stumbling attempts to explain what I wanted to do with a thesis on Milton's theodicy. To other teachers, friends, and acquaintances along the way whose lectures, conversations, or criticisms have been formative I am also grateful: John Hick in Victoria; Basil Mitchell, Alvin Plantinga, and John R. Lucas in Oxford; Milo Kaufmann and James Houston in Vancouver; Philip Sampson in too many places to mention; Norman Geisler in Los Altos, California. I want to thank, respectively, two of my colleagues and my research assistant: David Staines, for his great kindness in initiating my contact with Jane Majeski and her colleagues at Cambridge University Press; John Hill, for his advice on my use of Greek terms, as well as for his ongoing Miltonic fellowship; and Tony Cummins, for his valuable and uncomplaining help in preparing the index. I especially want to express my appreciation to Janis Bolster for the skill, hard work, and downright intelligence she displayed in copyediting my manuscript. And I would also here like to honor the memory of my late friend Henry Banman; our conversations about the problem of evil on the banks of the Nechako in 1974 have often come back both to humble and to inspire me.

In preparing the Ph.D. dissertation upon which this book is based, I had the rare privilege of being advised by two outstanding Milton scholars at two great universities. From October 1975 to July 1977 my work at Oxford was supervised by John Carey, whose keen, open-minded, and generous criticism encouraged me immensely in the earlier stages. Then for my last two years of doctoral research, at Stanford, I worked under the direction of J. Martin Evans, whose personal kindness and generosity encouraged me almost as much as did his advice on all matters Miltonic. He remains for me a model of supervision and scholarship. I am also grateful to Ronald Rebholz, whose friendly criticism and advice, beyond what one could expect of a reader, served as an invaluable lesson in the scholarly uses of "adversity." Finally, I owe an immeasurable debt of gratitude to my wife, Janet Henshaw Danielson, who for over eleven years has been the music and the anchor of my life. She has read and critiqued the entire manuscript, and has shared with me in the knowledge, without which this project could never have been begun, that

> Dominus ipse est Deus;
> Ipse fecit nos, et non ipsi nos.

The Social Sciences and Humanities Research Council of Canada (formerly the Canada Council) supported me from 1975 to 1979 with doctoral fellowships and enabled me through a further grant in 1980 to complete the research of which this book is the culmination; to the council I extend my sincere thanks. Chapter 3 is a revised version of my article "Milton's Arminianism and *Paradise Lost*," in *Milton Studies*, Volume 12, edited by James D. Simmonds and published in 1979 by the University of Pittsburgh Press; it is used by permission. Parts of Chapters 4 and 5 appeared in my article *"Imago Dei*, 'Filial Freedom,' and Miltonic Theodicy," in *ELH*, Volume 47, published in 1980 by Johns Hopkins University Press; it too is used by permission.

I should add only that I have no one but myself to thank for all the gaps, errors, and crudities that remain.

Ottawa   D. R. D.
8 May 1981

1

The contexts of Milton's theodicy

"Milton's object . . . was to justify the ways of God to man! The controversial spirit observable in many parts of [*Paradise Lost*] . . . is immediately attributable to the great controversy of that age, the origination of evil."[1] This pithy comment made by Samuel Taylor Coleridge in 1818 suggests three overlapping contexts that will be the terrain of the present study, Milton figuring in each of them. First, there is the conceptual context: the so-called theological problem of evil. Secondly, there is the historical context in which Milton tackled the problem: seventeenth-century England, "that age" and its controversies. And thirdly, there is the context in which Coleridge's remark itself arises: that of the literary criticism of Milton and his writings, particularly *Paradise Lost*. My purpose will be to describe Milton's contribution to the first two of these contexts and in so doing to attempt my own contribution to the third. However much may have been written on Milton, I know of no major work that sets out to elucidate both conceptually and historically the immediate issues of theodicy – of the justification of God's ways – with reference to the great literary achievement that is *Paradise Lost*. My aim here is to fill that gap. The literary-critical relevance of my project I shall attempt further to justify at the end of this chapter; but first I must introduce contexts one and two, the conceptual and the historical.

The problem of evil

The importance of the theological problem of evil for an understanding of *Paradise Lost* will be argued implicitly and explicitly

1

throughout this study. All I mean to do now is to describe the problem. Not all of what is said will find critical consummation in the discussion of Milton that follows, partly because Milton's theodicy is not exhaustive and has little to say about some issues raised by the problem of evil. However, the details I shall now lay out are all relevant to the problem as a whole; and the problem as a whole is relevant to an understanding of Milton. For the moment, I think, one can simply take Coleridge's word for that.

The *theological* problem of evil does not specifically concern the task we all share of dealing with pride, hatred, cruelty, deceit, adultery, envy, and covetousness (both in ourselves and in others), or with disease, flood, famine, and drought in the world at large. That task is fundamentally practical, whereas the theological problem of evil is theoretical in character, even though it does of course have practical implications. It begins with two claims made by orthodox Christians and by certain other theists, namely, that (1) there is a God who is omnipotent, and (2) this God is wholly good. These claims are considered together with a third claim – accepted not only by theists – that (3) the evil of hatred, disease, and so on, which I have just mentioned, does really exist in the world. Hence, in its barest form the theoretical problem is this: If (1) and (2) are true – if God is both omnipotent and wholly good – how is it that evil can in fact exist in the world? If (2) and (3) are true – if God is wholly good and evil does exist – how can God be said to be omnipotent? And if (1) and (3) are true – if God is omnipotent and there is evil in the world – how can God be wholly good? The word "theodicy," although it has entered English since Milton's time, is virtually synonymous with his phrase "to justify the ways of God."[2] Deriving from the Greek *theos* ("god") and *dike* ("justice"), it denotes any attempt to show the consistency and truth of (1), (2), and (3); or, more minimally, to support the claim that the conjunction of (1), (2), and (3) is not contradictory.

One of the oldest and most famous formulations of the question is that of Epicurus (341–270 B.C.), as quoted by Lactantius (A.D. 260–330):

> God . . . either wishes to take away evils, and is unable; or He is able, and is unwilling; or He is neither willing nor able, or He is both willing and able. If He is willing and is unable, He is feeble, which is not in accordance with the character of God; if He is able and unwilling, He is envious, which is equally at variance with God; if He is neither willing nor able, He is both envious and feeble, and therefore not God; if He is both willing and able, which alone is suitable to God, from what source then are evils? or why does He not remove them?

Lactantius adds, understatedly, "I know that many of the philosophers, who defend providence, are accustomed to be disturbed by this argument."[3] I shall say much more about Milton's reaction to this section from Lactantius in Chapter 6, but for now it serves the purposes of this study simply by stating the issue, and by suggesting a long-standing connection between the assertion of providence as such and the justification of God, given the fact of evil.

Traditionally, three kinds of evil have been distinguished: "metaphysical," natural, and moral. It is the last that will demand most of my attention, as it did most of Milton's. One can provisionally define it simply as any evil directly resulting from or consisting in a rational agent's wrong act, choice, or habit, or the wrong acts, choices, and habits of a group of rational agents. Included in this category are the evils mentioned earlier, such as hatred, cruelty, and so on. For the purposes of this discussion, "moral" will be used in a very broad sense to refer to right and wrong not only in human and angelic matters, but also in matters that concern God himself. To some it may sound impious to apply the category of morality to God. But all I am saying is that I shall take cardinal proposition (2), that God is wholly good – to which anyone concerned with piety will presumably assent – as involving, not necessarily exclusively, the category of moral goodness. It is important to insist on that category's applicability to God at this stage because clearly what a challenge such as Epicurus's demands is a *moral* justification of God's ways, even though the challenge pertains to the existence of evil of every kind.

The category of natural evil is usually taken to include diseases, floods, famines, volcanoes, toothaches, and any evil not directly attributable to the wrong acts, choices, or habits of rational agents. Milton and his age had relatively little to say about this kind of evil so far as it concerns theodicy, partly, as will become clearer, because of what they saw as its connection with moral evil. I shall argue in Chapter 6 that Milton's position has important implications for a view of natural evil, even if that aspect of his theodicy is not explicit. For now I would simply emphasize that, although most seventeenth-century theodicists did not see it as lying at the core of their task, the problem of physical suffering in general was not lost sight of. Indeed, a number of modern introductions to the subject borrow Milton's vivid description of the "lazar-house" that appears to Adam:

> wherein were laid
> Numbers of all diseased, all maladies
> Of ghastly spasm, or racking torture, qualms
> Of heart-sick agony, all feverous kinds,
> Convulsions, epilepsies, fierce catarrhs,
> Intestine stone and ulcer, colic pangs,
> Demoniac frenzy, moping melancholy
> And moon-struck madness, pining atrophy,
> Marasmus, and wide-wasting pestilence,
> Dropsies, and asthmas, and joint-racking rheums.
> Dire was the tossing, deep the groans, despair
> Tended the sick busiest from couch to couch;
> And over them triumphant death his dart
> Shook, but delayed to strike, though oft invoked.
>   [*PL*, 11.479–92]

The question now arises, if such suffering constitutes natural evil, and if natural evil is defined as that evil which is not obviously moral evil, then have we not already precluded any definition of "metaphysical evil" that does not overlap the other two kinds?[4] It is true that the distinctions quickly become blurred once the discussion of theodicy gets going in earnest; that is why I am trying to make them as clear as I can now. However, the answer to the question is essentially yes, for metaphysical evil is not properly actual evil at all. If God is the absolute Good, it is argued, then everything else must be less good than the Good; and to be less good is in some sense evil. In this manner, then, metaphysical evil can simply be taken as denoting the essential dependency, finitude, imperfection, and limitation of all created things.

This category, of course, is most at home in the ontology associated with the so-called Great Chain of Being, that essentially Neoplatonic, hierarchical view of reality according to which each thing participates (in the Platonic sense) in Being to either a greater or lesser degree than that which is adjacent to it in the chain. In this system, furthermore, a thing is good precisely in accordance with its degree of participation in Being, so that the farther down something is in the chain, the less good and hence the more metaphysically evil it is. Plotinus, the great third-century advocate of this scheme, nevertheless emphasizes that no one, neither God nor creature, is to be blamed for metaphysical evil – "nothing is to be blamed for being inferior to the First" – for "since higher exists, there must be the lower as well. The Universe is a thing of variety, and how could there be an inferior without a superior or a superior without an inferior? . . . Those that would like evil driven out from the All would drive out Providence itself."[5]

Plotinus's argument in fact might well suggest, at least to someone not committed to the Great Chain of Being, that evil of a metaphysical sort is not evil at all. I would like to retain the category, however, even while questioning its label's accuracy. For, first, it provides a basis for an etiology of evil. Even if creaturely finitude is itself not properly an evil, it does help to explain how natural and moral evil might have come about in a good creation. As St. Augustine put it, "All things that exist, . . . seeing that the Creator of them all is supremely good, are themselves good. But because they are not, like their Creator, supremely and unchangeably good, their good may be diminished and increased. But for a good to be diminished is an evil."[6] God could not logically have created another absolutely perfect and immutable being, another God; so if he was to create anything at all, it had to be to some degree imperfect and mutable. If it were imperfect and mutable, then the conditions would exist for evil to come about. One can see how such an argument could be developed in order to justify God, given the *possibility* of evil. And although Augustine was greatly influenced by Neoplatonism,[7] there is no need to consider his account of the metaphysical conditions for the ingress of evil into the creation as being necessarily grounded in a Neoplatonic cosmology. Perhaps that is where it first sprang forth; but it has shown enough vitality of its own to be capable of thriving in other soil. However, I shall leave further discussion of the metaphysical conditions for the existence of evil until Chapter 2.

The other reason for retaining the category of metaphysical evil, together with some of its initially Neoplatonic baggage, is simply that it has provided not only an etiology but also, and even more importantly, an ontology of evil for almost the entire history of Christian thought since Augustine. In his *Confessions,* Augustine declares: "You [God] have made all things good, nor are there any substances at all which you have not made. And because you did not make all things equal, therefore they each and all have their existence."[8] Whereas Plotinus, as we have noted, saw evil ontologically as a thing's being "inferior to the First," Augustine would see a thing's existence at the level of "inferiority" at which it was created as being good, its finitude and mutability notwithstanding. What constitutes evil, therefore, according to this Augustinian view, is not something's "inferiority" in Plotinus's sense but rather its *being diminished:* "For a good to be diminished is an evil." In other words, evil is not the absence of a goodness that a thing has never and could never possess, but rather the *lack* of a goodness in some sense original to it – in the words of Thomas Aquinas,

a goodness "which it ought to have but has not."[9] Metaphysi-
cal-evil-as-limitation is thus transformed in Christian thought
into actual-evil-as-*privation*. The importance of this conception
in avoiding dualism will be touched on again in Chapter 2. But
for now it is enough to recognize the role the notion of metaphysical evil has played in suggesting that, ontologically, evil
might be seen as privative. Hence, of course, the famous and
influential conception of evil as *privatio boni*.

Having briefly considered kinds of evil and, before that, the
three propositions that basically define the theological problem
of evil, we must now ask what forms a theodicy might take and
what the criteria for its success might be. I say *might*, because I
do not intend to lay down strict guidelines.

The most ambitious theodicy conceivable, one supposes,
would set out to establish with absolute certainty the truth of
the three propositions – (1) that God is omnipotent, (2) that he
is wholly good, (3) that evil exists in the world. (From their
truth, of course, their consistency would follow automatically.)
By contrast, the most modest theodicy would merely attempt to
demonstrate that there is an interpretation of the three cardinal
propositions such that their conjunction implies no contradiction. I know of no attempt to accomplish the former; there is in
modern philosophical circles a major attempt to accomplish the
latter, though its main spokesman denominates it a *defense*
rather than a theodicy, in that it concerns itself with matters of
mere consistency rather than actual truth.[10] However, I think
we can assume that most theodicies will attempt something in
between, something consciously less ambitious than apodictic
demonstration but also less formal than a logical defense of consistency. They will seek to establish for their solutions not only
a bare possibility, but also some degree of probability or plausibility. In so doing they must avoid farfetched interpretations
of "omnipotent," "good," and "evil" that might nevertheless
guarantee a consistent solution, and must instead seek a consistency in accordance with an interpretation of the terms that
is reasonable or at least not contrary to their ordinary sense. For

it is that sense which constitutes the problem as a problem in the first place.

Given these general guidelines, we are in a position to say, if nothing more, what form a successful theodicy shall not take. For the sake of brevity, let me simply present a stereotype of the three forbidden forms, which correspond respectively to theodicy's three cardinal propositions.

The advocate of theodical "heresy" number one, although claiming to accept propositions (1), (2), (3), seeks to solve the problem of evil in one way or another that involves a de facto denial of (1), God's omnipotence. Of course omnipotence does need to be defined and qualified; otherwise we leave the way open for nonsense of the sort that claims God is able to create rocks so heavy he cannot lift them. But neither must it be qualified beyond recognition. Where that happens, the result is generally some form of *dualism*.

Heresy number two assents to the proposition that God is wholly good, but defines goodness in such a way that it is meaningless as applied to God. The common form of this error in the history of Christian thought views what God wills as being good and just merely in virtue of the fact that he wills it. In effect, God himself is thus made "good" by definition alone, and proposition (2) is accordingly rendered devoid of content. This I shall refer to as theological *voluntarism*.

The third heresy, finally, qualifies proposition (3) in such a way that it loses its meaning. Most obviously, *illusionism* declares the unreality of evil and thus treats the problem of evil as primarily a subjective or psychological matter.[11] In a Christian context, however, this heresy has mainly taken a somewhat more subtle form, declaring that the evils we see around and within us combine with the good to form a beautiful whole, like the dark and light shades of a master painting. Partial evil somehow constitutes universal good, and in the final analysis whatever is, is right. In this system, as Voltaire sarcastically says, "everything is for the best," and, as Karl Barth puts it, "the wolf not only dwells with the lamb . . . but actually

becomes a lamb."[12] Such is the position known as *optimism* –
not, of course, in the popular sense of a cheery outlook on life
but in the philosophical sense of viewing this world as *optimus*,
the best. One of the many forms of optimism will be the concern of Chapter 7. Dualism will be discussed in Chapter 2, voluntarism in Chapters 3 and 5.

To summarize, then, a successful theodicy will avoid these
three heresies, will give an interpretation of the three cardinal
propositions that is plausible, if not demonstrably certain, and
will do so in a way that also supports their mutual consistency.
Such criteria, of course, represent necessary rather than sufficient conditions for success; and I suppose that in the final analysis *plausibility* is the term that will cause most difficulty,
because it concerns not only a theodicy's inward workings and
relations to its own subject matter, but also the dispositions and
prior convictions of various human beings to whom the theodicy is presented. This is to say that a further necessary condition of a theodicy's convincingness – indeed, of that of any
theory that does not absolutely compel belief – is an open-
mindedness on the part of its audience. It is hard to imagine a
convinced solipsist being moved by any argument for the existence of the external world. Without in the least minimizing the
seriousness of the problem it raises, I think we all recognize
that a question such as Epicurus's is often uttered insincerely,
sneeringly, with one's mind already made up. When such is the
case, no answer will suffice, because no real question has been
asked. We have just considered how the terms of Epicurus's
question can be tampered with so as to make an answer easy.
What I am warning against now is a putting of the question in
a way that of itself makes an answer impossible.

There are two good reasons, I think, for emphasizing this
"subjective" dimension of theodicy. The first is that honest discussion is facilitated by a recognition of presuppositions all
round. As a Christian, I believe that there is a God who is
omnipotent and wholly good, and thus also believe that ultimately the theological problem of evil can be solved. I therefore

have, as it were, a vested interest in making theodicy work and ought to be on my guard against an accordingly tendentious treatment of the theodicy that is the object of this study. But we likewise need to recognize that someone with different religious and philosophical presuppositions might, in a similar way, have a vested interest in the problem's *not* being solved. It is the nature of theodicy that none of us are perfectly disinterested spectators; and that, I dare say, is one of the reasons the topic continues to provoke so much discussion, even on the frontiers of logic and literary criticism. In short, I shall attempt a treatment of Milton's theodicy that is not unduly sympathetic and simply ask in return a hearing that is not unduly antipathetic.

The second reason for drawing attention to theodicy's subjective dimension, and the one more germane to the actual topic of this book, is that Milton's is a largely poetic theodicy; and poetry, more than other literary forms, is adapted to engaging and exploring the reader's response. Theodicy is no *Ding an sich*; it cannot be adequately considered within an empirical model of radically distinguished observer and thing observed, subject and object; and in this respect it lends itself to poetic treatment, in which, arguably, intentionality of both text and reader is of the essence. This general thesis is familiar enough since the work of Stanley Fish, and the notion of "the reader in *Paradise Lost*" is now willy-nilly part of our critical machinery. In any case it bears no exclusively phenomenological patent. I myself would question as potentially reductive Fish's dictum that "the poem's centre of reference is its reader."[13] However, Milton does recognize the importance of his audience's "fitness," does "entangle" his reader, and does, in short, seek to justify the ways of God *to men.*[14] In Chapter 4 I shall discuss specifically some of the means Milton uses to implicate his reader in the issue; but the literary dimension of his theodicy generally is something I think we ought to be aware of throughout. If such an awareness can be achieved and sustained, then perhaps literary criticism and philosophical theology will be seen to enjoy a relationship of mutual illumination. That, in any event, is what my discussion will aim at.

Prolegomena to a historical approach

The historical context of this study requires less introduction than the conceptual or the literary, and for the most part it can be filled in as we go along. But a few words are needed to justify my historical method, such as it is.

Let me say first that, in an interdisciplinary study like this, no one discipline can be entirely at the service of another. I would not have undertaken this study unless I thought knowledge of history and theology could enhance one's appreciation of literature. Yet one must avoid treating the disciplines of history and theology as merely functional; for otherwise one runs the risk of undermining the interdisciplinary enterprise itself, which must, I believe, be predicated on some sort of partnership of disciplines rather than on the sovereignty of one. This independence or mutual relationship of the various disciplines corresponds to the fact that the men and women who practice them are not, except in a secondary, artificial, and theoretical way, only literary, historical, or theological beings. Simply recognizing this can obviate the tendency to theoretical reductionism: Just as it will prevent us from trying to reduce literature to its theological or historical "content," so it will discourage the scholarly patronizing of other times or disciplines as if they had no right to demand our attention except as they can provide oil for our literary machine.

These points have two general applications. First, the basis for much of my argument in this book is seventeenth-century theological discussions that in themselves do not immediately strike one as being of any profound literary import; and the antireductionist principles I have just sketched help to explain why I intend to address theological issues qua theological issues even while trying to show their helpfulness in understanding *Paradise Lost*. They might also account for what may appear to be the inefficiency of such an approach. For the reasons I have given, it is quite possible that not all of the specific historical and theological details I present will be relevant to *Paradise Lost* qua literature. That is simply to be expected, given the nature of the study; and yet I hope that such dangling details might prove interesting nonetheless, because (as has been premised) no reader either of this essay or of *Paradise Lost* is a purely literary animal.

Moreover, just as my brief antireductionist credo explains a certain "irrelevancy" between disciplines, so it recognizes – and this is the second, more important point – a philosophical basis for the relation that does exist between them. If a thing's meaning involves some sort of pointing beyond itself, then any scheme that reduces, let us say, literary, theological, economic, psychological, and every other sort of meaning to historical meaning runs into a very serious difficulty with regard to its own absolutized theoretical sphere, in this case history: namely, what is *its* meaning? It is hard to see how the truly historicist answer could be anything but merely self-referential, hence circular, and so finally tautological. However, if we treat no such theoretical sphere as sovereign or absolute, and if we recognize that we, Milton included, transcend those spheres, involved in them though we are, then we can see that "sciences" such as the historical, theological, and literary are related to each other at least by way of the relationship of each of them to ourselves – that is to say, to you, to me, and, once again, to Milton.

Now the fairly naive recognition that Milton was a person like you or me actually encourages an intellectual-historical model less naive than one often encounters in studies of Milton. For ourselves, I believe, we generally posit unity of mind and creative personality; and we should therefore be wary of radically distinguishing Milton the poet from Milton the thinker. (I shall return to this point in a moment.) We would also surely deny that a recognition of the sources and parallels of our own thought and expression somehow explained it all away, and we must likewise avoid thinking that, once we have presented analogues or demonstrated influences of Milton's thought, we have "said it all." While admitting that we ourselves are influenced, moreover, do we not also recognize that our conceptual and pistic landscape is like a patchwork stitched together from various scraps of conversation, reading, experience, and disposition, the dye from each scrap bleeding into the one adjacent to it in the quilt, so that the hue of each is subtly altered by virtue of its now integrated relation to the whole? If this picture is not entirely inaccurate, then the sort of scholarly doing-as-one-would-be-done-by that I am trying to advocate will not allow us to employ a simplistic model of influence so far as Milton is concerned, either. In particular, it might curb the academic urge to treat written texts (especially written texts available to us) as if they were the only sorts of things by which Milton could have been influenced. Of course it may be that texts are all we have; but in studying the textual foreground, as it were, we can at least be aware of the existence of the nontextual background and allow it to temper, even render more sophisticated, our use of the written evidence that we do possess.

To this extent, I support Christopher Hill's attempt to exorcise what he refers to as the "prevalent donnish assumption that ideas are transmitted principally by books." He argues Milton's immersion in the ferment of his own day, and postulates Milton's familiarity with radical seventeenth-century thought through his contact, for example, with the milieu of taverns and alehouses.[15] Hill's own, perfectly reasonable assumption is that books which made it past the strict censorship of the years before 1640 and following the Restoration in 1660 can provide no accurate picture of the range of ideas that flourished in the minds and conversations of real people. In the chapters that follow, much of the primary material presented will be drawn from works published between those years and therefore arguably more representative of the diversity and debates that were a part of Milton's life and milieu.

However, I do not entirely agree with Hill's advocating a redirection of the energy of Milton studies "away from the classics and the Christian Fathers to Milton's contemporaries and immediate predecessors"[16] It is true that "traditional" aspects of Milton's work have at times been variously overemphasized, overgeneralized, even downright invented. But there is no doubt that Milton did read, and was influenced by, the church fathers; and even where he diverges from them, that divergence (as I hope to show, for example, in Chapter 6) can be of great significance. There is no reason why the importance of Milton's "radical" milieu should render less important his relationship to traditional Christianity, so long as that is discriminatingly conceived. Surely a balanced view will have to take account of both.

My aim, then, historically, will be to present enough material relevant to theodicy from the Christian tradition and from the contemporary seventeenth-century milieu (Milton being an inhabitant of both) to create a sense of what issues and answers were articulated – in short, to outline a historical context or landscape in which Milton's handling of the problem of evil can be seen for what it is, and for what it means.

The critical issues

The question of meaning quite naturally leads us on from history to criticism. By criticism I do not mean essentially the activity that Hill ascribes to what he calls the "Milton industry," "a great part of whose vast output appears to be concerned less with what Milton wrote (still less with enjoyment of what Milton wrote) than with the views of Professor Blank on the views of Professor Schrank on the views of Professor Rank on what Milton may or may not have written."[17] Although this is to a certain extent an Englishman's caricature of what he sees across the Atlantic, it does describe a tendency I shall do my best to avoid. Instead, I shall try to establish for my discussion as it goes along a critical context that is typical rather than comprehensive. For example, in Chapter 7, I shall use Arthur Love-joy's work on Milton as the critical jumping-off point for con-sidering the so-called Fortunate Fall in Milton, because it is Lovejoy whose views on the matter have been of greatest criti-cal influence. Some of the many others who have concerned themselves with that subject I shall mention but not consider in any detail.

I shall take the task of Milton criticism as involving primarily description and discussion of what, and how, Milton's writings mean. I say "Milton's writings" rather than "Milton" because I would prefer not to be accused of committing the intentional fallacy; yet one must speak of intentionality, and that of a text appears at least to be accessible in a way that that of a person who died three hundred years ago is not. This, in a way, is a tactical maneuver. Inevitably we do ascribe intentions to people long dead; it is just that for purely theoretical purposes we probably need not.

And of course texts use language – in the case of Milton's major poetry, English. However, here the problem is often that Milton and we are "divided by a common language," to echo the popular transatlantic quip. Surely one of the most com-monsensical justifications of historical criticism is that it can help span this natural gulf. In Chapter 3, for example, I shall show how the term "prevenient grace" was used in Milton's time by Calvinists and Arminians alike, and therefore in a seventeenth-century context implies no particular view of pre-destination – a point, it will be argued, important to our under-standing of books 10 and 11 of *Paradise Lost.* And in general much of the criticism in which I engage will be aimed at reveal-ing meaning simply by means of enriching our lexicon of sev-enteenth-century terms and issues.

This scholarly aspect of criticism naturally leads into some-thing that is more centrally critical in nature, namely, interpre-tation of the text. Supposing we know what the words mean and what the issues are, the job of explaining the text's being and meaning still lies ahead of us. In a poem as long as *Paradise*

Lost, our question will, initially at least, have to be broken down: What is the meaning of this book or that pair of lines? Are our interpretations of these consistent with each other? If not, is it the fault of the poem as a whole, or of our interpretations?

I shall return to the matter of interpretation later in this chapter. However, here I want to emphasize that criticism ends in judgment. As C. Q. Drummond has put it in a recent series of articles entitled "An Anti-Miltonist Reprise," of *Paradise Lost* we must finally ask: "Is the poem any good?"[18] Drummond charges that that question is often avoided; Miltonists, he complains, try to give the impression "that Milton and his poem [can]not be touched by adverse criticism" (pt. I, p. 29). Drummond confesses his own emancipation from that notion through reading F. R. Leavis and A. J. A. Waldock, the former leading the attack on the style of *Paradise Lost,* the latter, that on "the narrative structure and the theme of the poem."[19] It is Waldock's cause that Drummond's articles are primarily concerned to advance, and that I, in general, shall be primarily concerned to oppose. I shall recognize with Drummond that Milton "needs defending," something he accuses Miltonists of failing to recognize or admit (pt. I, p. 33); but I shall not concede that the task is hopeless.

Drummond's recapitulation of the case against the narrative integrity of *Paradise Lost* is worth considering on account of some critical distinctions that, typically, it fails to make. His first move is to point out that the style of Gen. 2 and 3 conforms to Erich Auerbach's description of narrative style elsewhere in the Old Testament as characterized by a " 'background' quality" and "multiplicity of meanings."[20] As Drummond says, in the Genesis account of the Fall, "God's thoughts and feelings are unexpressed"; the story's meaning, "far from being clear and unmistakable, calls out for interpretation" (pt. II, p. 42). And the interpretation Milton gives it "in *Paradise Lost* is only one of many interpretations" (pt. II, p. 45). However, Drummond goes on in effect to blame Milton for the fact that epic style is not Old Testament style, and so to imply that *Paradise Lost* cannot be an acceptable interpretation of Genesis. Epic, says Drummond, is fiction, and "we demand from our fiction writers . . . the illusion of a consistent, real action. But Genesis must not be illusion at all: it is . . . absolute truth." Hence, "two antagonistic modes" create "contradictory demands in *Paradise Lost*. The narrative demands of a self-consistent story about believable characters are opposed to the theological demands of an absolutely and tyrannically true scripture" (pt. II, p. 50). Fiction is illusion; Gen. 2 and 3 must be believed true and unillusory; therefore, Gen. 2 and 3 cannot consistently be fictionalized. *Paradise Lost* is (much of it) a fictionalization of Gen. 2 and 3; therefore, *Paradise Lost* is inherently inconsistent.

But the argument is unsound. First, "illusion" is used equivocally. Of course, when we read a story we do imagine events and characters; yet that has nothing to do with the truth or fictitiousness of the story. For example, suppose we read a historical novel based on the life of Charles I: We have in one of Drummond's senses an illusion of Charles; but that is in no way inconsistent with the fact that a very nonillusory Charles did reign in England from 1625 to 1649. The historical novelist, more or less convincingly, fills in the details of Charles's life in a way that he or she hopes is consistent with the historical truth about him and yet that is not itself, properly speaking, historical. Moreover, the resulting mixture of fact and illusion (this time the illusion that invents, and not only imaginatively depicts, states of affairs) does not compromise the historical truth on which the story is based; nor does the fact that the story is historically based ipso facto compromise the integrity of the historical novel qua novel. Although they are certainly not the same thing, it would simply not make much sense to speak as if straightforward historical account and historical fiction writing were somehow "antagonistic modes."

Secondly, however, it is not only kinds of illusion that Drummond's argument fails to distinguish. We must also differentiate between *theology* and *truth*, as a sophisticated view would differentiate between history and fact. Genesis may indeed claim to present "absolute truth," but first-order truth has to be distinguished from theology and history as such, which are "sciences" in the broad sense that each is a branch of knowledge. Whereas truth, being, reality may in some sense be absolute, epistemology, science, knowledge *of* the truth are not absolute but relative. The historian may claim to know the truth about the past, just as the theologian claims to declare the truth about God and his ways. Yet both history and theology thus consist of *claims about* the truth; they are not the truth itself. Therefore, even if Scripture is "absolutely and tyrannically true," its truth is not to be confused with what Drummond, as we have seen, refers to as "theological demands." In writing *Paradise Lost*, Milton had to make his story comport with truth, as Scripture revealed it; but in so doing he was acceding to the demands of *truth*, not theology or some putative "set doctrine."[21] If one fails to make that distinction, one quite unfairly prejudices the chances of defending Milton and his major epic.

There is, nevertheless, an element of truth in Drummond's suggestion that "the demands of epic force on Milton certain attitudes toward his material that he did not anticipate, or perhaps . . . even recognize" (pt. II, p. 45), although it is patronizing and gratuitous to insinuate that Milton was in some undesirable way compelled and unaware. A theme to which I shall recur in the chapters that follow is that theology is indeed impinged upon by literary considerations, that, for Milton, not only does theology inform poetry, but poetry informs theology. In fact, the demands (if we want to call them that) of literary, dramatic, narrative, imaginative, and characterological coherence in part make the theology of *Paradise Lost* what it is.[22] And to the extent that Milton succeeds in submitting to those demands for coherence, he can be said, I think, to be doing theology well.

If these claims are true, furthermore, then the oft-trumpeted disjunction between Milton's poetry and Milton's theology

denial; in other words, both positive and negative analogy are present. For metaphors, as for models, it is the *neutral analogy* which invites exploration, and which prevents reduction to a set of equivalent literal statements." Both are in this way "open-ended" (p. 42). In Chapter 4, in connection with the "Free Will Defense," I will present one of Milton's models that exemplifies the tension and, in a literary context, the irony that can be produced by the sort of positive-and-negative analogy Barbour here refers to. And in keeping with what he says about literal reduction, I shall assume throughout this study that Milton's poetic models, like any literary images, have, as it were, their own organic existence within the literary context, yet are not necessarily violated through being critically analyzed. Both metaphor and model are by nature multilayered and irreducible. Yet we need not murder to dissect.

In what follows, then, I shall try by the means I have indicated to piece together the conceptual and historical contexts of Milton's theodicy, and try to show indeed how Milton added to them. The process, because the contexts overlap, must be cumulative rather than linear. The unity of my literary subject – namely, *Paradise Lost* – and of the problem of evil itself will be primarily what establishes any unity that this essay might possess.

And it will be, I must stress, an essay – only an attempt, yet one that has not hitherto been made. If it can add to our knowledge of discussions of theodicy in the seventeenth century, if it can show how these in turn enhance our appreciation of *Paradise Lost,* and if it can also show how understanding the particular theodicy of *Paradise Lost* enhances in its own way our understanding of theodicy generally, then the attempt will not completely have failed. For in doing that it will have furthered our awareness of what, after all, as Coleridge recognized, was Milton's object.

2

God and Chaos

In the beginning God created the heaven and the earth. And the earth was without form, and void; and darkness was upon the face of the deep.

Gen. 1:1–2[1]

An obvious criticism of any theodicy that bases itself on a doctrine of the Fall, as Milton's by and large does, is that the Fall is an arbitrary place to start one's etiology: It may explain the *post-lapsarian* condition, but how do you explain the Fall itself? That question leads us back to creation – as it did Milton.

Historically, and perhaps more generally, it is imperative, too, that the Fall be seen in the context of the biblical and more specifically the Reformed pattern of creation, Fall, and Redemption.[2] To cite only one prominent acknowledgment of this pattern, the first page of the Geneva Bible (1560) prefaces Genesis with the following "Argument":

> Moses in effect declareth the things, which are here chiefly to be considered: First, that the worlde and all things therein were created by God, and that man being placed in this great tabernacle of the worlde to beholde Gods wonderful workes, and to praise his Name for the infinite graces, wherewith he had endued him, fel willingly from God through disobedience: who yet for his owne mercies sake restored him to life, and confirmed him in the same by his promes of Christ to come, by whome he shulde ouercome Satan, death and hel.[3]

It is also imperative, therefore, to consider Milton's theodicy not only in relation to the Fall, but also in relation to creation and Redemption. These last two will be touched on a number of times throughout this study; in the present chapter I would like to focus mainly on the doctrine of creation, without which the doctrines of the other two are inevitably deficient.

It is appropriate, moreover, to begin a detailed discussion of Milton's theodicy by considering creation, not only because it is the starting point for the Bible, the Apostles' Creed, Reformed theology,[4] the world, and so on, but for two additional reasons. First, as indicated in Chapter 1, one of the three great "heresies" one must avoid in producing one's theodicy is dualism; and dualism, as I shall show presently, was historically the first major heresy that had to be opposed by orthodox Christian theology in connection with the problem of evil. Indeed, it was primarily in this battle that the church's position on the metaphysical status of good and evil was first worked out. And second, there are very significant parallels between evil in its metaphysical and in its moral dimensions, and between the relations each of these sorts of evil has to the sovereignty of God – parallels that have been recognized and explored since very early in the history of human thought. Most importantly for *Paradise Lost*, these parallels include an extremely rich and suggestive connection between Chaos and free will.

I would like therefore to begin by tracing some connections of this kind in biblical, patristic, and modern writings; then to return to the seventeenth century in order to get a sense of how connections among creation, Chaos, and evil were treated by Milton's contemporaries; and finally to consider Milton's own versions of creation and Chaos and how they figure in his theodicy as a whole.

Chaos and creation: literary and metaphysical roots

Typical of the pagan, dualistic characterization of creation and Chaos that early Christian apologists reacted against is that of Plato's *Timaeus*, which presents a "likely account" of how the world began. "God," says Timaeus in the dialogue, "wishing that all things should be good, and so far as possible nothing be imperfect, and finding the visible universe in a state not of rest but of inharmonious and disorderly motion, reduced it to order from disorder."[5] In this way, God is conceived to have done the best he could with preexisting and disharmonious materials, so that, as Timaeus says later in his account, "this world came into being from a mixture and combination of necessity and intelligence."[6] Such a view is contrary to the biblical teaching that "there is but one God, . . . of whom are all things" (1 Cor. 8:6), for it supposes that something other than God alone is primordial, that something apart from him existed in the beginning, which limited his creativity.[7] Even if Plato's God achieves a high degree of success in imposing his will on Chaos, the very assumption that the latter is primordial entails an inadmissible limitation of the divine power, and so seriously undermines cardinal proposition (1), that God is omnipotent.

Perhaps I need to say a few words about omnipotence before proceeding. It must not be taken to mean power without any limits of any sort whatsoever. As Alvin Plantinga puts it, "What the theist typically means when he says that God is omnipotent is not that there are *no* limits to God's power, but at most that there are no nonlogical limits to what he can do."[8] As suggested in Chapter 1, some such qualification of omnipotence is needed in order to obviate self-contradictory statements about God, like those that have him creating rocks so heavy he can't lift them. As Milton has Adam say in *Paradise Lost*, "contradiction . . . to God himself / Impossible is held, as argument / Of weakness, not of power" (10.799–801). The limitation imposed by the principle of noncontradiction qualifies the definition of omnipotence but does not in so doing diminish omnipotence per se. The Bible itself says that God cannot lie (Titus 1:2; Heb. 6:18); and the intention, far from being apologetic, is clearly to extol thereby God's greatness and goodness. The point is that consistency and truthfulness are inherent in God's character and are not independently primordial entities limiting God's creativity after the manner conceived by Plato in the *Timaeus*.

Nevertheless, there is a sort of biblical analogue to the pagan notion of Chaos, indeed a near enough analogue to have encouraged perennial efforts to syncretize pagan and biblical accounts. What one might call the passive aspect of the biblical analogue is represented by darkness and water: "The earth was without form, and void; and darkness was upon the face of the deep. And the Spirit of God moved upon the face of the waters" (Gen. 1:2). Not totally unlike the *Timaeus*, this account suggests that creation was accomplished over against its contrary. And as Bernhard W. Anderson points out, at the end of history, "when God's victory is complete the sea will be no more and there will be no more darkness (Rev. 21:1, 22:5)." Moreover, "just as the apocalypse of Daniel had represented the world empires as evil beasts emerging from the sea [Dan. 7:3], so the Christian Apocalypse portrayed the beast (Rome) as coming up from the sea" (Chap. 13).[9]

The beasts, of course, introduce the active side of what appears as God's opposition – opposition that is not only, as it were, an anticreational state, but an anticreational force. As Bruce K. Waltke has shown, "At least in a dozen texts of the Old Testament, reference is made to the LORD's conflict with the dragon or sea monster variously named as Rahab, 'The Proud One,' or Leviathan, 'The Twisting One,' or Yam, 'The Sea.' Moreover, at least five of these texts are in a context pertaining to the creation of the world."[10] And in the apocalypse of Isaiah it is "leviathan that crooked serpent; . . . the dragon that is in the sea" that the Lord will slay (Isa. 27:1) – "that old serpent" being in the book of Revelation explicitly identified as "the Devil, and Satan" (Rev. 12:9).

My intention here is simply to point out the biblical counterpart to the pagan version of Chaos, so that we might have some understanding of why the pagan version has been so eagerly taken up by Christian writers through the ages, and to consider the two main theodical questions raised by the biblical presentation of Chaos (if one can call it that): First, what is the connection between the evil of Chaos and that evil which is traceable to human or angelic agency? and secondly, is it possible to cling to any notion of evil ultimately transcending creaturely agency without lapsing into dualism? As Anderson puts it:

> We must face the question of the theological implications of the myth of Satan with respect to the problem of evil, especially as the myth came to be fused with the myth of chaos. Does the chaos myth merely provide imagery which adds richness and depth to the presentation of a dramatic conflict which . . . is essentially historical, that is, rooted in creaturely opposition to the Creator? Or does this imagery intend to locate evil not only outside of man but even before creation?[11]

I shall argue later that, in facing these questions, Milton was most concerned with avoiding any ontological dualism, yet that even while avoiding dualism he produced a view of Chaos that also provides "imagery which adds richness and depth" to his presentation of evil, including the role of Satan. First, however, I would like to consider further how dualism and the notion of Chaos have been treated by other Christian thinkers.

In the early church, Gnosticism and, somewhat later, Manichaeism were the forms of radical dualism that presented the greatest threat to the Christian doctrine of creation – the latter being succinctly asserted against the Gnostics by Irenaeus near the end of the second century:

> It is proper . . . that I should begin with the first and most important head, that is, God the Creator, who made the heaven and the earth, and all things that are therein . . . , and to demonstrate that there is nothing above Him or after Him; nor that, influenced by any one, but of His own free will, He created all things, since He is the only God, the only Lord, the only Creator, the only Father, alone containing all things, and Himself commanding all things into existence.[12]

Contrasted with this view is that of Manichaeism, which arose in the third century and, itself actually a form of Gnosticism, posited a primordial opposition of Good and Evil, Light and Darkness, God and Matter. It was this "heresy" (more properly, a separate religion) which St. Augustine spent the first stage of his career as a Christian theologian attacking. Like Irenaeus, Augustine reasserted that there is but one God, and that "of him, and through him, and to him, are all things" (Rom. 11:36). In order to do so, as was noted in Chapter 1, Augustine adopted certain aspects of Neoplatonic thought and developed the conception of evil as privation. Because evil by its very nature is thus parasitic, it cannot be seen as being in any way primordial or original.

Four points in connection with Augustine's position on creation and evil will be seen to have relevance to Milton's theodicy. First, as was also noted in Chapter 1, Augustine espouses a notion of "metaphysical evil" in the limited sense that created being is less good than absolute being – than God himself. In a similar vein, against the Manichaeans Augustine argues that natures (created things) are corruptible, not because of a mixture of good and evil principles, but because they are created *ex nihilo:*

All corruptible natures . . . are natures at all only so far as they are *from* God, nor would they be corruptible if they were *of* Him; because they would be what He himself is. Therefore of whatever measure, of whatever form, of whatever order, they are, they are so because it is God by whom they were made; but they are not immutable, because it is nothing of which they were made.[13]

This application of the doctrine of *creatio ex nihilo* became a theodical commonplace – one that Milton did his best, for the sake of theodicy, to undercut.

Secondly, lest the Manichaeans should resort to the familiar conception of a primal, formless matter and identify that with their evil principle, Augustine asserts that matter, too, is from God the creator:

Neither is that material, which the ancients called *Hyle,* to be called an evil . . . By *Hyle* I mean a certain material absolutely formless and without quality, whence those qualities that we perceive are formed . . . Nor is that *Hyle* . . . to be called an evil which cannot be perceived through any appearance, but can scarcely be thought of through any sort of privation of appearance . . . If form is some good, . . . even the capacity of form is undoubtedly something good . . . And because every good is from God, no one ought to doubt that even matter, if there is any, has its existence from God alone.[14]

Thus, in the most orthodox of writers, we find at least a hint of how the formless matter of the ancient pagan cosmogony might be syncretized with a Christian, nondualistic view of creation and the goodness of God. How Milton portrays that which "can scarcely be thought" we shall see presently.

The third point is tangential to a consideration of creation and Chaos but will be relevant when we arrive at Chapter 6; I mention it now because it arises as part of Augustine's polemic against the Manichaeans. In arguing yet again the parasitic, dependent character of evil, Augustine gives expression to what I shall continue to refer to as the principle of contrariety. "We should not know darkness," he says, "if we were always in darkness. But the notion of light does not allow its opposite to be unknown."[15] We shall have to ask whether this peculiar version of the principle contradicts or complements Milton's claim that in this fallen world we know good *by* evil.

And fourthly, the rejection of the dualistic explanation for the existence of evil brings us back to an emphasis on creaturely agency. The "metaphysical evil" that follows from things' being created *ex nihilo* may explain the possibility of evil, but the actuality of evil is the result of wrong human or angelic choice. Confesses Augustine: "Free will is the cause of our doing evil and your just judgment [, Lord,] the cause of our suffering it." "I asked: 'What is wickedness?' and found that it is not a substance but a perversity of the will turned away from you, God, the supreme substance, toward lower things – casting away, as it were, its own insides." And thus "it was by his own perverse will that the devil himself, after having been a good angel, became a devil."[16]

Before following such themes into the seventeenth century, I would like to consider briefly a modern discussion of freedom and Chaos that is remarkable for its fusion of philosophic and mythic elements and that gives a strong sense of the hardiness of this particular strain of theodical writing. I refer to the work of the Russian existentialist philosopher and theologian Nicolas Berdjaev.

Berdjaev's chapter entitled "The Origin of Good and Evil" in his book *The Destiny of Man* takes clear aim at voluntarism and optimism (although he does not use those terms). The former, in the person of Calvin, he opposes only very briefly; the latter, in the form of what he calls "positive theology," he systematically attacks.[17] "The ordinary theological conception of the creation of the world and the Fall," he complains, "turns it all into a divine comedy, a play that God plays with Himself. One may disagree with . . . the Gnostics and the Manichees, but one cannot help respecting them for their being so painfully conscious of the problem of evil" (p. 23).

Although he teeters on the brink of dualism, as exemplified by the heretics he mentions, Berdjaev provides an interesting discussion of the concept of Chaos in its relation to freedom. What he seems to be opposing in his criticism of the traditionally "comic" conception of human history and all its evil is the idea that freedom "in the last resort is determined by God." If such were the case, he recognizes, then man would not be truly free and God would really only be "playing with Himself."[18] To avoid this consequence, Berdjaev invokes the old negative concept of "meonic freedom" – in its essentials the notion we have just looked at in connection with Augustine, that the mutability of creaturely freedom is a necessary consequence of its possessors' having been created *ex nihilo*, out of nothing ($\tau\grave{o}$ $\mu\grave{\eta}$ $\mathring{o}\nu$). As Berdjaev startlingly restates it, God's "act of creation . . . cannot avert the possibility of evil contained in meonic freedom. The myth of the Fall tells of this powerlessness of the creator to avert the evil resulting from freedom which He has not created." For "freedom is not created by God: . . . it is part of the nothing out of which God created the world."[19]

Berdjaev in this way makes one of his chief contributions to Christian theodicy by drawing attention to the possibility – which, as I hope to show in Chapter 4, is not necessarily tied to a dualist formulation – of God's facing a genuine dilemma. "It is impossible," he says, "to deny that the Christian God is first and foremost, the God of sacrificial love, and sacrifice always indicates tragedy. . . . To deny tragedy in the divine life is only possible at the cost of denying Christ, His cross and crucifixion, the sacrifice of the Son of God." Thus it is, declares Berdjaev, that "the Lamb is slain from the foundation of the world. The Divine sacrifice forms part of the plan of creation from the first."[20] The problem of evil is a problem for God himself! God suffers. And yet herein lies not only tragedy, but also, according to the Christian message, the hope of mankind.

Chaos and creation: the Miltonic context

When one comes to the seventeenth century, one is amazed, I think, to find how clearly that century's apologists and polemicists articulated the connections among creation, evil, and omnipotence. I hope that a brief examination of a few seventeenth-century treatments of this aspect of the problem of evil not only will obviate any suspicion that the categories I apply to Milton are arbitrary or borrowed only from patristic and twentieth-century discussions, but also will lay a basis for appreciating how theologically bold Milton really was in carrying out his theodical task.

In the preface to a work entitled *The Originall Cause of Temporall Evils*, Meric Casaubon (1599–1671), son of the more famous Isaac Casaubon, sets himself to oppose the two theories concerning the origin of evil that, he says, the devil, before the time of "Epicurisme," introduced into men's opinions: (1) "that God was of an envious nature: . . . which was . . . the very argument he [the devil] used to our first father and mother . . . to make them transgress"; and (2), an error they fell into later, "not altogether so impious, but more absurd, that God is not omnipotent, and wanted not will, but power to amend what they conceived to be amiss in the world: or, that there were two Authors and Creators of all things, the one good, and the other evill."[21] Of course it is the second error that concerns us here – the denial of omnipotence and the resulting slide into dualism. As Casaubon recognized, one is faced with an apparent dilemma concerning God's power and goodness, with the result that "among them [i.e., those of the ancients] that were agreed concerning the goodnesse of God, there was no small controversie concerning his power. For, said they, were God as omnipotent, as he is good, why hath he not made all things as goodnesse would have prompted?" This sort, among whom Casaubon lists Seneca and Epictetus, "did put all the fault of all that was done amisse in the world upon the ὕλην [*Hylēn*], or, *materiam,* that God was to work upon, and was not able (so they) to rectify." Casaubon adds, "I cannot excuse *Plato,* though some have taken great pains to doe it; . . . his words are plain, that ἀνάγκη [the "necessity" discussed at the beginning of this chapter], or, *materia prima,* as eternall as God himselfe, did concurre with him, to the making of all things" (pp. 28–9). Clearly, one must not attempt to solve the problem of evil by means of a denial of divine omnipotence; genuine theodicy is incompatible with dualism.

Such a position, however, does not automatically rule out any notion of Chaos or original matter whatsoever. This point is made by Charles I's physician, Walter Charleton (1619–1707), in a chapter ambitiously entitled: "That God created the world *ex nihilo,* proved by Arguments Apodictical." Charleton focuses his attack on Epicurus, whom he singles out "as the most notorious *Patron,* though not the Father of [the] execrable delusion" that the universe was not created by God but resulted fortuitously from "an infinite Chaos of Atoms."[22] The view is epitomized by a poem Charleton translates from Lucretius, who, says Charleton, "was deplorably infected with this accurst contagion of Epicurus":

> The Worlds *Materials* having first been tost,
> An infinite *Time,* within an infinite Roome,
> From this to that uncircumscribed coast,

And made by their own Tendency to roame
In various *Motions;* did at last quiesce
In these *Positions,* which they now possess.

[P. 42]

Yet – despite his execration of what he calls "this old Romance
of the spontaneous result of the World from . . . that Abysse of
Atoms, which rowled up and down, to and fro, by an impetu-
ous and continual inquietude . . . or civil war" – Charleton very
carefully distinguishes those elements of the Epicurean view
that make it unacceptable to the Christian. Expressly to be
rejected are the claims "(1.) that the *Chaos of Atoms was non-
principiate,* or as antient as Eternity: (2.) that they were not created *ex nihilo,* . . . by God: (3.) that they were not becalmed,
separated, ranged, and disposed into their proper stations . . .
by the artifice of any other *Cause,* but the blind Ordination
. . . of *Fortune"* (p. 43). "Notwithstanding," Charleton goes on
to say, "I have never yet found out any justifiable ground, why
Atoms may not be reputed *Mundi materies,* the Material Principle of the universe, provided that we allow, that God created
that first *Matter* out of *Nothing"* (p. 44).

Suppose we, in short, that God in the first act of his Wisdome and
Power, out of the *Tohu,* or nothing, creates such a . . . mass of Atoms,
as was necessary to the constitution of the Universe: . . . and then will
all the subsequent operations of nature remain so clear and easie, that
a meer *Ethnick* by guidance of . . . *Sense* and *Ratiocination,* may progress to a physical theory of them, and thereby salve all the Phaenom-
ena's [*sic*] with less apostasie from first Principles proposed, then by
any other hypothesis yet excogitated. [P. 47]

Thus Charleton, like Augustine and countless other Christian
thinkers, seeks to render pagan philosophy for its "Egyptian
gold," and, by using that refined substance for the saving of
appearances, actually to further the attack against paganism's
other, dualistic or antitheistic tenets.

That Milton similarly adapts pagan sources is not in dispute.
The pagan sources of his Chaos have been adequately noted by
his editors and commentators.[23] However, pagan ideas have
not always been accepted for their own sake – out of a merely

syncretistic urge of the Christian thinker in question – but have often been taken up in an effort to make the thinker's philosophy more radically Christian. This needs to be emphasized in the case of a Renaissance figure such as Milton, because the simple citing of a pagan source in connection with a work like *Paradise Lost* too easily calls to mind possible similarities with paganism, without their accompanying contrasts. Charleton's discussion, at least, makes explicit the attempt to separate out the dross. Yet at the same time, we must recognize that the use of pagan terminology in connection with the biblical account of creation was, in the seventeenth century, a commonplace, and that it therefore, so far as Christian theology was concerned, need not imply anything scandalous. Even Hobbes appears to intend nothing more than an insult against his opponent when he refers to Bramhall's "School-learning Jargon" as "that . . . which the Scripture in the first *Chaos* calleth *Tohu* and *Bohu.*"[24] And Hobbes's more Christian contemporary Thomas Goodwin (1600–80), with complete ingenuousness, declares that when "in *Gen.* I.1. it is said, that on the *first day* God created the heaven and the Earth, . . .* by Earth is meant the confused *Chaos,* the matter of Sun, and Moon, and Stars, and Men, and Beasts, and Fire, and Water, and Earth, and all."[25] However, Milton's treatment of Chaos, I shall argue, transcends both its to some extent pagan roots and the commonplace, uncritical syncretizing of those roots with Christian theology. It may also be seen, in its literary and theological boldness, to stand apart from even his contemporaries' more critical efforts at saving appearances of creation, Chaos, and evil.

In some ways, Milton, as a poet, was ideally equipped to deal with what Karl Barth calls the "necessary brokenness of all theological thought and utterance," and to present that which, as Berdjaev says, "can only be expressed in myths and symbols."[26] However, before examining the poetic presentation of Chaos in *Paradise Lost,* let us consider some of that theodicy's more prosaic assumptions. I have already emphasized the importance of defining omnipotence in accordance with the principle of noncontradiction. If theodicy is to make any sense at all, we must agree that if God is absolutely good he cannot also be evil, and so on. In the *Christian Doctrine* Milton recognizes that, although God is "omnipotent and utterly free in his actions," he must be considered as it were subject to laws of logical consistency: "The power of God is not exerted in those kinds of things which, as the term goes, imply a contradiction."[27] As Henry Hammond (1605–60) put it, *"Omnipotence* is not only the power of doing all things that any or all creatures can do, but more than so, the doing all things that imply not a *contradiction,* (as the same thing at once to be and not to be, the doing of those being as impossible to God, as it is to lye)."[28] Or as Britomart puts it in Spenser's *Faerie Queen,* "neither God of loue, nor God of sky / Can doe . . . that, which cannot be donne."[29]

However, this principle raises another question that is often overlooked: What is the origin of something's capability or incapability of "being donne"? Put another way, what is the metaphysical status of logical possibility? Is the impossibility of a married man's being at the same time a bachelor primordial, or is it merely something God has decided shall be impossible? It is an apparent dilemma. For if possibilities and impossibilities are primordial, wherein do they inhere? If we accept their primordiality, are we not veering off in the direction of Plato's dualistic view of cosmogony as involving a mixture of necessity and intelligence? But on the other hand, if we assert that God decided what would be possible and not, then we must conclude that he could have decided somehow to make sins such as lying and murder morally good. And this, of course, leads us directly into voluntarism.

The issues involved here are recognized very clearly by Milton's famous Scottish contemporary Samuel Rutherford (1600–61), who opts for the voluntarist horn of the dilemma and opposes the dualist essentialism he considers to be the only other alternative. "The question is not," he declares, "whether God causes the same thing at the same time to be able to be and not be, or causes contradictories to be true both at the same time; for such things God cannot bring about."[30] The question, rather, is whether God himself is the source of possibilities and impossibilities: "an DEVS sit Origo et Causa impossibilium et possibilium." In considering the question, Rutherford rests heavily on Aristotle's discussion of potentiality and actuality in the *Metaphysics*, chapter 9 of book nine (which can in fact itself be seen as a rejection of Platonic dualism). Aristotle, as quoted by Rutherford, asserts, "Prior est actus quam potentia" – actuality is prior to potentiality. And God being wholly actual, therefore, Rutherford concludes that God is "prior omni possibili," prior to all possibility. Thus God's omnipotence determines what is possible and not; it is not itself delimited by any essential possibility or impossibility. "Neither things external to it nor even the possible essences of them are the origin, cause, and source of Divine Omnipotence – as if indeed the rivulets were the cause of the fountainhead!"[31]

However, we may question whether Rutherford needs to go as far as he does in order to avoid dualism and the compromise of omnipotence. For if we suppose that possibilities and impossibilities inhere not in some separate essence but in the very nature of God, then it is simply not a question of priority or posteriority, and dualism can be avoided without resort to voluntarism. God can still be seen as the source of possibility and impossibility even if we deny that they originate specifically from God's *will*. Omnipotence will accordingly be seen as *potentia ordinata*, not merely power that is arbitrary and absolute. And yet the impossibility or necessity we ascribe to God – as when we say it is impossible for him to lie, necessary for him to speak truly – will by no means imply dualism. For as Milton puts it in his *Christian Doctrine*, "In God a certain immutable internal necessity to do good, independent of all outside influence, can be consistent with absolute freedom of action."[32] Therefore, assuming that God's goodness is no slur on his omnipotence, the question concerning the origin of possibility and necessity need not, as first appears, create a dilemma. Failing to see this, Rutherford flees to a position that ultimately entails abandoning the task of theodicy altogether.

Rutherford's defense of omnipotence, nevertheless, follows a pattern similar to one we have already seen in Augustine, who, we recall, in opposing the dualism of the Manichaeans, denies the primordiality of *Hylē,* matter. Unless omnipotence is to be compromised by something outside itself, matter must be seen as having been created, as having "its existence from God alone." What Rutherford does is similarly to see the "substance" implied by necessity or possibility as entailing a threat to omnipotence unless it too is conceived of as having been created. Milton's remarkable achievement, as I hope to show, is to create a poetic and theological model according to which neither matter nor the potentiality that concerns Rutherford are prior to or "beside" God, nor in the usual sense created by him. For God himself, Milton believes, is material; and it is in that material that all potentiality and necessity inhere.

Now despite materialism's being a heresy, in fact one of Milton's most famous, we need to consider the "orthodox," strongly theodical motivation for his adopting it. Augustine, as we have seen, propounds a doctrine of creation out of nothing, and he is followed by most of Christendom. Created things are corruptible not, as the Manichaeans taught, because they consist of a mixture of good and evil principles, but because they are created *ex nihilo.* Among Milton's contemporaries, we have already noted how Charleton qualifies his materialistic atomism by premising "that God created [the] first *Matter* out of Nothing." But others actually tended to conflate the ideas of matter and nothingness, even to a point verging on the Manichaean notion of creation as a mixture of light and darkness. Peter Sterry (d. 1672), Oliver Cromwell's chaplain, goes so far as to say that "man is composed of the light of God, and his own proper darkness; These two the Schools call the Act and Potentiality, the form and the matter, being and not being, which constitute every Creature; The darkness or nothingness, which is the Creatures own, is the proper ground of sin."[33]

Similarly, Thomas Goodwin declares that God "in making this Visible World . . . began with a rude Lump, . . . which was actually *Nothing,* potentially *All things;* therefore call'd *Earth and Waters;* but in truth a Darkness and deep Confusion without form." As I have already noted, elsewhere Goodwin explicitly refers to the "Earth" of Gen. 1:1 as "Chaos." And he too makes the connection between the "nihility" of man's origins and moral evil: "The Creature being made out of Nothing, tends to a Deficiency."[34] As Robert Harris puts it, "Man was made out of *Nothing,* and therefore apt . . . to return into his first princi- ples, and . . . prone to privations." Yet the fault, of course, is not God's; "man is the cause of his own naughtinesse."[35]

The term "naughtinesse" neatly fuses the moral and meta- physical implications of the doctrine of *creatio ex nihilo,*[36] impli- cations that Milton takes pains to reject. First, so far as meta- physics is concerned, Milton asserts that it was impossible for God to have created the world *ex nihilo,* "not because of any defect of power or omnipotence on his part, but because it was necessary that something should have existed previously" (*CD,* p. 307). This reasoning is based partly on what Milton con- ceived to be the exact meaning of Scripture. He argues that in Hebrew, Greek, and Latin, and throughout Scripture, the verb "to create" implies "to make of something."[37] Hence, con- cludes Milton, all things

were made not out of nothing but out of matter, [and] matter must either have always existed, independently of God, or else originated from God at some point in time. That matter should have always existed independently of God is inconceivable . . . There remains only this solution, especially if we allow ourselves to be guided by scrip- ture, namely that all things came from God. Rom. xi.36: *from him and through him and in him are all things;* I Cor. viii.6: *one God, the Father, from whom all things are, – from,* as the Greek reads in both cases. [*CD,* p. 307]

Of course this doctrine of *creatio ex deo* does not mean that God is material in the way in which the table I am writing on is material, for as Raphael says in *Paradise Lost* in his own enun- ciation of the doctrine:

> one almighty is, from whom
> All things proceed, and up to him return,
> If not depraved from good, created all
> Such to perfection, one first matter all,
> Indued with various forms, various degrees
> Of substance.
>
> [5.469–74]

Although this one substance includes what is usually distinguished as "body" and "spirit" (5.478), Milton's doctrine clearly separates him from the tradition that views these as radically different kinds of substance, just as it involves him in a rejection of the world's original "naughtinesse."[38]

That rejection, as I have suggested, is largely motivated by Milton's general concern for the interests of theodicy. For the meonic tradition, of which the doctrine of *creatio ex nihilo* is an outgrowth, being is essentially good, nonbeing essentially evil.[39] All created things, because it is out of nothing that they are created, accordingly retain a necessary element of nihility and are metaphysically evil in more than the merely technical sense of "less good than the Good." The problem for theodicy is that, given this doctrine, the creation and thus the individual creature are seen as coming from the hand of the creator in an already imperfect state; and he, therefore, not the creature, is responsible for it. Hence the moral dimension of this more generally metaphysical issue: Does the creation ipso facto entail "fallenness" in some sense? If so, how can God be justified? A theodicy tied to *creatio ex nihilo* must somehow explain why God would confine the human spirit in the base prison house of naughty corporeality – in what Milton himself, in his perhaps more Neoplatonic youth, called "a darksome house of mortal clay."[40] But Milton's later teaching that matter comes not from nothing but from God puts a radically different complexion on the problem. Matter is now seen as being essentially good; and no longer is doubt cast on the divine wisdom for creating a universe that, according to the meonic tradition, must exist in what can properly be called a metaphysically evil state from its very beginning. Rather, asserts Milton, the "original matter was not an evil thing, nor to be thought of as worthless: it was good, and it contained the seeds of all subsequent good. It was a substance, and could only have derived from the source of all substance" (*CD*, p. 308).

Milton's mention of "the seeds" of good, furthermore, indicates how he avoids the dilemma in which Rutherford seems to entangle himself. Just as the view of God as material entails the conclusion that matter is neither prior to nor beside God, nor created, so the view that potentiality inheres in such divinely originated matter implies the same thing for potentiality: It is neither independent of God nor created. Matter and potentiality are thus parallel with each other, as they are for Peter Sterry; but in contrast to the position Sterry represents, they are not parallel to darkness, nothingness, or sin. In the view Milton presents, therefore – in contrast to the cosmogony he rejects, and with profound implications for theodicy – the potentiality inherent in the stuff of creation is not prejudiced or weighted toward the actualization of evil. God is good, and so is the stuff he makes.

Two points remain to be made in connection with Rutherford, who as we have noticed follows Aristotle in seeing actuality as prior to potentiality. Rutherford applies this principle by way of proving that God himself is prior to all necessity, possibility, and impossibility. And of course his assumption in so doing is, as scholastic theology asserts, that God is "Actus Purus," wholly and purely actual. This assumption Milton explicitly rejects: "God cannot rightly be called Actus Purus, or pure actuality, as is customary in Aristotle, for thus he could do nothing except what he does do, and he would do that of necessity, although in fact he is omnipotent and utterly free in his actions."[41] Remarkably, Milton denies God's pure actuality, and so implies potentiality in God, for the very reason that Rutherford rejects the notion of eternally real possibilities:

namely, in order to safeguard divine freedom and omnipotence. Rutherford attacks those who postulate the existence of real beings coeternal with God ("entia realia coaeterna Deo"), because, he implies, such a postulation contradicts Gen. 1:1, which teaches that all things came about by the determination of God, by means of his free creation, and not by means of a coeternal or "natural" emanation.[42] But Milton, again, points to a third alternative. Because any primordial possibility and necessity are internal, whereas creation is external, Milton is able to claim, as we have seen, that "in God a certain immutable internal necessity to do good, independent of all outside influence, can be consistent with absolute freedom of action." He adds, "Nor, incidentally, do I concede the point that there is in God any necessity to act" (*CD*, p. 159) – and here he distinguishes himself from the sort of Neoplatonic notion of necessary emanation that Rutherford thinks only his own position avoids. In contrast to Rutherford, therefore (who insists that a possibility is not something real),[43] Milton establishes a metaphysical basis for conceiving of necessity and possibility as being real, even before creation; yet he does so in a way that not only avoids dualism but also positively enhances the freedom and omnipotence of God.

And finally, in order to ensure divine freedom, Milton seeks to purge terms such as "nature" and "fate" of their absolute or deterministic connotations. The etymology of both of these words, he contends, reveals that each is relative: Neither is "to be identified with [the] supreme being . . . Nature or *natura* implies by its very name that it was *natam*, born . . . Surely, too, fate or *fatum* is only what is *fatum*, spoken, by some almighty power." In this way Milton signals, virtually at the beginning of his treatise,[44] that even when he uses terms drawn from pagan philosophy, he does so undualistically – within the bounds, one might say, of the full sense of theodicy's cardinal proposition (1), that God is omnipotent.

Creation, new creation, and the theodicy of *Paradise Lost*

In *Paradise Lost* the themes discussed in this chapter are summed up by God himself just before the account in book 7 of the days of creation from Gen. 1. The Father declares:

> thou my Word, begotten Son, by thee
> This [creation] I perform, speak thou, and be it done:
> My overshadowing spirit and might with thee
> I send along, ride forth, and bid the deep
> Within appointed bounds be heaven and earth,
> Boundless the deep, because I am who fill
> Infinitude, nor vacuous the space.
> Though I uncircumscribed my self retire,
> And put not forth my goodness, which is free
> To act or not, necessity and chance
> Approach not me, and what I will is fate.
>
> [7.163–73]

Recognizing the philosophical and theological issues that this passage engages, we are now ready to examine Milton's poetic presentation of divine omnipotence and goodness in action.[45]

As a way of leading from general principles to a consideration of the poetic presentation of creation in *Paradise Lost*, let me review some of the main similarities and differences between Milton's position, as stated in the *Christian Doctrine,* and that of his more orthodox contemporaries. For the sake of simplicity, I would like to take William Pemble's chapter "Of Creation," which opens his *Treatise of the Providence of God,*[46] as representative of the latter. Pemble says that "creation . . . is the action of God, whereby out of nothing he brought forth Nature, and all things in Nature" (p. 265); Milton, although agreeing about the relative status of nature, declares that "God produced all things not out of nothing but out of himself" (p. 310). With Pemble, Milton would agree that there can be no "eternal substance, which is not God" (p. 266), but he avoids the doctrine of *creatio ex nihilo* by assuming that God *is* that eternal substance, from which all other derive. Pemble, incidentally, believes "the world was created . . . *in the beginning,* that is, in the beginning of time, or together *with time,* rather than *in time*" (p. 267); but Milton sees no reason why time and motion, "according to our concepts of 'before' and 'after,' " could not "have existed before this world was made" (pp. 313–14). Pemble distinguishes the creation of "spiritual . . . substances, as the Angels, . . . which are void of matter," from "all corporall and materiall substances" (p. 267); Milton, as we have seen, teaches – from the mouth of an angel – that all things derive from "*one* first matter" (*PL,* 5.472). Both would agree that God created, as Pemble says, "of his good pleasure, no necessity urging him, no power of the matter he took helping him" (p. 268). But whereas Milton describes the initial production of matter "in a confused and disordered state" (p. 308), Pemble describes the same thing only to reject it: "The first Matter, that huge lump, a rude and indigested heape, darke and obscure, . . . the *Chaos* . . . seemes not fit to be admitted." For, among other reasons, God "is not the Author of Confusion" (p. 267). Milton, I believe, would see this objection as part of the problem of evil as a whole: "You will say, how can something corruptible result from something incorruptible?" But the answer, he points out, is no easier even if one accepts *creatio ex nihilo.* And indeed, the same problem presents itself on the moral level: "How can anything sinful have come . . . from God?" (pp. 308–9). Milton's bold presentation of creation and Chaos in *Paradise Lost,* I want to suggest, is an integral part of his answer to both questions.

In examining that presentation we must return to Gen. 1, particularly verses 1 and 2, with which this chapter began and which most Christian discussions of creation have likewise taken as their starting point. Exegetically, it might be argued that Milton's assumption of a preexisting material of any sort goes beyond what the Scriptures teach. However, the question is not whether he goes beyond it but whether he goes against it. The fact that Gen. 1:2 does seem to suggest some state that preceded the six days' creation, but does not fill in any details, has allowed, indeed fueled, Christian speculation concerning what was "before the beginning." I trust I have already established that the notion of some preexisting stuff of creation need imply no slur on God's creative freedom. It is certainly hard to see what evidence there is for Patrides' claim that "the Mosaic narrative . . . is essentially dualistic."[47] In fact the Mosaic account is silent on the question what that which is "without form, and void" implies; and it is precisely this that puts the onus on the interpreter of Genesis to make his account undualistic.

Of course, as Patrides clearly shows, in order to accommodate cosmogonies such as Plato's without incurring the charge of dualism, apologists as early as Irenaeus and Tertullian "proposed that God had created . . . formless matter in advance of the six day's [*sic*] work," and other, later apologists went even further and "postulated *two* creations: a first creation that resulted in the *ex nihilo* production of chaos ('from Absolute Notbeing to Being'), and a secondary creation during which order was imposed upon the 'first matter' ('from Potentiality to Actuality')."[48] It is just such a twofold creation that Charleton envisages in his antidualistic version of materialistic atomism, and that Pemble, as we have seen, rejects.[49] However, Patrides goes on to claim that *"Paradise Lost* sustains unreservedly the secondary creation," and that the " 'first matter' is . . . described . . . in broadly traditional terms."[50] I should not like to deny that Milton's account exhibits traditional characteristics. However, we must not allow generalized notions of what is traditional, nor Milton's prose, either, to prevent his poetry from speaking for itself. And if we do let it speak for itself, what in fact it tells of is not a twofold, but broadly a threefold, creation.

In the *Christian Doctrine* Milton does not distinguish various stages of creation as such; in describing the "original matter" that came from God he simply says that "it was in a confused and disordered state at first, but afterwards he made it ordered and beautiful" (p. 308). But in *Paradise Lost* we can discern a first stage – not yet creation proper – in which prime matter is in some way "alienated" from God, rendered external to him; a second stage in which some but not all of that matter is chosen to be the stuff of this visible world; and a third stage in which that stuff receives its actual forms. The result of the first stage is Chaos; and we first meet it in book 2, where Satan, Sin, and Death look out from the gates of hell[51] onto

> the hoary deep, a dark
> Illimitable ocean without bound,
> Without dimension, where length, breadth, and highth,
> And time and place are lost; where eldest Night
> And Chaos, ancestors of Nature, hold
> Eternal anarchy, amidst the noise
> Of endless wars, and by confusion stand.
>
> [2.891–7]

And we meet with Chaos again in book 7, where this time from heaven's gates the Father, Word, and Spirit view the same "immeasurable abyss / Outrageous as a sea, dark, wasteful, wild" (7.211–12). If our minds are concerned only with "traditional" notions, then the temptation will be to identify that which is viewed from the gates of heaven and hell with "the deep" or "the abyss"[52] of Gen. 1:2 – which would be a mistake. For so far as Milton is concerned, these two terms are generic; and the fact that they can describe Chaos does not mean that whenever Milton uses them it is Chaos to which he must be referring.

The distinction between Chaos and the deep of Gen. 1:2[53] first emerges at the beginning of book 3, where the poet invokes that holy light which "as with a mantle [did] invest / The rising world of waters dark and deep, / Won from the void and formless infinite" (3.10–12). Chaos is consistently acknowledged to be "infinite," "illimitable," "immeasurable," "without bound";[54] the world that Gen. 1:1 speaks of God as creating is not so. As we read in the account of creation in book 7, God commands his Son to "ride forth, and bid the deep / Within appointed bounds be heaven and earth, / Boundless the deep"

(7.166–8). Heaven and earth are bounded; Chaos – the "deep" referred to here – is bound*less*. What takes place in the second stage of creation broadly conceived (actually the beginning of this world per se, as in Gen. 1:1) is precisely the establishing of limits. What is asserted in the first sentence of the Bible Milton depicts as the work of God's "golden compasses" in Chaos:

> One foot he centred, and the other turned
> Round through the vast profundity obscure,
> And said, Thus far extend, thus far thy bounds,
> This be thy just circumference, O world.
>
> > [7.228–31]

God dubs that which he has demarcated "world," despite the fact that there is as yet nothing else to distinguish it from the rest of Chaos. For as Milton continues:

> Thus God the heaven created, thus the earth,
> Matter unformed and void: darkness profound
> Covered the abyss.
>
> > [7.232–4]

Hence the matter mentioned here cannot be coextensive with that "one first matter," mentioned by Raphael (5.472–4), of which all things, in various forms and degrees, consist, although it may be the same sort of stuff; and likewise the "matter unformed and void" that composes the newly circumscribed world contrasts, by virtue of its finite bounds, with "the void and formless *infinite*" known as Chaos. In this sense, then, Chaos is, as it were, "before the beginning"; the beginning itself involves merely a demarcating of territory within Chaos, territory that is then warmed and vitalized by the spirit (7.234 ff.); and the third stage consists of the six days' work of which we read in Gen. 1:3–31, and which Milton describes in the rest of book 7.

Now the fact that Milton in *Paradise Lost* expands the creation from two stages to three, so going beyond both tradition and his own prose treatise, is of more than merely technical importance. The traditional two-stage theory has the limitation that

all of Chaos gets used up in the second stage. But just as Milton
needed the doctrine of *creatio ex deo* in order to establish that
the "original matter . . . was good, and . . . contained the seeds
of all subsequent good" (*CD*, p. 308), so, in order that he might
do justice also to the fact of *evil*, he needed to retain an infinite
Chaos even after the world was created.[55] In *Paradise Lost*, as in
the *Christian Doctrine*, God is omnipotent, free, and wholly
good. He is also fundamentally material. To allow the seeds of
good to grow and bear fruit beyond himself, God had first to
make a "beyond." Moreover, if all this is conceived spatially,
and if the "beyond" is not to be surrounded by God, then it,
like God, will be infinite. As God is its origin, however, no
dualism follows. In *Paradise Lost*, coming from the very mouth
of God, that point is emphatic: The deep (in this case Chaos) is
"boundless" only as a result of God's own infinitude. God's
omnipotence is compromised by no pagan fate, no Platonic
"necessity" – not by any internal "pure actuality," not even by
an infinity which he himself creates (7:168–70). For the deep is
boundless only *because* God himself is both boundless and free,
if he chooses, to place certain limits on himself for the sake of
putting forth what amounts to a vast ocean of potentiality. Furthermore, although Milton undoubtedly believes that his
account is "true," he also quickly reminds us that it is not literal, but accommodated to "process of speech," "told as earthly
notion can receive" (7.178–9). In this way he makes his presentation of Chaos and creation consciously mythic, even while
recognizing that symbol and myth have literal implications,
and presenting therefore – from the mouth of God himself – a
remarkable case for the consistency of Chaos with divine
omnipotence.

Now the symbolic aspects of Milton's Chaos, like the more
literal aspects that have been emphasized so far, have an inti-
mate connection with theodicy, particularly in its literary form.
In the *Christian Doctrine,* as we have seen, Milton's assertion of
the essential goodness of matter leads him to ask how "anything sinful [can] have come from that virtue and efficiency

which themselves proceed from God." He answers with another question:

Really it is not the matter nor the form which sins. When matter or form has gone out from God and become the property of another, what is there to prevent its being infected and polluted, since it is now in a mutable state, by the calculations of the devil or of man, calculations which proceed from these creatures themselves? [P. 309]

In *Paradise Lost*, Milton goes further and gives to the relationship between Chaos and freedom, between metaphysical and moral good and evil, poetic life and shape.[56] For one thing, the poem provides a vehicle for dramatic parallels between divine and creaturely creativity. As we have seen, God dissociates himself from necessity and chance; his goodness is free to act or not (7.171–3). In book 3 he has also dissociated his creatures' freedom from fate or necessity: He "ordained [men's] freedom, they themselves ordained their fall" (3.127–8). God is responsible for man's having freedom in the first place; man is responsible for how he uses it. God, as it were, provides the matter, and it is up to the creature to give it form. Just as God "retires" himself in order to provide the matter, the potentiality, which will receive form in his positive act of creation, so creaturely freedom involves a self-limitation of God as a means of providing the stuff of that freedom which man himself is to exercise. God in creation actualizes possible goods that exist in Chaos in a state of mere potentiality; and man, if he obeys God, will be creative and free after the pattern that God has thus set for him.

However, in the preactual abyss of Chaos there are evil possibilities as well, and likewise man's freedom to create and enjoy is accompanied by the possibility of destruction and self-enthrallment (3.125). As Aristotle says in his section on actuality and potentiality, mentioned earlier, "Every potency is at the same time a potency of the opposite."[57] In Chaos this results in the menacing appearance of its "inhabitants." In God's new world it results in the possibility of disobedience and moral disintegration. Such is the nature of potentiality. And yet the existence of Chaos and of creaturely freedom, undetermined by the sovereign will of God, is itself something that he has sovereignly decreed, and for a good purpose.[58]

Opposed to that good purpose, of course, is Satan; and as we follow his career in *Paradise Lost* we see how Chaos and creaturely freedom not only parallel each other in important ways, but at times actually intersect. As has been noted, we first meet Chaos as Satan looks out on it from the gates of hell; and with great irony Milton intertwines its symbolic and literal roles. What we see is a confusion where

> Hot, Cold, Moist, and Dry, four champions fierce
> Strive . . . for mastery, and to battle bring
> Their embryon atoms.
>
>   .   .   .
>
> To whom these most adhere,
> He rules a moment; Chaos umpire sits,
> And by decision more embroils the fray
> By which he reigns: next him high arbiter
> Chance governs all. Into this wild abyss,
> The womb of nature and perhaps her grave,
> Of neither sea, nor shore, nor air, nor fire,
> But all these in their pregnant causes mixed
> Confusedly, and which thus must ever fight,
> Unless the almighty maker them ordain
> His dark materials to create more worlds.
>   [2.898–900, 906–16]

Literally, of course, as Walter Clyde Curry says, Chaos can "logically be identified with that which . . . the Deity has prepared for the reception of forms in creation,"[59] although one should add that only what God marks out with his compasses will in fact receive form from him. For in this infinite receptacle of unformed matter are entire possible worlds that, one infers, God leaves forever merely possible and uncreated.

But less literally, we see Chaos as what Roy Daniells calls "a wild amoral ocean from which God has in some sense . . . retracted his controlling power."[60] The "rulers" of the domain are Chaos and Chance: What a fine picture of any world without God! The scene is certainly Satan's view in more ways than one. Concerning his "world view" in the philosophic sense, it is significant that Satan alone in *Paradise Lost* speaks in dualistic terms, referring to his voyage through "*unoriginal* Night and Chaos wild" (10.477) and implying thereby the pagan view of some primordial state that is uncreated and without origin. Moreover, considering that his project is to cross Chaos in order to corrupt the newly created pair in Paradise, we are not unjustified in viewing Satan's activities themselves as the moral equivalent of what God originally purges from the still chaotic earth in the process of creation: "cold infernal dregs / Adverse to life" (7.238–9).

Now Satan, who has already been explicitly likened to "that sea-beast / Leviathan" (1.200–1), makes his voyage across the deep to this world; and we can hardly fail to recall this and other biblical images of evil beasts emerging from the sea. Yet without in the least minimizing the nefariousness of Satan, Milton keeps reminding us that the deep Satan has navigated[61] continues to present both evil and good possibilities, which in Chaos as well as in creaturely freedom exist in poignant proximity.

The natural geography of Eden itself emphasizes this proximity of good and evil. Milton in fact presents earth as being built on the abyss and Paradise in turn as being planted on the earth, in the east of Eden (4.208–10), on a plateau circled round by trees and by a wall, which together form a natural amphitheater. The elevated garden, of course, needs a water supply, and Milton describes the following hydrological system that God has devised for its irrigation:

> Southward through Eden went a river large,
> Nor changed his course, but through the shaggy hill
> Passed underneath ingulfed, for God had thrown
> That mountain as his garden mould high raised
> Upon the rapid current, which through veins
> Of porous earth with kindly thirst up drawn,
> Rose a fresh fountain, and with many a rill
> Watered the garden.
>
> [4.223–30]

Here we see a glorious life-giving fountain, ordered by God. Yet the description of it follows hard after Milton's account of the trees that grow near the fountain, in the center of the garden:

> in this pleasant soil
> His far more pleasant garden God ordained;
> Out of the fertile ground he caused to grow
> All trees of noblest kind for sight, smell, taste;
> And all amid them stood the tree of life,
> High eminent, blooming ambrosial fruit
> Of vegetable gold; and next to life
> Our death the tree of knowledge grew fast by.
>
> [4.214–21]

Now just as the proximity of these two trees reminds us of the precariousness of Paradise, given man's freedom, so later in *Paradise Lost* it becomes clear that the life-giving fountain itself opens up a possibility for the entrance of evil and death. In book 4, Satan enters by leaping over the garden walls, but then is discovered spying on Adam and Eve and expelled by the guardian angels who were sent to protect them. He therefore must find a more secret way of entering the garden. In book 9, Milton describes the scene and reminds us of the trees, of the fountain, and of their potentiality for good or ill:

> There was a place
> Now not, though sin, not time, first wrought the change,
> Where Tigris at the foot of Paradise
> Into a gulf shot under ground, till part
> Rose up a fountain by the tree of life;
> In with the river sunk, and with it rose
> Satan involved in rising mist, then sought
> Where to lie hid.
>
> [9.69–70]

Satan enters through the very fountain that God placed there for the purpose of supporting life in the garden – of feeding "flowers worthy of Paradise" (4.241). Is it not also thus with Chaos and with the freedom God has given to his creatures? Ordered and actualized in obedience to God, in accordance with his good will, the waters of the abyss and of freedom can be a life-giving current bubbling with ever-new possibilities of growth and creativity. But harnessed by an evil will they lead to destruction.

And, of course, harnessed by an evil will they are. As a result of Satan's journey across Chaos and his success in tempting Adam and Eve to disobey God, the entrance of Sin and Death into the world is now much more than a mere possibility. After the Fall

> in Paradise the hellish pair
> Too soon arrived, Sin there *in power* before,
> Once *actual*, now in body, and to dwell
> Habitual habitant; behind her Death
> Close following.
>
> [10.585–9; italics added]

As a result of God's circumscribing his own control over man's freedom, sin has been a potential inhabitant of Paradise from the moment of man's creation. But now that sin has taken place, some of those inhabitants of Chaos that are "adverse to life" have been actualized in Eden.[62]

However, although God has withdrawn his controlling power from Chaos and from human freedom, this does not imply that he no longer cares what happens to his creatures. On the contrary, God reveals his concerned opposition to evil both in the commands he gives and in the action he himself takes to counter evil. Indeed, in important respects, Milton's portrayal of God's response to sin exhibits what Berdjaev has characterized as divine tragedy. In Chapter 4 I shall examine the dilemma involved in man's creation: Either God makes him free and so capable of allegiance, faith, and love, and accordingly also prevents himself from determining men's choices; or else he does determine their choices, so preventing the entrance of sin, but also thereby precluding the existence of genuine creaturely freedom and those profound values which presuppose it. God elects the first alternative. Furthermore, as we shall see in Chapter 3, God, foreseeing man's fall, announces his

purpose of extending grace to lapsed mankind (3.130 ff.); and
the Son himself volunteers to be the means of that grace, to take
on himself the punishment of death (3.227 ff., 236 ff.).

It might be argued that on a subordinationist view such as
Milton's the Son does all the suffering, whereas the Father in
no meaningful sense engages in the kind of self-sacrifice
required by the notion of tragedy. But this objection underes-
timates the extent to which Milton is scriptural and orthodox in
his presentation of the relationship between Father and Son.[63]
Not only is the Son the Father's "chief delight" (3.169) and "sole
complacence" (3.276), but, so far as the creature is concerned,
he is also the very

> divine similitude,
> In whose conspicuous countenance, without cloud
> Made visible, the almighty Father shines,
> Whom else no creature can behold; on thee
> Impressed the effulgence of his glory abides,
> Transfused on thee his ample Spirit rests.
> He heaven of heavens and all the powers therein
> By thee created.
>
> [3.384–91]

By thus echoing the epistle to the Hebrews – "his Son . . . [God]
hath appointed heir of all things, by whom also he made the
world; Who being the brightness of his glory, and the express
image of his person" and so on (1:2–3) – Milton emphasizes that
the Son's agency in redemption parallels his agency in creation;
and in both cases it is the Father's power and character that are
made manifest.

The theme of the divine countenance (3.385) soon recurs in
the angels' song:

> No sooner did thy dear and only Son
> Perceive thee purposed not to doom frail man
> So strictly, but much more to pity inclined,
> He to appease thy wrath, and end the strife
> Of mercy and justice in thy face discerned,
> Regardless of the bliss wherein he sat

> Second to thee, offered himself to die
> For man's offence. O unexampled love,
> Love nowhere to be found less than divine!
>
> [3.403–11]

Although the creature cannot behold it except as mediated through the Son, God's countenance, the expression of his person and character, reveals strife. Presenting as he does this conflict of mercy and justice within the Godhead, occasioned by man's sin and resolved by the sacrificial death of the Son, Milton would appear to agree with Berdjaev that "tragedy exists within the Divine life itself."[64]

Milton also, it seems, would agree with Berdjaev that "the Divine sacrifice forms part of the plan of creation from the first."[65] At the beginning of book 1, chapter 4, of the *Christian Doctrine*, Milton says that predestination is the decree by which God, "BEFORE THE FOUNDATIONS OF THE WORLD WERE LAID, HAD MERCY ON THE HUMAN RACE ... ACCORDING TO HIS PURPOSE or plan IN CHRIST" (p. 168). And later in the same chapter, Milton emphasizes that "except for Christ, ... who was foreknown, no grace was decided upon, no reconciliation between God and man who was going to fall" (p. 175). Furthermore, in *Paradise Lost*, when the Son, anticipating his mediatorial role, suggests that man should not finally be lost, because he fell "circumvented ... by fraud, though joined / With his own folly" (3.150–1), God declares that the Son has "spoken as my thoughts are, all / As my eternal purpose hath decreed" (3.171–2). Clearly God's purpose, given the foreseen Fall, involved Christ's sacrifice from the beginning.

The relation of redemption to creation is emphasized again at the end of *Paradise Lost*. Having been given a series of visions covering Old Testament history and culminating in an account of the work of Christ, Adam responds, "Replete with joy and wonder":

> O goodness infinite, goodness immense!
> That all this good of evil shall produce,
> And evil turn to good; more wonderful

> Than that which by creation first brought forth
> Light out of darkness![66]

Redemption is here explicitly paralleled with creation and declared to continue and augment its work. Just as Chaos was reduced through the act of creation, so through redemption darkness is replaced with light, and "the abyss" itself takes on a new and positive meaning. At the end of time, as Michael recounts, Christ shall return

> to dissolve
> Satan with his perverted world, then raise
> From the conflagrant mass, purged and refined,
> New heavens, new earth, ages of endless date
> Founded in righteousness and peace and love
> To bring forth fruits joy and eternal bliss.
>
> [12.546–51]

And Adam replies to this glimpse of the new creation by exclaiming:

> How soon hath thy prediction, seer blest,
> Measured this transient world, the race of time,
> Till time stand fixed: beyond is all abyss,
> Eternity, whose end no eye can reach.
>
> [12.553–6]

Purged of the influence of evil by the redemptive power of God, the abyss is now identified with eternity itself, an infinite storehouse of creativity and meaning.

Finally, in *Paradise Lost*, Satan and Adam present contrasting pictures of the results of a journey through Chaos, which each of them in some sense endures.[67] Satan journeys through that realm where Chaos is umpire (2.907); arrives at the new creation, where "conscience wakes despair" (4.23) and where he experiences the hell within himself (4.20–1, 73–4); and yet refuses to repent (4.79–80). Adam, like Satan, experiences a fall; and the conscience that God had promised to place within fallen man as "umpire" (3.195) drives Adam, as he complains, into an "abyss of fears / And horrors . . . out of which / I find no way, from deep to deeper plunged" (10.842–4). And yet

God's promise that if men will listen to conscience, "Light after light well used they shall attain, / And to the end persisting, safe arrive" (3.196–7), is fulfilled. For despite the mazes in which his thinking wanders, Adam is led at least to an acceptance of his own responsibility (10.829–33). And although he and Eve court despair, they are led through it by the light of God's promise (10.1028–32) and by the remembrance of the mercy he has already shown them (10.1058 ff., 1093 ff.). By grace they come through the abyss; and, having acknowledged Christ as redeemer, Adam in book 12 is promised a "paradise within" (line 587) – the complete antithesis of the state at which Satan arrives.

Meanwhile, of course, for Adam and his race, the "ever-threatening storms / Of Chaos" will bluster round (3.425–6). But even in this fallen world, Chaos can be exploited for good by God, and by man in obedience to God. As Adam comes to recognize through Christ's example (12.561–79), suffering itself can be infused with meaning for the one who serves truth and is conscious of providential purpose. In this way all things can indeed be meaningfully asserted to "work together for good to them that love God, to them who are called according to his purpose" (Rom. 8:28). For although evil does exist in the world, God is omnipotent and wholly good, and so both able and willing to overcome evil. And yet this is genuine optimism, not the sort that survives at the cost of denying that evil actually and potently inhabits the world.

In *Paradise Lost*, the presence of Chaos helps obviate that theodically heretical sort of optimism. Both conceptually reinforcing and symbolically enriching his account of the origin and nature of evil, even while supporting a view of the omnipotence and goodness of the creator, Milton's presentation of Chaos deserves to be recognized as a highly important and highly original aspect of his justification of God's ways.

3

Assertion and justification: providence and theodicy

In the last chapter, one of my main concerns was how Christian theology could conceive of creation in such a way as to avoid dualism and retain a high view of divine omnipotence. Moreover, the discussion of theodicy led from creation to redemption – indeed, to a view of redemption as new creation. With that parallel in mind, I would like in this chapter to continue my account of the conceptual context of Milton's theodicy by examining more closely an important, soteriological aspect of the justification of God's ways. Just as Milton produced a cosmogonic model designed to safeguard divine goodness and sovereignty even while actually heightening his readers' awareness of evil's scope, character, and reality, so, I shall argue, the requirements of theodicy led him toward a soteriological model that aimed at emphasizing the mercy and power of God while retaining that creaturely agency without which evil could scarcely be accounted for in the first place.

So far as the historical context is concerned, I began in Chapter 1 with a few words of Coleridge's on Milton's object and on "the great controversy" of Milton's age, "the origination of evil"; Coleridge immediately continues his pronouncement by remarking: "The Arminians considered it a mere calamity. The Calvinists took away all human will."[1] Despite his possible oversimplification on this point, Coleridge nevertheless rightly draws attention to the central connection between Milton's great interest in theodicy and the major rift in seventeenth-century Reformed theology. This chapter will introduce that rift, indicate its connections with theodicy, and argue its relevance to a correct reading of *Paradise Lost*.

Milton and Arminianism: prolegomena

That Milton's later theology is Arminian, I take it, is not on the whole a controversial claim. The adjective has long been applied to his views. Samuel Johnson noted two centuries ago that Milton's theological opinions can be said "to have been first Calvinistical, and afterwards, perhaps when he began to hate the Presbyterians, to have tended toward Arminianism."[2] And Maurice Kelley, in his edition of Milton's *Christian Doctrine*, shows very clearly how Arminian that work is.[3] Nor, I take it, does Milton's direct knowledge of Arminius or lack thereof have much bearing on the validity of using the term Arminian to describe Milton's work. How many Marxists there must be who have scarcely read a word of Marx.

Just the same, terms such as "Arminian" – and "Calvinist," too – are capable of various meanings, and certain distinctions need to be made between them. Strongest in early seventeenth-century England was the so-called Arminianism of the right, associated primarily with the ecclesiastical policies of Archbishop Laud and unquestionably eschewed by Milton. This kind of Arminianism in fact made it difficult at first for Milton and his contemporaries to gain a clear understanding of Arminianism proper, of "Arminianism of the left."[4] In the earlier part of the seventeenth century, anything smacking of Arminianism of any sort was likely to be dismissed, by Puritans particularly, as popish and Pelagian; and it would seem that Milton himself, as I shall show more fully later, initially accepted this caricature, implying in 1642 that Arminians "deny originall sinne."[5]

In the present discussion, however, I shall for the most part ignore those who might in fact have deserved the charge of popery and Pelagianism, and take Arminianism to be the theology, especially as it concerns free will and grace, of Arminius and his followers condemned at the Synod of Dort, none of whom, so far as I can tell, denied "originall sinne." In so doing, I believe I follow most closely what Milton himself finally saw Arminianism as being. In 1673 he declared: "The *Arminian* . . . is condemn'd for setting up free will against free grace; but that Interpretation he disclaims in all his writings, and grounds himself largely upon Scripture only."[6] This, as I hope to show, is an accurate description of Arminius and his immediate followers. It also represents the nearest thing we have to an explicit declaration by Milton of his Arminian sympathies, because to say that a theologian "grounds himself largely upon Scripture only" was perhaps the highest compliment he could pay. Indeed, it was the claim he made for his own *Christian Doctrine:* "I devote my attention to the Holy Scriptures alone. I follow no other heresy or sect. I had not even studied any of the so-called heretical writers, when the blunders of those who are styled orthodox, and their unthinking distortions of the sense of scripture, first taught me to agree with their opponents whenever these agreed with the Bible" (pp. 123–4). It is the nature of Milton's agreement with some of these "so-called heretical writers" that I wish to explore.

The task is necessary because insufficient account has been taken of the nature of Milton's Arminianism and in particular its implications for *Paradise Lost.* Though few have gone as far as Joseph M. McDill, who claims that "there can be no doubt that in *Paradise Lost* Milton teaches the five points of Calvinism,"[7] a major tendency amongst some Milton critics has been tacitly to presuppose that Milton's view of God and his ways agrees with that of orthodox Calvinist theology. William Empson, for example, assumes that Milton conceives of a God who "was working for the Fall all along"[8] – a conception that belongs to a good deal of Calvinist, but not Arminian, teaching. Although Empson recognizes that Milton "came to give up" Calvinist predestination, he insists on referring to Milton's attempt "to make *his* God appear a bit less morally disgusting" (pp. 202, 200; italics added). It is difficult to see what point there is in holding Milton responsible for a conception of God he had decided to reject.

A more specific difficulty is alleged by Thomas Greene's account of what he considers to be one of the seeds of destruction for the epic genre, namely, "the questioning of the hero's independence":

> Heroic independence in *Paradise Lost* is weakened by Milton's juggling with the theological categories of grace and merit. If we were to grant "the better fortitude of Patience and Heroic Martyrdom" as a proper notion of epic heroism, we should still want to feel that fortitude to be the painful achievement of the hero. But Milton in more than one passage suggests that this fortitude is the gift of God. It is a little anticlimactic for the reader, after following tremulously the fallen couple's gropings toward redemption in Book Ten, to hear from the Father's lips that he has decreed it – that all of this tenderly human scene, this triumph of conjugal affection and tentative moral searching, occurred only by divine fiat. One might have been tempted to alter his ideas of heroism to include Adam's contrition, did he not encounter God's own curt dismissal of it:

> > He sorrows now, repents, and prayes contrite,
> > My motions in him, longer then they move,
> > His heart I know, how variable and vain
> > Self-left.[9]

Now if Greene were right – if Adam and Eve's repentance were the result merely of "divine fiat" – then we would indeed seem to be presented in *Paradise Lost* with a version of the theological determinism that accompanies Calvinist predestinarianism, as well as with the severe dramatic inconsistency or anticlimax Greene suggests. The same problem is alleged by Patrides, who, while denying that Milton presents the God of Calvinism, still feels that the passage referred to by Greene represents what he calls "the traditional 'inconsistency' of the Bible and St. Augustine": "upholding man's free will at one moment and denying it the next." The repentance we have witnessed, Patrides argues, accordingly seems "odd as well as unnatural," particularly "when we reach Milton's explanation of the episode":[10] "Prevenient Grace descending had removed / The stony from their hearts" (11.3–4). However, I propose that if we understand the Arminian character of the position Milton holds, then the beginning of book 11 will be seen as neither theologically nor dramatically inconsistent with what precedes it.

John Peter has complained that a common fault "in Milton criticism is to wrench the characters and incidents of *Paradise Lost* from their artistic context, and then to consider them as if they were autonomous or as if they were simple copies of their doctrinal or traditional equivalents, disregarding the significance which has been conferred upon them by the poem."[11] Though this charge can, I believe, be laid against those who uncritically read Calvinism into *Paradise Lost*, their errors will not be remedied by a similarly uncritical imposition upon the poem of Arminian doctrine. Therefore, I shall try at the outset simply to show what Arminianism is and what motivated its development, and then to indicate how the hypothesis of Milton's Arminianism can be supported by the artistic context in question. As we have seen, Patrides traces Milton's alleged brilliant "inconsistency" at least as far back in history as St. Augustine, and it is with him that we must begin.

Grace and free will: Augustinian roots

Consider briefly Augustine's teaching on grace and free will. The latter developed within the context of his doctrines of creation and the Fall. As we saw in Chapter 2, Augustine believes that man was created perfect, yet mutably so. That mutability was reflected in free will, according to which, if man chose, he could turn from God "toward lower things."[12] Sin being thus seen in terms of man's agency, God is absolved of direct responsibility for the existence of evil. "Of course," says Augustine,

no one would dare to believe or declare that it was beyond God's power to prevent the fall . . . But, in fact, God preferred not to use His own power, but to leave success or failure to the creature's choice. In this way, God could show both the immense evil that flows from the creature's pride and also the even greater good that comes from His grace.[13]

That grace, Augustine teaches, is to be considered a prerequisite to the accomplishment of any good; in fact, even in Eden good acts were possible only through divine assistance, whereas to go wrong was completely within man's own power. Augustine illustrates this claim with an analogy from living:

The act of living in a body is a positive act which is not a matter of choice but is only possible by the help of nourishment; whereas the choice not to live in the body is a negative act which is in our human power, as we see in the case of suicide. Thus, to remain living as one ought to live was not a matter of choice . . . but depended on the help of God, whereas to live ill, as one ought not to live, was in man's power; therefore, man was justly responsible for the cutting short of his happiness and the incurring of the penalty that followed.[14]

On the surface, this position may appear to make a mockery of human freedom, as if the latter rendered man an agent culpable of all sin but capable of nothing but sin. Although man can clearly be an instrument of good, Augustine may seem to imply that if a person's actions are good, the agency is God's; if evil, the agency is the person's own. However, if we examine the matter more closely, we see that there is an interpretation of Augustine's words quite in keeping with the task of theodicy. It is not really relevant here that man is independently capable of sin, any more than, in the analogy, a person's freedom either to carry on living or to commit suicide is nullified by the hypothetical possibility of starving to death. Rather, the important question is this: *Given the means* of avoiding starvation, does one's carrying on living truly depend upon one's decision about whether or not to commit suicide? If it does, then one's free will is indeed decisive with respect to one's living or dying; and, in the same way, Adam's free will would have operated as meaningfully in deciding not to eat of the forbidden fruit as it did in his act of disobedience, even though obedience, according to Augustine, presupposed divine assistance. What certainly would be inimical to theodicy is a situation in which God had withdrawn his grace and then accused Adam of willful disobedience – something that would amount to claiming that one who starved to death unwillingly was a suicide. But, at least in the chapter of the *City of God* just quoted, Augustine does not go that far; and we ought to recognize in his analogy a coherent model of how man can be innately incapable of good and yet responsible for evil.

The notions of free will and responsibility will be explored further in the next two chapters; however, a few points concerning grace and choice need to be interjected now. First, "grace" is a term that primarily concerns matters of salvation – "by grace are ye saved through faith" (Eph. 2:8) – although many theologians, Augustine included, extend it to apply to any good work. The picture is further complicated by the fact that there are also many theologians who deny that salvation or the choice to accept salvation can be considered a good *work*. In the present short discussion, I see no possibility of disambiguating the term "grace" in this regard, and simply hope that acknowledging its relative imprecision will itself help to prevent confusion. In any case, as we have already seen, the crux in *Paradise Lost* has to do with salvation and how it occurs.

Secondly, this recognition that grace and free will primarily concern matters of salvation and damnation will discourage the uncritical acceptance of the pagan, ethical model of choice as involving fundamentally a decision between vice and virtue. That sort of choice, traditionally, is like the one Hercules faced when he came to the fork in the road and was counseled by Pleasure (or Vice) to follow her into the left fork and by Virtue to follow her into the right.[15] This parting of the ways (*bivium*) is symbolized by "the Pythagorean letter," *Y*;[16] and the general picture is that of a person standing in neither the way of vice nor the way of virtue but having to choose between these ways. However, it is also a model of choice that has been rejected by Christian thinkers from very early on, its continued influence notwithstanding.

An example of that rejection, and incidentally one that Milton was almost certainly familiar with, is Lactantius's discussion of the *duae viae* in his *Divine Institutes.*[17] As he acknowledges, pagan poets and philosophers "say that the course of human life resembles the letter Y, because every one of men, when he has reached the threshold of early youth, and has arrived at the place 'where the way divides itself into two parts' [*Aeneid*, VI, 540] is in doubt, and hesitates, and does not know to which side he should rather turn himself." Although admitting an element of truth in such accounts, Lactantius complains that they are limited by their authors' pagan, fundamentally secular perspectives; and he asserts that "we . . . speak better and more truly, who say that the two ways belong to heaven and hell." Moreover, the pagans

do not represent any as entering upon that way except boys and young men . . . We, on the other hand, lead those of each sex, every age and race, into this heavenly path . . . The shape also of the ways themselves is not as they supposed. For what need is there of the letter Y in matters which are different and opposed to one another? But the one which is better is turned towards the rising of the sun, the other which is worse towards its setting.[18]

In a Christian view, there is not one "neutral" road with two ways forking off it in the divergent directions of virtue and vice; there is but one road, which can be traveled in two opposite directions, toward light or toward darkness, toward heaven or toward hell. Furthermore, everyone is on that road, and the crucial question is in what direction they are moving. The point of Augustine's analogy of suicide is that one can travel downward on one's own, whereas to travel upward one needs help. Yet given the availability of that help, one is free to choose one's direction. And if one is traveling toward death, one will find no fork in the road: The only way to change direction is precisely to be turned around, *converted*.

There is, nevertheless, real difficulty in evaluating Augustine's doctrine of grace, for there are places in his writings where he does indeed seem to imply a denial of the concept of free will upon which his theodicy depends. In arguing against the Pelagians, who "confide rather in [free will] for doing righteousness than in God's aid, and to glory every one in himself,

and not in the Lord,"[19] Augustine tended to depreciate free will
to the point where it could no longer be seen as meaningfully
decisive. In *On Grace and Free Will* he says that "God works in
the hearts of men to incline their wills whithersoever He wills,
whether to good deeds according to His mercy, or to evil after
their own deserts."[20] If this claim is correct, then a theodicy
based on man's responsibility for sin is surely not possible; for
once man's will is seen as determined by the prior will of God,
it can no longer be said in the case of any particular sin that the
sinner could have chosen otherwise, and one is reduced to
seeing all human actions, both good and evil, as the result of
sheer divine will.[21] Thus it can appear, as N. P. Williams has
put it, that Augustine tries "to run with the hare and hunt with
the hounds. He wants to keep freedom in order to reserve
man's responsibility for actual sin, and yet he wishes to throw
it overboard in order to provide scope for irresistible grace."[22]
The term "irresistible grace" anticipates the development of
Augustine's thought by Reformers such as Luther and Calvin.
Nevertheless, as suggested earlier, Augustine is not consistently predestinarian in the later, Calvinist sense, and this dis-
crepancy allowed his support to be enlisted on opposite sides
of disputes that were to arise in the future. As Williams says in
a slightly different context, "The Reformation . . . was in great
measure the posthumous rebellion of Augustine with Augustine" (p. 321).

Reformation theology and the battle for theodicy

The classic instance of this Augustinian conflict in the early Reformation is the debate on free will between Erasmus and
Luther. Erasmus opposes Luther's determinism primarily in
the interests of theodicy, saying in *The Free Will* that "care
should be taken not to deny the freedom of the will, while
praising faith. For if this happens, there is no telling how the
problem of divine justice and mercy could be solved."[23] He
agrees with Augustine insofar as "Augustine challenges the

view that man, subject to sin, can better himself or act to save himself. Only undeserved divine grace can spur man supernaturally to wish that which will lead to eternal life. This is known to some as prevenient grace" (p. 28). Such teaching is, as I have argued, consonant with the purposes of theodicy so long as the gift of prevenient grace is in fact bestowed: One is culpable or not in respect to a given act only if one's own choice is meaningfully decisive in respect to that act, regardless of the origin of the power by which what one chooses is actually effected or enabled – just as the potential suicide will be responsible for his dying or not dying only if he has the means to avoid starving to death, regardless of the origin of those means. Accordingly, Erasmus avoids rejecting the necessity of prevenient grace (thereby avoiding Pelagianism, with which Luther unjustly charges him), but, in order to safeguard theodicy, simply adds the assumption that "the goodness of God does not refuse to any mortals this . . . grace" (p. 29). Such a provision curbs the (determinist) predestinarian tendency of the doctrine of grace in Augustine (who "gained a more unfavorable view of the free will, because of his fight with Pelagius than he had held before" [p. 85]), a tendency that, as Erasmus recognizes, leads in some Reformers to the opinion that he considers "worst of all": "that the free will is an empty name and . . . that rather God causes in us evil as well as good, and that everything happens of mere necessity" (p. 31).

In responding to Erasmus, Luther in *The Bondage of the Will* confirms and in a way fulfills the dangers that his opponent has pointed out, preferring to imperil the notion of divine justice rather than deny, as he thinks Erasmus's position does, divine prescience and omnipotence. Arguing that these two attributes of God entail our being under necessity,[24] Luther claims that God "foresees, purposes and does all things according to His immutable, eternal and infallible will. This thunderbolt throws free will flat and utterly dashes it to pieces" (p. 106). But Erasmus would maintain that such a position is inconsistent with any conception of either the goodness of God or the responsibility of man: "Everybody would judge . . . [a] lord cruel and unjust . . . were he to have his servant flogged for his stature, or protruding nose, or some lack of elegance. Would he not be justified in complaining against the lord who had him flogged: why should I suffer punishment for something that is not in my power to change?" (p. 83). Erasmus, recognizing the difficulty of reconciling foreknowledge with free will, suggests that possibly it is one of those things that "God wishes to remain totally unknown to us" (p. 9), although elsewhere he proposes that the matter has been explained sufficiently by Lorenzo Valla (who recapitulates Boethius): "Foreknowledge does not cause what is to take place. Even we know many things which will be happening. They will not happen because we know them, but vice versa" (p. 49). However, this was not a position that had much influence on Luther.

The necessitarianism that Luther defended became fully worked into the system of Reformation theology, again with apparent disregard for the interests of theodicy, in Calvin's doctrine of double predestination. Predestination, says Calvin in his *Institutes of the Christian Religion,* is "the eternal decree of God," by which "some are preordained to eternal life, others to eternal damnation."[25] Calvin denies, moreover, that this decree is in any way contingent upon the foreseen free acts or choices of men, there being no such freedom as might be presupposed by those who would see predestination as a conditional decree. Rather, Calvin teaches, in giving an account of predestination "we must always return to the mere pleasure of the divine will, the cause of which is hidden in [God] himself" (3.23.4). "Nor ought it to seem absurd . . . [to say] that God not only foresaw the fall of the first man, and in him the ruin of his posterity; but also at his own pleasure arranged it" (3.23.7). And to Adam's posterity "there is a universal call, by which God . . . invites all men alike [to come to him], even those for whom he designs the call to be a savour of death, and the ground of a severer condemnation" (3.14.8).

Thus, Calvin's doctrine of predestination can indeed appear

to make God as cruel and unjust as the lord in Erasmus's little parable who had his servant flogged for something that he had no power to do anything about. It also thereby threatens to undermine the assumption (as Samuel Hoard put it in 1633) that "Justice, Mercy, Truth, and Holinesse in God are the same in nature with these virtues in men, though infinitely differing in degree" – an assumption without which "we may not safely imitate God, as we are commanded, Be ye perfect as your heavenly Father is perfect."[26] For the only way of preventing one's theology from throwing open the possibility of "devil-worship" is, as D. P. Walker has said, "to make the ideas of goodness, justice, etc., anterior to . . . God's decrees."[27]

Yet Calvin does face up to the charge that his position entails a denial of divine justice, though he rejects the charge on the basis of what he sees as the impossibility of man's in any way judging the will of God; for "truly does Augustine maintain that it is perverse to measure divine by the standard of human justice" (3.24.17); "the will of God is the supreme rule of righteousness, so that everything which he wills must be held to be righteous by the mere fact of his willing it" (3.23.2). In this connection, it is also important to note that Calvin would deny that he is a voluntarist. He does *not* say that something *is* righteous by the mere fact of God's willing it; nor will he be numbered among those who declare God to be "exlex."[28] However, when he says that men "are not to seek for any cause beyond [God's] will" (3.22.11), one inevitably wonders whether this is not because the divine will is fundamentally arbitrary. With other "foolish men," one may indeed be inclined to "ask why God is offended with his creatures, who have not provoked him by any previous offence," or to suggest that "to devote to destruction whomsoever he pleases, more resembles the caprice of a tyrant than the legal sentence of a judge," as Calvin himself puts it (3.23.2). But so long as the divine will alone is considered the highest rule of justice, in practice it will follow that what God does is just, merely by definition, and the doubt concerning the meaningfulness of any assertion of God's goodness will thus be rendered insoluble. By placing the reason for God's will quite beyond human ken, Calvin ends up being a voluntarist in practice if not in theory, so that any argument he presents for the justice of God becomes circular and hence meaningless. And in this sense, I would suggest, Calvin begs the theodical question.

We can see, in any case, why Calvin's doctrine of predestination might have become the occasion for so much controversy. Although it was not the main emphasis of his theology – he does not propound it until the third book of his *Institutes* – it was nevertheless that which was most strenuously attacked and so also that which Calvin's followers had most strenuously to defend. Indeed, it was in response to doctrinal rebellion from within the Reformed confession itself that *orthodox* Calvinism as such developed.

In 1591 a Dutch Reformed pastor by the name of Jacobus Arminius was called upon to refute the errors of two Delft ministers who had been assigned to argue against Coornhert, the humanist critic of Calvinism, but who in so doing had modified their own position to such an extent that it, too, deviated from what was considered acceptable Reformed teaching.[29] Arminius was a likely choice to represent Calvinism, as he had studied in Geneva with Theodore Beza, Calvin's successor. However, either the domino effect continued, with Arminius falling away from the position he was trying to justify, or else he secretly had disagreed with his former teacher for some time.[30] In any case, his refutation never appeared, and his deviation from the Calvinist norm became known. In 1603 he was installed as professor of divinity at the University of Leyden, where he began to come under fire for his views. The controversy grew, though Arminius himself died prematurely in 1609, and in 1610 his followers organized themselves under the leadership of a man named Uitenbogaert. These "Remonstrants" published in the same year "Five Arminian Articles," also known as the Remonstrance of 1610.[31] The Synod of Dort of 1618–19 was convened expressly to deal with the views of Arminius and the Remonstrants. The result, ecclesiastically and politically, was a great victory for orthodox Calvinism, with the Remonstrants being forced into one form of exile or another. Theologically, the upshot was the formulation of "Five Heads of Doctrine" to correspond to the Remonstrant articles, the former being better known as the "five points" of Calvinism: namely, (1) unconditional election, (2) limited atonement, (3) the total depravity of man, (4) God's irresistible grace, and (5) the perseverance of the saints through God's preserving grace. These points thus enshrined the doctrine of predestination as the most dominant feature of orthodox Calvinist theology in the seventeenth century and have remained its shibboleth ever since.

Arminius's ideas seem to have developed in the first place primarily out of an attempt to bring Reformed theology into line with the requirements of theodicy. Like Erasmus before him, he placed emphasis on human freedom, while at the same time insisting that "free will is unable to begin or to perfect any true and spiritual good, without grace":

That I may not be said, like Pelagius, to practice delusion with regard to the word "grace," I mean by it that which is the grace of Christ and which belongs to regeneration. I affirm, therefore, that this grace is simply and absolutely necessary for the illumination of the mind, the due ordering of the affections, and the inclination of the will to that which is good. It . . . infuses good thoughts into the mind, inspires good desires into the affections, and bends the will to carry into execution good thoughts and good desires. This grace [*praevenit*] goes before, accompanies, and follows; it excites, assists, operates that we will, and co-operates lest we will in vain.[32]

However, Arminius recognizes the problem that such a view of grace seems to entail in Augustine and almost certainly entails in Calvin – namely, that one's salvation depends on a sort of divine caprice. And, like Erasmus, he avoids the problem by positing that sufficient grace is offered to all: "Were the fact otherwise, the justice of God could not be defended in his condemning those who do not believe."[33] Furthermore, in contrast to the orthodox Calvinists, Arminius claims that grace is resistible rather than irresistible, and again he clearly is theodically motivated. In opposing those who represent grace "as acting with such potency that it cannot be resisted by any free creature," Arminius says:

> It is not our wish to do the least injury to Divine grace, by taking from it any thing that belongs to it. But let my brethren take care, that they themselves neither inflict an injury on Divine justice, by attributing that to it which it refuses; nor on Divine grace, by transforming it into something else, which cannot be called GRACE.[34]

Put in another way, if sufficient grace were not offered to all, then those to whom it was not offered would be incapable of willing to accept salvation, and so in this regard would in no meaningful sense be free; God alone, in withholding grace, would be responsible for those who perish without salvation. This state of affairs clearly being inconsistent with divine justice, a universal and sufficient grace must be assumed. Furthermore, if grace were irresistible, then all those to whom it was offered would become regenerate. But not everyone becomes regenerate, so that either grace is resistible or else it is not universally offered. As shown in the preceding argument, we must assume sufficient grace to be offered to all, and must therefore conclude that grace is resistible.

Thus Arminius reasoned, opposing Calvinist predestinarianism and, within the context of Reformed theology, trying to work out the implications of the view that goodness and justice are anterior to God's decrees. Arminius's followers, as has already been mentioned, published a list of these implications in 1610 in the form of five articles. The first, in accordance with the conviction that the human will plays a decisive role in accepting or rejecting salvation, declares that "God, by an eternal, unchangeable purpose in Jesus Christ his Son, before the foundation of the world, hath determined . . . to save . . . those who, through the grace of the Holy Ghost, shall believe on his Son Jesus, and shall persevere in his faith, through this grace."[35] This is conditional election, as opposed to the Calvinist assertion of unconditional election, by which God inexplicably decrees from eternity, without respect to any prior consideration of belief in men, that certain shall be saved, the rest damned. The second Arminian article, in accordance with the first, asserts that Christ "died for all men and for every man." For the Calvinist, on the other hand, because the decree of election to salvation preceded the decree of the means of salvation – namely, the sacrifice of Christ – the efficacy of that sacrifice was limited to the elect. Hence the doctrine of the "limited atonement," explicitly asserted at Dort.[36]

The third Arminian article is one that has occasionally been misunderstood. Seeing that the Calvinist tenet of the total depravity of man, as restated at Dort, was supposedly formulated in response to the third article, one might assume, as one modern writer has put it, that this article expressed "man's partial depravity and the co-operative ability of his fallen will."[37] But in fact what the third article states is this:

> That man has not saving grace of himself, nor of the energy of his free will, inasmuch as he, in the state of apostasy and sin, can of and by himself neither think, will, nor do any thing that is truly good; . . . but that it is needful that he be born again . . . and renewed in understanding, inclination, or will, and all his powers, in order that he may rightly understand, think, will, and effect what is truly good.

Such teaching is clearly in the tradition of Reformed theology, which, as we have seen, has its roots in Augustine's doctrine of grace. It resembles not at all the Pelagianism of which the Remonstrants were accused. And, as it stands, the Calvinist could scarcely find any objection to this article short of misrepresenting it, although this is what the third head of doctrine appears in fact to do. For the list of errors that the Synod of Dort claims to reject includes the teaching that "a corrupt and naturall man can so rightly vse common grace (by which they [the Remonstrants] meane the light of nature) or those gifts, which are left in him after the fall, that, by the good vse thereof, he may attaine to a greater, namely Euangelicall, or sauing grace, and by degrees at length saluation it selfe."[38] This, however, is not an opinion found in the statements of the Remonstrants, and appears rather to be a conveniently Pelagian-sounding version of the Arminian insistence on the importance of free will – packaged, as it were, for easy disposal.[39]

One must therefore take care not to join the detractors of Arminianism in misrepresenting it. Its teaching on divine grace, except for the insistence that grace is universally, sufficiently, but not irresistibly bestowed, is scarcely to be distinguished from that of Augustine or even of Calvin. The exceptions just mentioned have far-reaching implications, certainly; but they do not alter the view of the essential necessity of divine grace. The fourth Arminian article, for example – the one famous for its rejection of irresistible grace – is devoted primarily to reiterating the weakness of man and accordingly his need for the power of grace:

> This grace of God is the beginning, continuance, and accomplishment of all good, even to this extent, that the regenerate man himself, without prevenient or assisting, awakening, following and co-operative grace, can neither think, will, nor do good, nor withstand any temptations to evil; so that all good deeds or movements, that can be conceived, must be ascribed to the grace of God in Christ.

It is vital that we recognize this emphasis, for otherwise we shall be liable either to accept a caricature of Arminianism as Pelagian[40] or else to see as Calvinistic a teaching that is in fact not necessarily allied with Calvinist predestinarianism.

The fifth Arminian article is connected with the fourth: If grace is resistible, then the Christian may be free to reject his salvation even after it has first been accepted. However, the article avoids dogmatism and expresses only an uncertainty about whether those who have once received God's offered grace "are capable . . . of forsaking again the first beginnings of their life in Christ, . . . of becoming devoid of grace."[41] The Remonstrants declared that this is something that "must be more particularly determined out of the Holy Scripture, before we ourselves can teach it with full persuasion of our minds." And yet a doubt is all that was needed to mitigate the sense of security that often accompanied Calvinist predestinarian teaching and had in certain cases encouraged antinomianism such as that of the Ranters in England. In this sense, the fifth article (though the least theoretically developed of the five) may be seen as the one of greatest practical importance, because it took away the overconfidence that could lead to moral laxity and irresponsibility. I mention this aspect of Arminianism, not because the fifth article is very important for the present discussion of *Paradise Lost,* but because it completes the picture we have of the moral motives that informed Arminian teaching: Arminianism was concerned to produce good and righteous people, as well as to make theology conform to the view that there is a good and righteous God.

Milton amid the battle

Milton rejected the same aspects of Calvinism as did Arminius and the Remonstrants; and he did so, it seems, out of a similar concern for righteousness, particularly divine righteousness. Milton's main expression of this rejection is found in his *Christian Doctrine,* where, in the interests of theodicy, free will is asserted in opposition to the doctrine of absolute predestination. "We must conclude," declares Milton, "that God made no absolute decrees about anything which he left in the power of men, for men have freedom of action. The whole course of scripture shows this" (p. 155). Elsewhere in the treatise he says that

as a vindication of God's justice, especially when he calls man, it is obviously fitting that some measure of free will should be allowed to man . . . and that this will should operate in good works or at least good attempts . . . For if God . . . turns man's will to moral good or evil just as he likes, and then rewards the good and punishes the wicked, it will cause an outcry against divine justice from all sides. [P. 397]

As we have seen in the case of the Remonstrants, such a position entails a rejection of the doctrine of "limited atonement," and Milton accordingly affirms that God "has omitted nothing which might provide salvation for everyone" (p. 175;

cf. pp. 447, 455). This general conviction leads in turn to the doctrine, already discussed in connection with Erasmus and Arminius, that each individual is granted sufficient grace. God "considers all worthy of sufficient grace, and the cause is his justice" (p. 193; cf. p. 446). The doctrine is important for the present discussion because, like his Arminian predecessors, Milton held that God's grace is necessary in every stage of salvation and sanctification, even in the act of will by which one accepts God's gift in the first place, so that if all persons are to be free to accept or reject God's salvation, enabling grace must be withheld from no one. At the same time, an insistence that the power to will comes from God prevents any tendency to Pelagian self-reliance. Milton's doctrine is thus "absolutely in keeping with justice and does not detract at all from the importance of divine grace. For the power to will and believe is either the gift of God or, insofar as it is inherent in man at all, has no relation to good work or merit" (p. 189).

This consistent restatement of the basic Arminian position is significant not only in itself but also in relation to the main theological concerns of Milton's English contemporaries. Calvinist teaching was a powerful force in English politics and religion of the seventeenth century, and even James I had sent a delegation to the Synod of Dort, where they added their votes in denunciation of the Remonstrant articles. As indicated already,[42] Arminianism when it first came to England took on a "Romish" aspect: The grace offered to all became closely associated with the sacraments administered to all, and "hence the preoccupation under Archbishop Laud with altars and private confessions before receiving communion, as well as a belief in the absolute necessity of baptism."[43]

The reaction against this trend was vehement and highly political. For example, William Prynne (1600–69), Milton's fellow Puritan and one of the great polemicists of the age, in one of his works urges Parliament "to further . . . the discouery and suppression of those Hereticall and Grace-destroying Arminian nouelties, which haue of late inuaded, affronted, and almost shouldered out of doores, the ancient, established, and resolved Doctrines of our Church."[44] Given that view of Arminianism, it is not surprising that in the early 1640s Milton should style himself an anti-Arminian. As I have noted, in his *Apology against a Pamphlet* (1642) he implies that Arminians "deny originall sinne." In the *Doctrine and Discipline of Divorce* (1643) he mentions that "the Jesuits, and that sect among us which is nam'd of *Arminius*, are wont to charge us of making God the author of sinne."[45] And then in 1644, in *Areopagitica*, he refers to the circumstances of Arminius's coming to doubt certain points of Calvinism, as mentioned earlier: "The acute and distinct *Arminius* was perverted meerly by the perusing of a namelesse discours writt'n at *Delf*, which at first he took in hand to confute."[46] Although he indicates here almost an admiration for the man, Milton clearly accepts the Calvinist caricature of Arminianism; and, even though in *Areopagitica* his argument concerning the nature of freedom actually assumes an Arminian view, Milton would appear to be oblivious to that, as well as to his corresponding disagreement with the Calvinist theology of men such as Prynne.

However, the number of works defending or attacking orthodox Calvinism during the mid-seventeenth century must have given Milton ample opportunity to decide just where he himself stood. Put simplistically, the Calvinists saw in free will a kind of moral equivalent to the dualistic notion of primordial *Hylē*, or matter, which God could not quite control; and accordingly, of course, they sought to oppose it. The Arminians likewise wanted to emphasize grace and the sovereignty of God, but sought to retain free will because of moral and theodical considerations. The Calvinists thought the Arminians would deny proposition (1), that God is omnipotent; the Arminians thought the Calvinists would render meaningless proposition (2), that God is wholly good. The Calvinists wanted above all to assert eternal providence; the Arminians considered it their task to do so while justifying God's ways.

In order to sketch the outlines of the controversy as it

stretched into the mid-seventeenth century, I will simply mention a number of the writers who can be seen as participating in it, some of whom will be met with again in the chapters that follow. The titles alone of the main works indicate how closely bound up with the problem of evil the Arminian question was. I have already mentioned Prynne and his *Anti-Arminianisme*, which was published in 1629 and again in 1630. He published in addition a title that sums up some of the issues I have mentioned: *God, No Imposter nor Deluder; or, An Answer to a Popish and Arminian Cauill, in the Defence of Free-Will, and Vniversal Grace* (also 1629 and 1630). We have also in the last chapter already met William Pemble, whose *Vindiciae Gratiae: A Plea for Grace . . . Wherein . . . the Maine Sinewes of Arminivs Doctrine Are Cut Asunder* appeared in 1627, 1629, 1635, and 1659. And I have likewise cited Robert Baillie's *Antidote against Arminianisme* (1641 and 1652) and Samuel Rutherford's *Disputatio Scholastica de Divina Providentia . . . adversus Jesuitas, Arminianos, Socinianos, . . .* (1650). Both of these latter men are mentioned dyslogistically in Milton's poem "On the New Forcers of Conscience under the Long Parliament" (1646), Rutherford by name (line 8), Baillie as "Scotch What-d'ye-call" (line 12).[47]

Among the most extreme of orthodox Calvinists was William Twisse, prolocutor of the Westminster Assembly, an outright voluntarist[48] and amazingly prolific writer. His *Vindiciae Gratiae, Potestatis, ac Providentiae Dei* (1632) was directed against Arminius's examination of William Perkins; and his *Riches of Gods Love . . . Consistent with His Absolute . . . Reprobation* (1653) was intended as a reply to perhaps the most notorious Arminian work in English in the mid-seventeenth century, Samuel Hoard's *Gods Love to Man-kinde* (1633 and 1656). (Twisse takes 299 folio pages to answer Hoard's 103 pages in quarto!) Another main Calvinist spokesman was John Owen, who became vice-chancellor of Oxford University, and whose *Display of Arminianisme: Being a Discovery of the old Pelagian Idol Free-will* appeared in 1643 and 1649. Significantly, this was followed in 1653 by his *Diatriba de Justitia Divina,* which seeks to pull back from the scholasticism and voluntarism of Twisse and Rutherford. Owen declares "the justice by which God punishes sin, to be the very essential rectitude of Deity itself" and not, as "Rutherford . . . roundly and boldly asserts, '. . . a free act of the Divine will.' "[49]

Owen's was but one attempt to moderate orthodox Calvinism from within the ranks. On the continent, Moses Amyraldus (Amyraut) developed so-called hypothetical universalism, influenced in part by the Scottish theologian John Cameron; and yet he defended Calvin against Hoard, and God's justice against the Arminians generally.[50] Amyraldus himself was attacked on the one hand by Petrus Molinaeus (DuMoulin) in *Pro Dei Misericordia, et Sapientia, et Justitia Apologia,*[51] and on the other by the Arminian Stephanus Curcellaeus (de Courcelles), who sought to defend Arminius against Amyraldus.[52] Kelley says that there exist "provocative similarities" between Curcellaeus's *Opera* and Milton's *Christian Doctrine,* although the former appeared too late to have been borrowed from by Milton (*CD*, p. 86). In fact, Curcellaeus's defense of Arminius against Amyraldus appeared in 1645, and it therefore probably deserves to be examined closely in any future search for Milton's Arminian sources. Curcellaeus also knew Hugo Grotius,[53] perhaps the most famous Arminian of his time, who, having been sentenced to life imprisonment after the Synod of Dort and later escaping, was visited in Paris in 1638 by Milton on his way to Italy.

Back in England, Grotius was opposed by Richard Baxter's *The Grotian Religion Discovered* (1658), a work replying to Arminian Thomas Pierce and replied to in turn by him in *The New Discoverer Discover'd* (1659). Pierce, in 1657, one year after the appearance of Jeremy Taylor's *Deus Justificatus,* had published two similarly theodical works, *The Divine Philanthropie Defended* and *The Divine Purity Defended,* in the latter quoting Baxter's claim that Pemble and Twisse had "fought against Jesuites and Arminians with the Antinomian Weapons" (p. 49).

Baxter in fact did represent a much more conciliatory approach to Arminianism – for which, however, according to Pierce, Baxter's own party proclaimed him "a great Arminian"[54] – and Baxter's subsequent works, such as *Gods Goodness, Vindicated* (1671), and *Catholick Theologie* (1675), clearly sought to repair some of the damage the controversy between the Calvinists and Arminians had caused. Similarly irenic attempts were made from the Arminian side, notably by Henry Hammond in his *Pacifick Discourse of Gods Grace and Decrees* (1660).

Two other main figures who ought to be mentioned here, though they will be discussed in subsequent chapters, are John Goodwin, whose great work was *Redemption Redeemed* (1651), an attack on the orthodox Calvinist doctrine of the limited atonement; and Alexander More, a strict Calvinist and Milton's hated opponent. More's *Victoria Gratiae: De Gratia et Libero Arbitrio* (1652) Milton mentions with contempt in *Defensio Pro Se* in 1655, although the work had apparently not yet come into his hands. And More's would-be defense of Calvin[55] Milton likewise excoriates: "Pharisee that you are, you honor [Calvin] as a prophet . . . and yet you slay him with your life and manners."[56]

The summation of British Calvinist orthodoxy, of course, was the Westminster Confession, set forth in 1647. Like the Canons of Dort some thirty years earlier, it taught that grace is bestowed not universally but only upon "those that are ordained unto life." It followed that, because "God did, from all eternity, decree to justify all the elect," the atonement was limited, and "Christ did, in the fulness of time, die for their sins, and rise again for their justification."[57] However, Milton argues from an assumption of divine justice to the conclusion that "no one should lack sufficient grace for salvation. Otherwise it is not clear how [God] can demonstrate his truthfulness to mankind" (*CD*, p. 193).

Milton further contradicts Westminster by denying absolute predestination and asserting free will, lest "we should make [God] responsible for all the sins ever committed, and should make demons and wicked men blameless" (*CD*, pp. 164–5). Of course, this teaching is extremely important with respect to the Fall of Man, for on it hinges the question of God's responsibility for Adam's lapse, or even of his complicity in it. Calvinist theologians taught both absolute predestination and human culpability; Milton had trouble seeing this as anything but a bald assertion of contraries. The position that in some sense God, as Empson puts it, "was working for the Fall all along," though it is opposed by Milton, is clearly set forth in the Westminster Confession:

> The almighty power, unsearchable wisdom, and infinite goodness of God so far manifest themselves in his providence that it extendeth itself even to the first fall, and all other sins, . . . and that not by a bare permission, but such as hath joined with it a most wise and powerful bounding; . . . yet so as the sinfulness thereof proceedeth only from the creature, and not from God.[58]

In dealing with the same issue in his *Christian Doctrine*, Milton says: "Everyone agrees that man could have avoided falling. But if, because of God's decree, man could not help but fall (and the two contradictory opinions are sometimes voiced by the same people), then God's restoration of fallen man was a matter of justice not grace" (p. 174).

It is hard to tell exactly when Milton arrived at such a clearly Arminian position, particularly given his putatively anti-Arminian utterances in the early 1640s. Perhaps his great personal misfortunes of the 1650s and the decline of the revolutionary cause, ending finally in the Restoration, forced him to abandon the earlier optimism that accompanied English Calvinist theology.[59] Indeed, the possibility of "devil worship" lurking in voluntarist predestinarianism may have started to look like an actuality. Christopher Hill suggests that "Milton was not of the devil's party without knowing it: part of him knew"; and he had to make sure no trace of this element remained in his theology:

> If Milton had allowed himself consciously to accept the view of Winstanley, Erbery and some Ranters, that the God whom most Christians

worshipped was a wicked God, his life would have lost its structure, would have fallen in ruins about his head like the temple of the Philistines. He had to justify the ways of God to man in order to justify his own life.[60]

As Milton himself says of those who see God's decree or foreknowledge as shackling supposedly "free causes" with necessity, "To refute them . . . would be like inventing a long argument to prove that God is not the Devil" (*CD*, p. 166).

Milton's Arminianism and *Paradise Lost*

Whatever the answers to the biographical questions, a recognition of Milton's adoption of an Arminian solution to some of the problems concerning divine justice renders a great deal less problematical the utterances of God in *Paradise Lost* and the theme of regeneration in Milton's later poetry generally. Of course I do not suggest that the Arminian theology of Milton's prose should be imposed uncritically on his poetry; but it is surely fair to assume that where a Calvinist and non-Calvinist reading of a given passage are possible, the greater burden of proof will rest upon those who would argue the former.

Kelley has already shown how the Arminianism of the prose can illuminate potentially confusing statements in the poetry. For example, God's promise in book 3 of *Paradise Lost,* that "Man shall not quite be lost, but saved who will / Yet not of will in him but grace in me / Freely vouchsafed" (3.173–5), expresses both the decisive character of the will and the instrumentality of grace[61] – central points, as we have seen, of Arminian teaching.

Milton's rejection of the limited atonement and his definition of the elect as simply "all who shall believe" (*CD*, p. 183) lead Kelley likewise to declare Arminian God's famous lines "Some I have chosen of peculiar grace / Elect above the rest" (3.183–4).[62] Here, however, unless Milton really intended to speak, as it were, in code, it is hard to feel convinced by Kelley's interpretation. And yet the lines' Arminian context does seem to

preclude an orthodox Calvinist reading of them. I think it possible that Milton is attempting a sort of compromise solution,
such as that proposed by Baxter in a section of his *Catholick
Theologie* entitled "Of the sufficiency and efficacy of Grace."
Baxter posits not two but three categories in regard to the operation of grace. Summing up, he says:

> The Act of *faith* sometimes followeth this [divine] Impulse through its
> *invincible force;* And sometime it followeth it through its *sufficient force*
> . . . And sometimes it followeth it *not at all* . . . And if the question
> be, Why *sufficient Grace* which is *Effectual ad Posse* is not *effectual ad
> agere?* It is because (being but *sufficient,*) mans *Indisposition* and *wilful
> neglect* or *opposition,* maketh him an *unfit Receiver.* [Pp. 51, 52]

Perhaps Milton similarly posits some kind of "super-elect" (*PL*,
3.183–4), and then a generality who receive sufficient grace
(3.189), some of these availing themselves of it (3.195–7), some
neglecting and scorning the offer (3.198 ff.).[63] In fact, in *Christian Doctrine,* Milton seems at least to recognize the legitimacy
of a notion of election that comports with something like an
"elect above the rest." He distinguishes his general use of
"election" from "the election by which [God] chooses an individual for some employment, . . . whence they are sometimes
called elect who are superior to the rest for any reason" (p. 172).
And in *Samson Agonistes,* Samson refers to "such as thou [God]
hast solemnly elected, / With gifts and graces eminently
adorned / To some great work" (lines 678–80). The categories
are not the same as Baxter's, but similar. In any case, as these
different uses of "elect" suggest, Milton's "elect above the rest"
can reasonably be seen as a category with which he complements an otherwise generally Arminian position. Although the
two difficult lines should probably not be squeezed into a
tightly Arminian mold, neither should they be taken as signal-
ing a relapse into orthodox Calvinism.

The scene in heaven in book 3 of *Paradise Lost* nevertheless
repeats a number of the Arminian themes that have already
been discussed, and the important thing to notice here is that
it is primarily a concern for theodicy that informs their expres-

sion. Many readers have found the God of book 3 an unappealing figure. For example, as Peter has pointed out, "In representing God anthropomorphically and then obliging him to speak his own defences at some length, Milton has conveyed a most unfortunate impression of uneasiness."[64] Yet despite their arguably unhappy dramatic context, God's words deal frankly and effectively with the issue of divine justice as it concerns the Fall of Man and his need for salvation. God declares that he made man free, because otherwise man "had served necessity, / Not me" (3.110–11), and thereby dissociates himself from the theology of the Westminster Confession, which conceives of God's predeterminations as including "even . . . the first fall, and all other sins." And whereas for the orthodox Calvinist "the will of God is the supreme rule of righteousness," in book 3 of *Paradise Lost* the Son himself suggests that some more-than-self-referential justification of his Father's will is in order. His question is as blunt a challenge to divine benevolence and omnipotence as any posed by Empson, although the Son's use of the subjunctive shows that he has not closed his mind to the possibility of receiving an answer:

> should man finally be lost, should man
> Thy creature late so loved, thy youngest son
> Fall circumvented thus by fraud, though joined
> With his own folly? That be from thee far,
> That far be from thee, Father, who art judge
> Of all things made, and judgest only right.
> Or shall the adversary thus obtain
> His end, and frustrate thine, shall he fulfil
> His malice, and thy goodness bring to nought,
> Or proud return though to his heavier doom,
> Yet with revenge accomplished and to hell
> Draw after him the whole race of mankind,
> By his corrupted? Or wilt thou thy self
> Abolish thy creation, and unmake,
> For him, what for thy glory thou hast made?
> So should thy goodness and thy greatness both
> Be questioned and blasphemed without defence.
>
> [3.150–66]

What follows is essentially the Arminian teaching of sufficient and universal grace. Apart from that somewhat puzzling
"super-elect," who in any case receive "peculiar grace," everyone will be granted sufficient grace. God will, he promises,

> clear their senses dark,
> What may suffice, and soften stony hearts
> To pray, repent, and bring obedience due.
> To prayer, repentance, and obedience due,
> Though but endeavoured with sincere intent,
> Mine ear shall not be slow, mine eye not shut.
> [3.188–93]

And the grace of God manifest in the atonement of Christ is not
limited but universal, sufficient to save "the whole race lost"
(3.280). Provided one accepts and values man's freedom of
choice, one must admit that the Son's request for theodicy has
been met. For although those who freely "neglect and scorn"
God's grace will indeed be lost, "none but such from mercy" he
excludes (3.202).

Now it is important to understand the relationship between
man's freedom and the grace that is offered him, for when later
in *Paradise Lost* they are shown operating, their relationship to
each other is not spelled out so explicitly. Consequently, if one
fails to understand or remember what one has been told in book
3, one is liable to misread what happens. As we have seen, the
Synod of Dort asserted the depravity of man in response to
what it believed was the Remonstrants' teaching on man's only
partial depravity and the cooperative ability of his fallen will,
although in fact the Arminian articles taught that "man has not
saving grace of himself, nor of the energy of his free will, inas-
much as he, in a state of apostasy and sin, can of and by himself
neither think, will, nor do anything that is truly good," and
that accordingly there is a need for prevenient grace. It is precisely this doctrine, I would suggest, that the Son is expressing
when he refers to grace as something that is sent to all God's
creatures, "and to all / Comes unprevented, unimplored,
unsought." And it is "happy for man" that it does come in this

manner, since "he her aid / Can never seek, once dead in sins and lost" (3.230–3).

This prevenient grace, moreover, is granted universally and sufficiently, so that one's salvation depends on what one does with it once it has been granted. Grace is not, as it is in orthodox Calvinist theology, irresistible; rather, its efficacy depends, strictly speaking, on one's freely deciding not to resist it. As we recall from Augustine's analogy of suicide, human choice can in fact be decisive without being innately sufficient to produce any positive result, just as "the act of living in a body is a positive act which is not a matter of choice but is only possible by the help of nourishment; whereas the choice not to live . . . is a negative act which is in our human power." The distinction is subtle, but it provides an instructive parallel to the one God makes when he promises that "Man shall not quite be lost, but saved who will, / Yet not of will in him, but grace in me" (3.173–4): Will is decisive but not by itself efficacious; grace is absolutely necessary for salvation but does not overrule the human will. For the orthodox Calvinist, the divine will alone is decisive; for the Pelagian, the unaided human will can be efficacious.

By adopting the Arminian position on predestination, grace, and free will, therefore, Milton is able to avoid both Pelagianism on the one hand and the theodically dissonant aspects of Calvinism on the other. As Arminianism teaches, sufficient grace is offered to all human beings, so that their wills are truly decisive, even though they would be incapable of desiring or producing good without that grace. But at the same time, they are also meaningfully free with respect to evil, and so God is not made the author of sin. Such, it would seem, is the view presented in *Paradise Lost*, where it thus consistently furthers Milton's justification of the ways of God.

From this view, furthermore, there emerges a peculiar though significant conception of the nature of human virtue. Put briefly, divine agency accounts for good; human agency accounts for the evil of sin. But, given God's offer of divine grace, man is free either to reject it and use his own innate power to sin, or else to accept it and use the power received from God to refrain from sinning. The peculiarity of the view is that, so far as man is concerned, sin is by commission and moral virtue by omission, just as in Eden virtue was to be achieved through abstaining from eating the forbidden fruit, whereas sin consisted in the commissive act of disobedience.[65] As Milton says in commenting on Rom. 9:16 ("it does not depend on him that wills or on him that runs but on God who is merciful"), "I am not talking about anyone willing or running, but about someone being less unwilling, less backward, less opposed" to divine grace (*CD*, p. 187).

If such a view of virtue were to be presented in a piece of literature, the difficulty might be that the reader, failing to understand the respective functions of grace and free will, would suspect some essential inconsistency between being led to believe that certain actions are humanly virtuous and praiseworthy and being told that in fact they result from divine agency. Of course this is just what occurs at the end of book 10 and in the earlier part of book 11 of *Paradise Lost*, although any suspicion of inconsistency, I would argue, is unwarranted. Bewailing the results of fallenness and the evil prospects before her and her husband, Eve proposes suicide as a way of escape (10.1001). But Adam responds with counsels of hope, and he and Eve, acting upon them, penitent and remorseful,

> forthwith to the place
> Repairing where [God] judged them prostrate fell
> Before him reverent, and both confessed
> Humbly their faults, and pardon begged, with tears
> Watering the ground, and with their sighs the air
> Frequenting, sent from hearts contrite, in sign
> Of sorrow unfeigned, and humiliation meek.
> [10.1098–1104]

Thus ends book 10, and book 11 begins with what might look like a reductive explanation of the human drama we have just witnessed:

> Thus they in lowliest plight repentant stood
> Praying, for from the mercy-seat above
> Prevenient grace descending had removed
> The stony from their hearts, and made new flesh
> Regenerate grow instead, that sighs now breathed
> Unutterable.
>
> [11.1–6]

Then the Son, already fulfilling his role as mediator, presents to the Father Adam and Eve's humble request for pardon:

> See Father, what first fruits on earth are sprung
> From thy implanted grace in man, these sighs
> And prayers, which in this golden censer, mixed
> With incense, I thy priest before thee bring,
> Fruits of more pleasing savour from thy seed
> Sown with contrition in his heart, than those
> Which his own hand manuring all the trees
> Of Paradise could have produced ere fallen
> From innocence.[66]

How we understand these lines – which on their own admit of various interpretations – ought, I think, to depend finally on the context provided by the poem as a whole. And, as we have seen, the grace mentioned here in book 11 was in book 3 promised by God himself, even to those who, unlike Adam and Eve, would "neglect and scorn" his "long sufferance" and his "day of grace" (3.198–9): "I will clear their senses dark, / What may suffice, and soften stony hearts / To pray, repent, and bring obedience due" (3.188–90). It makes no sense to see this grace as the exclusive explanation for Adam and Eve's sighs and prayers when it clearly does not produce any such "fruits" in those who reject God's offer. God's grace explains how man's repentance is possible, once he is "dead in sins and lost" (3.233), but does not finally account for the fact that it actually takes place.[67] Grace is not irresistible, and we must recognize that the human will (although not on its own efficacious) is decisive, because it is free not to resist, as well as to resist, God's will.

In 1653 Robert Harris produced the following catechism for

those who might wonder, given that all "spirituall goodnesse" is accomplished by grace, what room there is for their own agency:

> *Quest.* What can we do toward [the softening of our hearts]? it is not in our power to soften our selves.
>
> *Answ.* True: but yet it is in our power to harden our selves . . . : Here therefore, take heed that when God speaks, you stop not your eares; when God shines upon you, that you shut not your eyes . . . ; do not receive the grace of God in vain; do not future your repentance, nor make delaies, . . . but when the Word findes you out in your sins, take Gods part against yourselves, stablishing your hearts in the assured truth of all the promises of God.[68]

Similarly, in *Paradise Lost*, Adam and Eve recall both the promise concerning the bruising of the serpent's head and the evidence they already have of God's pity (10.1028 ff., 1056 ff). Having refrained from hardening themselves, from stopping their ears, from shutting their eyes, they also avoid any "futuring" of their repentance: To the place of judgment they repair "forthwith" (10.1098). Moreover, when Adam counsels against suicide on the grounds that it "cuts us off from hope, and savours only / Rancour and pride, impatience and despite, / Reluctance against God and his just yoke" (10.1043–5), there is no reason for thinking him mistaken in assuming this possibility of "reluctance against God" to be real, even though we are subsequently told that the decision not to be reluctant was effected through God's grace.[69] For here Augustine's analogy is virtually the fact; mutatis mutandis, his words describe precisely the situation in which Adam and Eve find themselves: "To live was not a matter of choice . . . but depended on the help of God, whereas to live ill . . . [here, to cease living altogether] was in man's power."

The opening of book 11, therefore, does not deny the validity of the reader's feeling that what he has just seen is the righteous behavior of freely acting human beings; what it does is to place within the context of divine grace the limited but real freedom we have seen operating.[70] There is no need to doubt that Adam and Eve's contrition is truly their own; for as Michael implies

when he tells Adam he must leave Paradise, what God has provided is "grace wherein thou *mayst* repent" (11.255; italics
added). Although human freedom must be recognized as
meaningful and important, it is even more important that one
recognize God as the ultimate source of that power whereby
righteous deeds are possible. If one keeps in mind the context
provided by the rest of *Paradise Lost,* the passage in question
can be seen to complement rather than contradict what has
immediately preceded it. We may conclude that there is no justification for the charge that Milton "juggles" with grace and
merit, or that he upholds man's free will at one moment and
denies it the next. Certainly Patrides is right to point out that
"grace is no philosophical tenet to be dissected but an experience to be lived";[71] I am not suggesting that it can be reduced
to a simple formula. How God removes "the stony" from hearts
and makes "new flesh / Regenerate grow instead" must remain
a great mystery, and how the operation of such grace is experienced may be ineffable, even at times paradoxical. But human
experiences have philosophical implications, and an understanding of Milton's Arminian view of grace reveals that the
experience of grace he presents in *Paradise Lost* implies no contradiction.[72]

   Further, the foregoing analysis suggests that *Paradise Lost*
does indeed present a meaningful version of that notion which
Greene would seem to accept as fulfilling the minimum requirements of epic heroism, namely, something like "the better for-
titude / Of patience and heroic martyrdom" (9.31–2). Milton's
position seems to be, as already indicated, that righteousness
before God is, strictly speaking, more an omission of evil than
a commission of good. And to this extent, to serve God is, as it
were, but to stand and wait and to observe providence, because
it is by grace alone that evil is overcome with good.[73] Given
this notion of *patient* heroism, therefore, Adam and Eve's decision to repent is unambiguously as we have perceived it: a
heroically significant "painful achievement," and not the result
merely of divine fiat.

Finally, the view of grace and freedom that we encounter in *Paradise Lost* accords with a predominant motive of Milton's later theology, as well as of Arminianism generally: to show how God is good and just, as well as omnipotent. The reason of God's action is ultimately to be found, not in his will alone, but in the justice and goodness that are part of his nature. Just as God's bestowing prevenient grace on Adam and Eve fulfills an earlier promise, so, in the fallen couple's anticipation of God's response to their repentance, we are reminded of the promise in book 3 that the divine policy will be "mercy first and last" (3.134). In *Christian Doctrine,* Milton defines saving faith as divinely implanted persuasion, "by virtue of which we believe, on the authority of God's promise, that all those things which God has promised us in Christ are ours" (p. 471); and in *Paradise Lost* it is precisely such a recognition of God's gracious purpose that informs Adam's speech opposing suicide: "Remember," he urges Eve, "with what mild / And gracious temper he both heard and judged / Without wrath or reviling" (10.1046–8). If they do repent of their sin, God undoubtedly

> will relent and turn
> From his displeasure; in whose look serene,
> When angry most he seemed and most severe,
> What else but favour, grace, and mercy shone?
> [10.1093–6]

"Thus the excellence of faith appears," as Milton says in *Christian Doctrine,* "which is that it attributes the supreme glory of veracity and justice to God" (p. 473). In Adam and Eve's regeneration in *Paradise Lost,* Milton demonstrates the same divine qualities. In his presentation of the manner of God's gracious cultivation of the fruits of repentance, he affirms both God's sovereign purpose and man's genuine creaturely freedom. And in so doing he achieves a theologically consistent artistic fusion of both aspects of his poem's "great argument": to "assert eternal providence, / And justify the ways of God to men."

4

Milton and the Free Will Defense

Having considered the outlines of Arminianism and the historical context it provided for Milton's justification of God, we must now examine more closely the relation between theodicy and what Francis Tayler in 1641 referred to as the Arminian's "navell-string of free-will."[1] In particular, I would like in this chapter to present the so-called Free Will Defense and to emphasize its peculiarly literary roles in *Paradise Lost*.

As I have indicated, seventeenth-century orthodox Calvinists looked on Arminian teaching as a threat to the doctrines of divine providence and omnipotence. Samuel Rutherford, for example, claims to contend for the lordship of the creator against the Arminians, who contend for the lordship of the creature.[2] John Owen sees theodicy as merely an excuse for the Arminians "to free themselves from the supreme dominion of . . . all-ruling providence" and to worship "their idoll Free-will": "So it must be," they say, "or else . . . God is unjust, and his waies unequall." Owen later adds sarcastically: "Having robbed God of his power, they will yet leave him so much goodnesse, as that he shall not be troubled at it."[3] Milton's aim, as was suggested at the end of the last chapter, is to assert those two things which Owen here almost admits cannot both unequivocally be asserted: God's omnipotence *and* goodness.

Free Will Defense: the model and its uses

The Free Will Defense is a traditional model to explain how God's omnipotence and goodness might indeed both be

92

asserted, even given the fact that this world contains evil, particularly moral evil. The argument is one that continues to provoke a great deal of interest in philosophical circles; put simplistically, it runs as follows: Evil, at least a great deal of it, is caused by the misuse of free will by angels and humans. However, it is a very great good that there be angels and humans, and that they be free creatures rather than some sort of automata. Furthermore, angels and humans cannot be both free and fully automatic. Not being fully automatic, their choices cannot be wholly controlled by God. Hence it may be that God had no choice but to make no free creatures at all, or else to make ones who could cause evil. Given such a choice, God was justified in creating humans and angels as he did. And yet the fact that he faced a dilemma in so doing is no slur on his omnipotence, because omnipotence does not include the power to actualize two incompossibles, such as a person's being both fully automatic and free. Therefore, the argument concludes, the claims that God is omnipotent and wholly good and that evil exists in the world need imply no contradiction.

Clearly, each of this argument's constituent assertions needs clarification and support; but, in general, its plausibility as a whole will depend on the plausibility of the claims (1) that free creatures indeed cannot be wholly determined, (2) that the freedom of those creatures is finally "worth it," given the amount of evil they cause, and (3) that omnipotence cannot guarantee that what it creates will be the best of all possible worlds. The first of these three assumptions will be examined primarily in Chapter 5. The second and third I would like to examine in reverse order now.

J. L. Mackie, a modern critic of the Free Will Defense, argues that even if "it is better on the whole that men should act freely, and sometimes err, than that they should be innocent automata, acting rightly in a wholly determined way," and even if it is logically impossible for God to make a person whose choices would be both free and automatic, it *is* logically possible for persons to be free and always refrain from evil.[4] Therefore, an omnipotent good creator ought to have created a world in which there existed free creatures, and hence moral good, but no moral evil.

Alvin Plantinga, an opponent of Mackie's and a prominent "Free Will Defender," denies the validity of this conclusion, pointing out that if a world contains "creatures whose activity is not causally determined – who, like [God] himself, are centres of creative activity," and if those creatures do choose to do evil, then the possible world in which those creatures refrain from evil is one that God cannot create, even though it is better than the one in which they do choose evil. In other words, there are possible worlds in which the free creatures inhabiting them determine whether they will contain moral evil. Of course it is up to God whether to create such beings; but if he does decide to create them, then whether they will do evil is up to them, not God.[5] Therefore it is quite coherent to claim that this is not the best of all possible worlds even though omnipotence may have done all it logically could.

Now despite the fact that this account of the Free Will Defense uses the vocabulary of "possible worlds," which has been developed primarily since the time of Leibniz, the essential concepts on which that vocabulary is based were current in the seventeenth century – as we can see in the process of considering a major objection to the Free Will Defense and some implicit responses to it from seventeenth-century theology. The objection is put in twentieth-century terms by Mackie, who sees it as related to what he calls the "Paradox of Omnipotence": "There is a fundamental difficulty," he claims, "in the notion of an omnipotent God creating men with free will, for if men's wills are really free this must mean that even God cannot control them, that is, that God is no longer omnipotent" (p. 57). How, one might respond, is it paradoxical to claim that, if God decided to make creatures whose choices were not causally determined, then he could not causally determine them? Samuel Hoard, for example, does not see the self-limiting nature of choice to be any fundamental limitation on omnipotence: Citing Tertullian, he declares that "man is made by Gods own gracious constitution, a free creature, undetermined in his actions, till he determine herself: and therefore may not be hindred from sinning by omnipotency, because God useth not to repeal his own ordinances."[6] Even Rutherford, who as we have seen argues for a very comprehensive notion of omnipotence, acknowledges that God's power should not be taken to include "that which involves a contradiction, that which is simply impossible, or more correctly incompossible."[7] And Owen distinguishes two types of impossibility, the recognition of which, I think, dissolves Mackie's would-be paradox. Discussing Matt. 26:39, Owen notes that

Christ himself, in his agony, placeth *the passing away of the cup among things possible. All things,* (saith he) *Father, are possible with thee. Let this cup pass from me* . . . [However,] 'tis well known, that the word *impossibility* may be considered in a two-fold point of view: the first is in itself absolute, which respects the absolute power of God, antecedent to any free act of the Divine will; in this respect, it was not impossible that, that cup should pass from Christ. The Second is *conditional,* which respects the power of God, as directed in a certain order, that is, determined, and (if I might so phrase it) circumscribed by some act of the Divine Will; and in this sense it was impossible.[8]

Clearly, the impossibility of God's controlling men's wills, which Mackie thinks is a threat to omnipotence, is likewise an impossibility of this second, merely *conditional* sort; it results from a prior "free act of the Divine will." Or in Rutherford's terms, God's controlling men's wills is incompossible with God's decision to make man a free creature.

Another objection anti-theists raise against the Free Will Defense is that God, being good, will eliminate evil as far as he can; and, being omnipotent, he can eliminate evil completely.[9] Furthermore, if God is omniscient, why did he create man free, foreknowing as he must have that doing so would lead to sin? Plantinga's reply is that "surely a good person would not be obligated to eliminate a given evil if he could do so only by eliminating a good that outweighed it."[10] The Free Will Defense postulates that creaturely freedom, together with other goods of which creaturely freedom is a precondition, in the final analysis will be seen to outweigh all the evil that it has occasioned. And so long as the good thus overbalances evil, God is justified in permitting what he has permitted.[11]

This postulation is no doubt speculative, but again it represents an approach to the problem that was not uncommon in the seventeenth century. In general terms, Anthony Burgess affirms that, even given the sin that is in the world, good finally overbalances evil: "That [saying] of *Austins* is good, *God would not have suffered sin to be, if he could not have wrought greater good then sin was evill.*"[12] And Baxter speculates in more specific terms that if all angels and inhabitants of nonearthly realms, as well as human beings, are taken into account, then it is at least possible that good outweighs evil, in the sense that the number of the blessed might far exceed the number of the damned:

Certain it is, that Spirits are innumerable. And though some of these are fallen to be Devils, God hath not told us how many: Nor can we know that it is one to a Million of happier Creatures. And can that Man then, who is offended with God, not for damning a very few, but for the proportion of the Damned in comparison of others, tell what he saith? . . . It's true I cannot tell the Number; but it is as true that when our Foundation is sure, that God is infinitely wise and good, it is madness to accuse him as unwise, or evil, or cruel, for that which we must confess we do not know . . . Stay till you see who dwelleth in all the superior Regions, and then take your selves for fitter Discerners of your Maker's Ways.[13]

As we shall see shortly, Milton also recognizes, albeit in terms more earthly than those Baxter uses here, a certain quantitative dimension to the relation of good and evil, such that it makes sense to speak of the possibility that the one might outweigh the other.

Now in the Free Will Defense, a large proportion of the "weight" of goodness is seen to consist in the value of freedom as it pertains to man's relationship to the divine. The legal and what might be called the "familial" or genetic aspects of this relationship are summarized by Baxter's rebuttal of Peter Sterry:

I take the root of [Sterry's] error to be his overlooking and undervaluing Gods Design in *Making* and *Governing* free Intellectual agents, by his Sapiential Moral Directive way: He [Sterry] supposeth this way to be so much below that of Physical Motion and Determination, as that it is not to be considered but as an instrument thereof: As if it were unworthy of God to give any creature a Meer Power, Liberty, Law, and Moral Means alone, and not to Necessitate him Positively or Negatively to *Obey* or *Disobey*. And this looking only at Physical Good, Being and Motion, and thereby thinking lightly of Sapiential Regency, is the summ, as of his, so of *Hobbes, Spinosa's, Alvarez, Bradwardines, Twisses, Rutherfords,* and the rest of the Predeterminants errors herein . . . I think, that God made man a free self-determining agent, that he might be capable of such Sapiential Rule: And that it is a great Honour to God, to make so noble a *Nature* . . . : And though man be not Independent, yet to be so far like God himself, as to be a kind of first-determiner of many of his Volitions and Nolitions, is part of Gods Natural Image on Man.[14]

This "family resemblance," this creation of man in the image of God, is of profound importance for all of Christian theology; and of course its identification with human freedom is of particular significance to the Free Will Defense and in turn to theodicy as a whole. Connected with it is a third aspect of man's relation to God, namely, the personal. This aspect, along with the legal and the familial, is acknowledged by Robert Harris. Interestingly, he mentions "that private opinion of *Zanchy's* and others, who conceived that Christ assumed mans nature for a pattern whereby *Adam* should be made." Harris declines to comment on this opinion and simply asserts that "the text sufficeth us: *God made man in his own image according to his own likeness.*" However, when he later mentions the legal and personal aspects, he returns to a recognition of Christ's role in the relationship between God and man: If man had not "freedome of *choyce* . . . he were not *capable of a law* . . . . Nay, more; He would be uncapable of good or bad; as a stone is; and consequently uncapable of reward or punishment; nay, uncapable of *Christ,* or an Holy Ghost; which dwels not in stocks."[15] As we shall see, the personal aspect of man's relationship to the divine – implicit in any such recognition of the indwelling of the Holy

Spirit – is something Milton explores with theodicy in mind in *Paradise Lost*.

Among seventeenth-century Arminians, a favorite authority on the Free Will Defense, especially as it identifies freedom with the divine image, was Tertullian (160?–230?). As I have noted already, Hoard cites Tertullian in asserting that "man is made by God's own gracious constitution, a free creature." Pierce too, in discussing the Free Will Defense, follows Tertullian's work *Adversus Marcionem:*

> *Marcion* objected thus. *If God is good, and praescient of all the Evill which is to come, and withall able to prevent it, why did he suffer mankinde to fall?* . . . *Tertullian* answered, *That God made man in his own Image,* and that in nothing more *lively,* than in the *liberty of a Will.* . . . But (saith *Marcion*) Man ought to have been made of *such a frame,* as *not to be able to fall away.* Marry then (saith *Tertullian*) Man had not been a *voluntary,* but a *necessary Agent.* (which is as much as to say, *a Man should not have been a Man*).[16]

Tertullian's words are worth looking at more closely. As Pierce indicates, Marcion asks why God, if he is so prescient, good, and powerful, did not intervene to prevent man from falling, or else create him such that he could not fall in the first place.[17] Tertullian begins his answer by stressing that God is of course prescient, and moreover that "the Creator's works are evidence of both . . . his goodness in that they are good . . . and of his power in that they are so great." Even being prescient, good, and omnipotent, however, God could not intervene in the way Marcion says he should have, because "man was created by God . . . with power to choose, and power to act, for himself. I can think," declares Tertullian, "of no clearer indication in him of God's image and similitude than this, the outward expression of God's own dignity" (2.5). The *value* of man's being created free thus inheres in man's Godlike ability "to exhibit goodness as his own, by voluntary act" – this freedom being spoken of by Tertullian as the "primary postulate of goodness and reason" (2.6). And the impossibility of God's intervening to overrule Adam's free will is no slur on omnipotence, but rather follows from a choice that God himself had made and in accordance with the self-limiting character of such a choice:

For anyone who grants another something to use, invariably grants permission to use it according to that other's mind and choice. Therefore it followed that once God had granted the man freedom he must withdraw from his own freedom, restraining within himself that foreknowledge and superior power by which he might have been able to intervene to prevent the man from presuming to use his freedom badly, and so falling into peril. For if he had intervened he would have cancelled that freedom of choice which in reason and goodness he had granted. [2.7]

Of course the most famous exponent of this kind of argument is Augustine, who was also, as we have seen, the favorite non-scriptural authority for seventeenth-century opponents of free will. In *De Libero Arbitrio* he argues that free will is not fortuitous or accidental, but essential to the value of man as a moral creature: "If, indeed, man is something good and cannot do what is right unless he wills to, then he must have free will, without which he cannot do what is right."[18] Secondly, the gift of freedom did not in any way necessitate its misuse; hence man's maker is not directly to blame for man's going wrong:

When [some people] look at the sins of men, they are grieved not simply because men do not give up sinning, but because they have been created at all. God, they tell us, should have created us so that we would always will to enjoy His changeless truth but never will to sin.
    These men should put an end to their complaining and indignation. The fact that God has created men does not force them to sin just because He has given them the power to do so if they choose. Furthermore, there are angels who have never sinned and who never will sin. [3.5(14)]

Finally, even given the fact that man's freedom has been misused, the resulting state of affairs is preferable to that which would obtain if there were no such thing as creaturely freedom. Declares Augustine:

God has not withheld His bountiful goodness from making a creature which He foreknew would not only sin, but would persist in its will to sin. Just as a stray horse is better than a stone that does not go astray through a lack of self-movement and sense perception, so a creature which sins by its free will is more excellent than one that does not sin because it is without free will. [3.5(15)]

Certainly, one that does *not* sin by its free will would be more excellent than both; but, freedom being presupposed, it was in the power of the creature, by sinning, to limit God's choices to those which Augustine mentions here: in effect, to create man who could sin – and who, he foresaw, would sin – or else to create no man at all. And Augustine, along with other "Free Will Defenders," argues that God was justified in choosing the former option.

Before turning to Milton, I would like to consider briefly one further example of the traditional Free Will Defense, which we find in Sir John Davies's *Nosce Teipsum* (1599). Davies's claim that "the Soul were better so to be / Born slave to sin than not to be at all" recalls Augustine's argument that just as a wayward horse is better than an "obedient" stone, so it is better for a creature to be sinful than to be nonexistent. And Davies's attempt to express the Free Will Defense in a poetic way also provides us with a kind of doorway, however narrow, into theodicy's literary dimension, which will be my concern for most of the rest of this chapter. Almost immediately following the lines just quoted, he presents this concise version of the argument:

> Yet this the curious wits will not content;
> They yet will know: sith God foresaw this ill,
> Why His high Providence did not prevent
> The declination of the first man's will.
>
> If by His Word He had the current stay'd
> Of Adam's will, which was by nature free,
> It had been one as if His Word had said:
> "I will henceforth that Man no man shall be."
>
> For what is Man without a moving mind
> Which hath a judging wit and choosing will?
> Now, if God's power should her election bind,
> Her motions then would cease and stand all still.

And why did God in man this soul infuse
But that he should his Maker know and love?
Now, if love be compell'd and cannot choose,
How can it grateful or thankworthy prove?

Love must free-hearted be, and voluntary,
And not enchanted, or by Fate constrain'd;
Nor like that love which did Ulysses carry
To Circe's isle, with mighty charms enchain'd.[19]

Again we see the insistence that freedom, particularly freedom in relation to the creator, is an essential quality if man is truly to be man. Furthermore, Davies augments Augustine's account of the value of freedom with the suggestion – one that Milton develops even further – that freedom is necessary if love itself is to have any meaning. Thus in man and his relationships value is a function of freedom, and complaint against "high Providence" is accordingly unfounded.

Milton and the model: prosaic assumptions

Although in Augustine and in Davies the Free Will Defense is closely associated with a Neoplatonist cosmology, according to which a thing's value derives largely from its position or degree in the ontological hierarchy, this association should not be overemphasized, because the idea that in some sense meaning presupposes freedom has been held both by those who do and by those who do not subscribe to the theory of the Chain of Being. Neither Tertullian nor Pierce, for example, seems especially wedded to that cosmology. And although Milton is often quoted as a proponent of the Great Chain of Being,[20] the truth is that the main thrust of his thought is directed away from such a conception. In particular he rejects both the body-and-soul dualism that accompanies Neoplatonist theology[21] and the suggestion that creation was accomplished by necessity or in accordance with a necessary pattern. Proponents of the Great Chain of Being believe, as Pope puts it, that in the chain "There *must* be, somewhere, such a rank as Man."[22] Milton repudiates this view: In *Paradise Lost,* as we have already seen, God declares that his creative "goodness . . . is free / To act or not, necessity and chance / Approach not me" (7.171–3).

Now in Milton's earlier works, despite what he seems to have thought was their orthodox Calvinist tenor, we find the Free Will Defense sketched in its essential outlines. As indicated in the preceding chapter, *The Doctrine and Discipline of Divorce* contains a reference to "the Jesuits, and that sect among us which is nam'd of *Arminius,* [who] are wont to charge us of making God the author of sinne." Milton's reply to the charge is that "considering the perfection wherin man was created, and might have stood, no decree necessitating his free will, but subsequent though not in time yet in order to causes which were in his owne power, they might, methinks be perswaded to absolve both God and us." The opinion he approves, in short, is that quite apart from any consideration of fate, "mans own freewill self corrupted is the adequat and sufficient cause of his disobedience."[23] Of course, Milton later modified this position somewhat; in *Paradise Lost* it is Satan alone whose will is "self-corrupted, self-depraved," whereas man is first led astray by Satan, not by himself (3.129 ff.). Yet Milton's affirmation of free will as the sufficient cause of moral evil was something he did not go back on, and in subsequent writings he used it as a basis for his attempts to produce what in *The Doctrine and Discipline of Divorce* he refers to as "reasons not invalid, to justifie the counsels of God."[24]

In *Areopagitica,* published only a year later, Milton goes on to suggest why God should have bestowed free will on man in the first place. Like Augustine's and Davies's versions of the Free Will Defense, Milton's stressed that freedom is an essential quality for any moral or rational creature:

Many there be that complain of divin Providence for suffering *Adam* to transgresse, foolish tongues! when God gave him reason, he gave him freedom to choose, for reason is but choosing; he had bin else a meer artificiall *Adam,* such an *Adam* as he is in the motions. We our selves esteem not of that obedience, or love, or gift, which is of force.[25]

Like Davies, Milton implies that there must be freedom if love itself is to have any meaning.[26] And in order to strengthen his argument's plausibility, he refers not only to the principle's theological but also to its human application. We shall see that he does the same thing, with very interesting consequences, in *Paradise Lost*.

A further point relevant to the Free Will Defense that Milton enunciates in *Areopagitica* is that freedom must be more than a merely theoretical possession; there must be morally significant choices to make. Just as Adam without freedom would be no more than a puppet, so freedom without genuine trial or exercise would allow for the development of no more than a "blank vertue" (II.515–16). This is why God "set before [Adam] a provoking object, ever almost in his eyes; herein consisted his merit, herein the right of his reward, the praise of his abstinence. Wherefore did he creat passions within us, pleasures round about us, but that these rightly temper'd are the very ingredients of virtu?" (II.527). In Chapter 6 I shall consider at some length Milton's conception of the conditions required for the constituting of human virtue. For now it is enough to note that Milton thinks this need for real "triall of vertue" "justifies the high providence of God" in placing man in a situation where sin is much more than a merely theoretical possibility (II.528, 527).

The final point to be made concerning the Free Will Defense as *Areopagitica* presents it is that, as Plantinga has argued, "a good person would not be obligated to eliminate a given evil if he could do so only by eliminating a good that outweighed it." Milton declares, "Were I the chooser, a dram of well-doing should be preferr'd before many times as much the forcible hindrance of evill-doing. For God sure esteems the growth and compleating of one vertuous person, more then the restraint of ten vitious" (II.528). Again Milton seeks to strengthen his argument by means of the assumption that certain norms of meaningfulness are common to God and man alike. Neither esteems a compelled "virtue." Thus we can appreciate that God might deem the value of genuine human virtue, and so of the freedom that it presupposes, to *outweigh* that of a state of affairs which included total obedience to God's commands only at the expense of true freedom.

Free Will Defense: literary dynamics

We can now turn our attention to *Paradise Lost,* where in book 3 perhaps the most explicit and well-known expression of the Free Will Defense in Milton's writings is uttered by God himself. Foreseeing Satan on his way to "the new created world" and the Fall of Man, which Satan's temptations will occasion, God speaks in his own defense:

> I made [man] just and right,
> Sufficient to have stood, though free to fall.
> Such I created all the ethereal powers
> And spirits, both them who stood and them who failed;
> Freely they stood who stood, and fell who fell.
> Not free, what proof could they have given sincere
> Of true allegiance, constant faith or love,
> Where only what they needs must do, appeared,
> Not what they would? What praise could they receive?
> What pleasure I from such obedience paid,
> When will and reason (reason also is choice)
> Useless and vain, of freedom both despoiled,
> Made passive both, had served necessity,
> Not me. They therefore as to right belonged,
> So were created, nor can justly accuse
> Their maker, or their making, or their fate.
>
> [3.98–113]

The argument is, first, that free will alone is sufficient explanation for the Fall. No determination on the part of God need be assumed. Secondly, despite its misuse, free will was an intrinsically valuable gift. To repeat Mackie's formulation, "It is better on the whole that men should act freely and sometimes err, than that they should be innocent automata, acting rightly in a wholly determined way." Also, by invoking the idea of praiseworthiness (3.106–107), the argument reaffirms Augustine's claim that man cannot properly be said to do what is right "unless he wills to." And, thirdly, like both Davies's account and that given in *Areopagitica*, God's version of the Free Will Defense implies that freedom is in particular a prerequisite to any meaningful relationship between persons – any relationship involving allegiance, faith, or love (3.104). In sum, God's speech reaffirms that freedom, as Tertullian says, is the "primary postulate of goodness and reason."

God goes on to say that men and angels are

> authors to themselves in all
> Both what they judge and what they choose; for so
> I formed them free, and free they must remain,
> Till they enthrall themselves: I else must change
> Their nature, and revoke the high decree
> Unchangeable, eternal, which ordained
> Their freedom.
>
> [3.122–8]

This passage asserts in stronger terms what Hoard says, following Tertullian – that "man is . . . undetermined in his actions, till he determine himself," and that "God useth not to repeal his own ordinances." Moreover, it recognizes that what is at stake is the nature of man; without freedom, as Pierce comments, "Man should not have been a Man."

We must notice here that in addition to God's utterance of straightforward doctrine, Milton has worked into the very context of God's speech the commonplace but profoundly significant idea of man's creation in the image of God. That image Milton in his prose identifies with the creature's freedom;[27] and elsewhere in *Paradise Lost*, referring to Adam and Eve, he says that

> in their looks divine
> The image of their glorious maker shone,
> Truth, wisdom, sanctitude severe and pure,
> Severe but in true filial freedom placed.
>
> [4.291–4]

"Filial" reminds us of the genetic relationship between the characteristics of parent and child, creator and creature, and hence of their corresponding value. In book 3, in the invocation that precedes the report of God's speech, the last item the blind poet laments no longer being able to see is the "human face divine" (3.45). And when God, a few lines later, bends down his eye (3.58), it is for the purpose of viewing "His own works and their works" (3.59). Which of his works? "He first beheld / Our two first parents" (3.64–5). And what works of theirs? "Immortal fruits of joy and love" (3.67). Thus the works/works parallel reinforces and complements the commonplace notion of the divine image in man, drawing attention to the value of creatures whose activity, to echo Plantinga, "is not causally determined – who, like [God] himself, are centres of creative activity."[28] And in this way Milton sets the stage for God's propounding of the Free Will Defense in the speech I have already quoted.

Theodical paradigm: Father and Son
God's speech has appeared to many to raise more questions than it answers. God says Satan is winging his way toward Eden to see "If [man] . . . he can . . . By some false guile pervert; and shall pervert" (3.91–2). The arguably glib tone of this statement might make one wonder if perhaps Satan's success is not assured. "Man will hearken to his glosing lies, / And easily transgress the sole command" (3.93–4). So what chance has man got? Is what God says about men's and angels' sufficiency to stand consistent with the facts? Moreover, is free will really incompatible with predetermination?[29] Did God's foreknowledge really not render the Fall inevitable? Did God genuinely not will the Fall? Of course, at the level of a defense, one is concerned only with the possibility of answering these questions in the affirmative. But Milton, presenting a theodicy *based on* the Free Will Defense, must also establish at least the probability or credibility of its constituent claims. And if any of the questions I have mentioned can in fact be answered negatively, how can such a theodicy succeed?

Some of these questions I shall return to in the chapters that follow. Here, however, I should like to argue that the Free Will Defense as spoken by God in book 3 of *Paradise Lost* not only raises questions but is intended to raise them. That is to say, a theodical and distinctively literary technique that Milton uses in *Paradise Lost* is to present the reader, or a character, or both reader and character, with only a part of the truth, with only a limited view of reality, in such a way that questions are raised concerning divine justice or providence; and then, in one or more stages, to present further truths, a more complete view of reality, which serves at least in part to answer the question originally raised, and possibly to reevaluate the terms of that question.

One of the most prominent examples of this technique concerns the speech of God in book 3 that I have just been discussing. After reading the divine self-defense one is, according to my hypothesis, in a somewhat restless, questioning mood. One has followed the argument, all right, but one cannot shake off the suspicion that God might simply be disguising a sinister plan to ensure mankind's humiliation. One is also conscious, perhaps, that such thoughts are not altogether compatible with the piety and reverence that one ought to exhibit in the divine presence. Hence one's surprise at hearing one's own questions, or something very like them, raised by presumably the greatest exemplar of piety and reverence – the Son himself. Although the Son begins by acknowledging that the "sovereign sentence" is "gracious" (3.144–5), he goes on, as we saw in the last chapter, to declare in remarkably blunt terms that if mankind is finally lost, then God's "goodness and . . . greatness both" will "be questioned and blasphemed without defence" (3.165–6).

However, one's surprise at hearing the Son putting so boldly the basic question one has oneself, somewhat guiltily, been pondering is exceeded by what one experiences on hearing God's reply. For not only is the question now seen to be decorous and valid – how could it be otherwise given that the Son himself asks it? – but the intent of the question is revealed to have been the very purpose of God all along:

> O Son, in whom my soul hath chief delight,
> Son of my bosom, Son who art alone

My word, my wisdom, and effectual might,
All hast thou spoken as my thoughts are, all
As my eternal purpose hath decreed:
Man shall not quite be lost, but saved who will,
Yet not of will in him, but grace in me
Freely vouchsafed.

[3.168–75]

Whereas *our* attitude in asking for justification of God's ways presupposed possible disharmony between God's interests and man's, the effect of the Son's putting the question and of God's answering it as he does leads us, in a dramatic sort of way, to the conclusion that no such disharmony exists. Yet the question itself is nonetheless valid, because we genuinely did not know what God was going to do about the situation, and its being raised has provided an opportunity for the divine plan to be revealed. It is as if God replies: "I was hoping you would ask me that."

Now there are two patterns exemplified here that are significant for the theodicy of *Paradise Lost* as a whole, and that will recur in some of the other examples of theodical model-building that I wish to discuss in this chapter. The first is that the issue of divine justice is treated in a dramatic way. God's enunciation of the Free Will Defense by itself lacks originality, as I have shown; and, isolated from its literary context, it could conceivably be taken as evidence in support of Arthur Lovejoy's outrageous charge concerning "the amazing superficiality of Milton's theodicy."[30] I am suggesting, however, that the Free Will Defense of book 3 is but an early stage in a kind of theodical dialectic that takes place on a large scale over the length of *Paradise Lost*, and that is reinforced by smaller-scale theodical dialectics within the poem, the former involving dialogue between Milton and the reader; the latter, dialogue between characters within the poem. The Father–Son dialogue of book 3, by engaging and tempering the reader's response to God's self-defense, as I have tried to show, exemplifies both kinds of dialectic.

The second pattern set by the scene is paradigmatic of how

theodicy itself ought to be conducted. For in the issue of divine justice, it is important how the questions are asked, as well as how they are answered. I have already emphasized that Milton set out to "justify the ways of God *to men*";[31] the question of theodicy cannot be radically separated from the role and situation of the questioner. And in this regard the Son is exemplary. If he is imitated, then the problem will still be raised – it will not be declared impious per se – but it will be characterized by a proper attitude on the part of the person who raises it. As the chorus says in *Samson Agonistes*:

> Just are the ways of God,
> And justifiable to men;
> Unless there be who think not God at all,
> If any be, they walk obscure;
>
>   .   .   .
> Yet more there be who doubt his ways not just.
>   [Lines 293–6, 300]

The Son, in contrast to those the chorus mentions, asks for justification of God's ways, but does so in an attitude devoid of doubt or unbelief. Despite one's ignorance of *how* God's ways are justifiable, one would do well to begin, the Son's example suggests, with an assumption that they *are* justifiable. And this is an assumption whose importance we shall see stressed again in connection with other theodical models in *Paradise Lost*.

Theodical paradigm: Abdiel and Satan

As we saw in the last chapter, the Son's request for theodicy sets the stage for the Father's enunciation of the doctrine of sufficient grace: In accordance with the goodness and justice of God, fallen man is given a chance of avoiding damnation. However, something analogous is required for prelapsarian man. The unavoidability of the Fall for Adam and Eve would have the same negative implications for theodicy as would the unavoidability of damnation for their offspring. Seventeenth-century Arminians recognized both problems. Pierce's response, for example, is simply to apply Arminian categories of grace, resistibility, and so on to the prelapsarian situation: "Though the *working* of *Grace* in the *heart* of *Adam* was so *strong* and so *perfect*, as to *enable* him to *stand*, . . . yet was it also so *resistible*, as to suffer him to *fall*."[32] John Goodwin, recognizing that the Fall could appear inevitable, seeks to undercut such a view by means of distinguishing possibility from probability. The species of mankind in Adam were "made *upright*, . . . and *in the image of God* . . . The possibility of becoming miserable . . . imported neither danger, nor likelyhood, of their becoming miserable, being nothing else but an essential distinguishing badg of their Creature-ship." Moreover, "the greatest unlikelyhoods sometimes take place, when probabilities vanish"; and so "the miscarrying of all Men in *Adam* is no sufficient Argument of any deficiency in the foundation of their standing."[33] Theodicy, in short, must somehow make plausible the claim that man need not have fallen. "Learn . . . to *justifie* God in all his wayes," implores Robert Harris, and he quickly asserts that "God made [man] a most glorious, happy, sufficient creature."[34] As Baxter declares in *God's Goodness, Vindicated*, "*Adam* could have stood when he fell . . . He fell, not because he could not stand, but because he would not."[35]

The task of rendering this claim plausible is especially formidable if the Fall is to be presented in a piece of literature; for in any "believable" fiction the author must provide discernible reasons for characters' behaving as they do, and yet if these reasons are perceived as sufficient causes, the characters' actions will appear to be determined. In such a case the reader, unless he or she believes free will and determinism to be compatible, will be unable to accept any claim that the characters are free and so responsible for what they do. In order to make his characters' actions appear both believable and responsible, therefore, the writer must somehow chart a course between the Scylla of randomness and the Charybdis of determinism.[36]

Such is Milton's task in presenting the Fall in *Paradise Lost*. Scylla, no doubt, is the lesser problem, for the temptations of the devil are sufficient to render the Fall credible. The harder question is, given the wiliness of the tempter, what chance have Adam and Eve really got of remaining uncorrupted? Milton, of course, cannot absolutely prove that Adam and Eve were sufficient to have stood. The only really firm demonstration of that claim would be their actually standing in the face of Satan's temptations. However, there is something Milton can do to make more plausible the claim that temptation by the devil does not necessitate a free creature's falling. Augustine, as we have seen, points out that "there are angels who have never sinned and who never will sin." In the seventeenth century, Nathaniel Homes affirms that Adam was "absolutely able to stand" and argues that man's fallibility was not a sufficient cause of his falling; for God also "made the Angels in a mutable condition, yet Myriades of them never fell."[37] And God, in *Paradise Lost*, says he made man "Sufficient to have stood, though free to fall. / Such I created all the ethereal powers / And spirits, both them who stood and them who failed (3.99–101). What Milton does, accordingly, is to exemplify the nonfall of one such free spirit in a way that reinforces the claim, made both to prelapsarian Adam and to postlapsarian reader, that giving in to Satan's temptations is not necessary.

The example is provided by the story of Abdiel. God, knowing Satan's design "to ruin all mankind" (5.228), sends Raphael to Eden on a mission of warning, with orders to bring on such discourse

> As may advise [Adam] of his happy state,
> Left to his own free will, his will though free,
> Yet mutable; whence warn him to beware
> He swerve not too secure: tell him withal
> His danger, and from whom.
>
> .   .   .
>
> this let him know,
> Lest wilfully transgressing he pretend
> Surprisal, unadmonished, unforewarned.
> So spake the eternal Father, and fulfilled
> All justice.
>
> [5.233–9, 243–7]

We are thus reminded, though God sends his warning out of pity toward Adam and Eve (5.220), that nevertheless there is a juridical dimension to their situation that is not unconnected with matters of freedom and familial affection. The same theme is stressed by Raphael, who tells Adam and Eve that mankind can expect a glorious future "If ye be found obedient, and retain / Unalterably firm his love entire / Whose progeny you are" (5.501–3). He then goes on to repeat the main thrust of the Free Will Defense uttered by God in book 3.

Significantly, Raphael's use of the first person plural serves as a reminder that freedom is an essential quality of men and angels alike, and thereby further emphasizes the implicit parallel between things human and things angelic around which the theodical model of book 5 is about to be constructed:

> God made thee perfect, not immutable;
> And good he made thee, but to persevere
> He left it in thy power, ordained thy will
> By nature free, not over-ruled by fate
> Inextricable, or strict necessity;
> Our voluntary service he requires,
> Not our necessitated, such with him
> Finds no acceptance, nor can find, for how
> Can hearts, not free, be tried whether they serve
> Willing or no, who will but what they must
> By destiny, and can no other choose?
> My self and all the angelic host that stand
> In sight of God enthroned, our happy state
> Hold, as you yours, while our obedience holds;
> On other surety none; freely we serve,
> Because we freely love, as in our will
> To love or not; in this we stand or fall.
>
> [5.524–40]

Adam responds by saying that he knows he was created free, assuring Raphael that "we never shall forget to love / Our maker, and obey him whose command / Single, is yet so just" (5.548–52). Adam is aware, therefore, of the vital connection among freedom, love, obedience, and divine justice. And now that the reader, too, has been reminded of the connection, both

Adam and he are ready to see what happens when God's commands are challenged.

Raphael narrates the events leading up to and including Satan's revolt, which is occasioned by "envy against the Son of God," whom the Father has "proclaimed Messiah" (5.662–4). Satan's first words of rebellion are addressed to Beelzebub:

> Remember'st what decree
> Of yesterday, so late hath passed the lips
> Of heaven's almighty.
>   .   .   .
> New laws thou seest imposed;
> New laws from him who reigns.
>   [5.674–80]

In terms of the problem of evil, we see immediately that Satan's view takes in God's omnipotence but not his goodness. Satan is conscious of law, but his consciousness of love is either non-existent or suppressed. Thus when he addresses his assembled cohorts he refers to God as if he were sheer impersonal power. He complains that "by decree / Another now hath to himself engrossed / All power, and us eclipsed" (5.774–6). Moreover, what that (unnamed) one will require is their "prostration vile," and Satan asks if they cannot somehow "cast off this yoke" (5.782, 786). His argument, essentially, is that the glorification of the Son robs the other heavenly inhabitants of dignity, and that God's command to honor the Son imposes a kind of necessity that limits their freedom:

> Who can in reason then or right assume
> Monarchy over such as live by right
>   .   .   .
> And look for adoration to the abuse
> Of those imperial titles which assert
> Our being ordained to govern, not to serve?
>   [5.794–802]

But here Abdiel breaks in – Abdiel, who, we are told at the outset, *both* "adored / The Diety, and divine commands obeyed" (5.805–6). Thus Abdiel's presence itself is an immediate reminder of the neglected dimension of love, or adoration, without which questions of obedience inevitably appear legalistic in the worst sense. Furthermore, he wisely refuses to speak of the exercise of divine power without reference to divine justice: Undermining as it were Satan's voluntarist assumptions, he refers to the anointing of the Son, of which Satan complains, as "the just decree of God" (5.814).

Yet Abdiel does not beg the question. He carries on to defend divine justice by means of a broad appeal to creation:

> Unjust thou say'st
> Flatly unjust, to bind with laws the free,
> And equal over equals to let reign,
> One over all with unsucceeded power.
> Shalt thou give law to God, shalt thou dispute
> With him the points of liberty, who made
> Thee what thou art, and formed the powers of heaven
> Such as he pleased, and circumscribed their being?
> Yet by experience taught we know how good,
> And of our good, and of our dignity
> How provident he is, how far from thought
> To make us less, bent rather to exalt
> Our happy state under one head more near
> United. But to grant it thee unjust,
> That equal over equals monarch reign:
> Thy self though great and glorious dost thou count,
> Or all angelic nature joined in one,
> Equal to him begotten Son, by whom
> As by his Word the mighty Father made
> All things, even thee, and all the spirits of heaven
> By him created in their bright degrees,
> Crowned them with glory, and to their glory named
> Thrones, dominations, princedoms, virtues, powers,
> Essential powers, nor by his reign obscured,
> But more illustrious made, since he the head
> One of our number thus reduced becomes,
> His laws our laws, all honour to him done
> Returns our own.
>
> [5.818–45]

Abdiel does not attempt to answer, by reason alone, how the Son's monarchy consists with the freedom of God's creatures, which is the sort of explanation Satan seems to want (5.794 ff.).

Rather, he simply emphasizes thaᵗ the powers of heaven, and by implication their freedom, are not infinite, but circumscribed, limited, and so to be seen in relation to the creator himself, who alone is infinite and uncircumscribed. Moreover, that this insistence on the limitation of creaturely freedom and existence does not imply the vile, degrading servitude that Satan's speech conjures up is evidenced by Abdiel's direct reference, with no sense of incongruity, to the angels' "good" and "dignity" (5.827). The creature's good has a vital genetic relation to the creator's good, and so Abdiel is able to answer Satan's questions not by abstract reasoning but by means of an appeal to the angels' own experience of that divine goodness and providence which Satan's speech so carefully avoided acknowledging.

The second part of Satan's question, concerning "right" (5.794), can also be answered in the context of the doctrine of creation, for it was by the Word of God that all things, "even thee, and all the spirits of heaven," were made (5.837). It is from the Father *through the Son* that the angels' goodness originates, so how could there be any such conflict between him and them as Satan imagines? As Abdiel says later, in book 6:

> Unjustly thou deprav'st it with the name
> Of servitude to serve whom God ordains,
> Or nature; God and nature bid the same,
> When he who rules is worthiest, and excels
> Them whom he governs. This is servitude,
> To serve the unwise, or him who hath rebelled
> Against his worthier, as thine now serve thee,
> Thy self not free, but to thy self enthralled.
>   [6.174–81]

At issue again is the true nature of freedom. In Satan's view it must be relative to no one and no thing. Therefore, knowing that he is free, he alters the facts to fit his theory: He cannot remember his own creation, so illogically imagines himself "self-begot" in accordance with some remote, impersonal "fatal course" (5.860–1). What he is in fact, as Abdiel makes clear, is not self-created but self-enthralled. For true and lasting creaturely freedom must, in accordance with the truth about its own genesis, recognize its relationship, its relativity, to God and his commands, without which it is meaningless, self-defeating, and "alienate" (5.877).

In the encounter between Satan and Abdiel, therefore, we again see Milton employing the dramatic technique we considered earlier in connection with the scene in heaven in book 3. One character presents not necessarily an inaccurate but a limited or incomplete view of reality. In this case, Satan the manipulative propagandist reveals only part of the truth: God is very powerful and has anointed the Son to rule. Of course, the Son's speech in book 3 involves no sinister intentions or bad faith, as Satan's does here; but the effect, in both cases, is to raise questions concerning the goodness or justice of God. And then what happens is that another character puts the partial truth in its broader context so as to indicate the solution to the problems that were originally raised.

Accordingly, in the theodical dialectic of book 5 one begins, if one believes Satan's rhetoric, with the suspicion aroused by God's self-defense in book 3 – that God is somehow bent on humiliating his creatures, or at least that he has not really got their interests at heart. But Abdiel interrupts, exclaiming, "O argument blasphemous, false and proud!" and then echoing Rom. 9:20, "Shalt thou give law to God?" (5.809, 822). Perhaps at this stage we have begun to suspect him of begging the question. However, Abdiel is not finished. He goes on to appeal to the heavenly powers' experience of God's goodness and providence as it concerns their own interests and dignity, and to point out, furthermore, that the correspondence between the norms of God and angel (5.844) is no arbitrary or chance phenomenon, but results from the essential, genetic relationship between creator and creature that the Son himself, as the creating Word of God, has mediated. He, therefore, and through him the Father are the very source of that glory and honor which Satan pretends is threatened by the Son's being proclaimed Messiah. How absurd, seeing that "all honour to him done / Returns our own."

The final stage of Abdiel's reply to Satan, if we include his speech in book 6, has the effect, like God's reply to the Son in book 3, of challenging one's attitude to the issue of divine justice. The terms of the question themselves are not rejected; Abdiel does not deny that God has pronounced the Son Messiah and commanded all the inhabitants of heaven to serve and obey him (5.606 ff.), for that is a fact. However, Abdiel does present a radically different interpretation of the facts. Satan sees service to the Son as servitude and bondage (5.173). But Abdiel turns that interpretation on its head:

> Reign thou in hell thy kingdom, let me serve
> In heaven God ever blest, and his divine
> Behests obey, worthiest to be obeyed.
>   [6.183–85]

Satan has it all wrong. Given the true nature of creaturely freedom and a recognition of the source and nature of value, service to God is freedom's fulfillment, not its antithesis. For God himself *is* that source of value, and so "worthiest to be obeyed."

In addition to constructing another theodical dialectic, Milton has also, in Abdiel's response to Satan, provided us with a further theodical paradigm like the one represented by the Son's speech in book 3. Although answering a question rather than asking one, as the Son does, Abdiel, in his attitude toward the issue of divine justice, is nevertheless similarly exemplary. Just as the Son puts his question to the Father without any hint of doubt or impiety, so Abdiel in answering Satan first rebukes the blasphemy and pride he knows the question implies (5.809) and makes it clear that theodicy must not be a matter of impiously imposing creaturely standards on the creator (5.822). And yet the fact that Abdiel goes on to give a reasoned (though not a rationalistic) justification of God's ways as they pertain to his ordination of the Son as Messiah shows that a request for theodicy is not something impious in itself. Indeed, it is actually salutary in that it provides an opportunity for further assertion and appreciation of eternal providence. That "all honour" rendered to the Son "Returns our own" (5.844–5) is something we may not have fully realized before. Of course, Satan still will not allow himself to realize it; but at least our knowing it puts us in a better position to see his rebellion for what it is.

And of course the same goes for Adam and Eve. They, as well as we, are shown an example, in word and deed, of the folly of disobedience, on the one hand, and of liberty fulfilled in voluntary and loving obedience to God, on the other. That is the explicit purpose of Raphael's telling the story; it is for their own good (5.571–2). It warns them of what they might have to face, and shows them how they ought to act when they do face it. And perhaps most importantly, the story of Abdiel also shows them that it can be done; obedience can be achieved, even under severe temptation. For Abdiel's is no blank virtue. He is a shining example of sincerely proven allegiance, faith, and love. Abdiel is

> faithful found,
> Among the faithless, faithful only he;
> Among innumerable false, unmoved,
> Unshaken, unseduced, unterrified
> His loyalty he kept, his love, his zeal;
> Nor number, nor example with him wrought
> To swerve from truth, or change his constant mind
> Though single.
>
> [5.896–902]

This summary of Abdiel's achievement brings us back to the Free Will Defense. We have seen that God sent Raphael to advise man of his happiness, free will, and mutability (5.234–7). This errand, together with Raphael's and Adam's discussion of free will and the theodical dialectic involving Satan and Abdiel, keeps us aware throughout book 5 of the fact that what is being attempted in *Paradise Lost* is an assertion of providence and a justification of God's ways. That justification, I have been arguing, centers on the Free Will Defense as a model for the consistency of the claims that God is omnipotent and wholly good and that there is evil in the world. In presenting the Free Will Defense Milton must also do what he can to make its various claims plausible. One such claim is that man is genuinely free to make the right morally significant choice when tempted to make the wrong one. Lest anyone suspect that such freedom is merely theoretical, and that in practice man would fall if actually confronted with the devil's temptations, Milton exploits the parallel between human and angelic freedom. Was it not simply that those who were not tempted stood and those who were tempted fell? The story of Abdiel shows that the answer to this question is no. And although no firm demonstration is possible, by thus modeling the notable nonfall of one free creature, Milton lends plausibility to God's claim that man, too, was "sufficient to have stood."

Theodical paradigm: God and Adam

The Free Will Defense raises a further though perhaps less obvious question. In *Paradise Lost*, God says that prelapsarian man "had of me / All he could have" (3.97–8). What in fact does this mean, and what bearing does it have on the matter of human freedom? One might argue that God could have locked Adam and Eve up somewhere and seen to it that no temptation ever beset them. But obviously this is more than he was willing to do, though it certainly would have prevented the Fall. The claim that follows, therefore (the one we have just considered concerning man's sufficiency to stand and freedom to fall), must be seen as qualifying or explaining what exactly it was that man had from God: He had "All he could have" that was consistent with the requirements of genuine freedom.

The point is relevant to the story of the Fall as a whole. John Hick criticizes what he considers to be the traditional Christian theodicy on the grounds that "an angelic or human fall presupposes some temptation such as is not conceivable in finitely perfect creatures existing consciously in the presence of God." He argues that the sort of creative freedom the Free Will Defense assumes would require that man live in a world "in which the divine reality is not unambiguously manifest to him."[38] There must be some sort of "epistemic distance" between God and man; otherwise man will be so overpowered by the knowledge of what is right that his freedom will have no genuine opportunity to function and will in effect therefore cease to exist – to the detriment of, among other things, the Free Will Defense.

Now Hick's argument concerning this matter of freedom and an "epistemic distance," is, I believe, sound; yet in *Paradise Lost*, Milton provides a model which suggests that no criticism of the traditional story of the Fall need follow, as Hicks thinks it must. The model is contained in book 8, in Adam's account to Raphael of his own first experiences upon being created. The account presents, too, a theodical dialectic and a paradigm of theodicy such as we have already considered in the cases of the Father–Son dialogue of book 3 and the Satan–Abdiel encounters in books 5 and 6.

Adam, after hearing the story of the war in heaven and receiving a lesson in cosmology and cosmogony, offers to tell Raphael his own story. Raphael responds by assuring Adam of his and all the angels' interest in matters human. His comment sets the tone for what is to follow:

> Nor less think we in heaven of thee on earth
> Than of our fellow servant, and inquire
> Gladly into the ways of God with man:
> For God we see hath honoured thee, and set
> On man his equal love.

[8.224–8]

Already we have seen the Son himself raising the matter of theodicy; now it is a good angel who inquires into God's ways. Raphael thus provides us with another reminder that such inquiry has no necessary connection with the kind of impiety that Satan displayed. Indeed, the initial emphasis here is on God's love toward mankind.

In response to Raphael's encouragement, Adam recounts what he knows of his creation. However, in contrast to Satan's proud and illogical conclusion that because the angels cannot

remember their making they must be "self-begot, self-raised /
By [their] own quickening power" (5.857–61), Adam begins by
expressing a fit modesty with respect to the extent of creaturely
knowledge: "For man to tell how human life began / Is hard:
for who himself beginning knew?" (8.250–1). Nevertheless, we
soon gather that Adam's cognitive and ratiocinative powers are
considerable, for as his account makes clear, from his own existence and from the wonders of creation that he beheld round
about him after having waked for the first time, he was immediately able to deduce the existence of an omnipotent and
wholly good God. He exclaims:

> fair creatures, tell,
> Tell, if ye saw, how came I thus, how here?
> Not of my self; by some great maker then,
> In goodness and in power pre-eminent.[39]

Adam's intellectual life thus begins with an acceptance of the
first two of the three propositions that, as we have seen, define
the theological problem of evil in its most basic form.

Yet having met God and given further evidence of his mental
powers by naming the animals, Adam somewhat surprisingly
begins what appears to be a complaint against the ways of God,
and initiates a case for his being provided with a "human con-
sort" (8.392). Although any sense we might have of the impro-
priety of Adam's request is lost when we see that God answers
"not displeased" (8.398), nevertheless Adam is not given satisfaction, and so must develop his case further. The basic charge
he advances is that, because he has no one with whom he can
share "collateral love," he has not been made perfect (8.426,
415–16, 423). And one wonders, I think, if perhaps Adam has a
point, particularly in view of Raphael's assertion earlier on that
God did make man "perfect," though mutable (5.524).

And of course God's final response reveals that indeed Adam
does have a point. As Adam tells Raphael:

> I emboldened spake, and freedom used
> Permissive, and acceptance found, which gained
> This answer from the gracious voice divine.

> Thus far to try thee, Adam, I was pleased,
> And find thee knowing not of beasts alone,
> Which thou hast rightly named, but of thy self,
> Expressing well *the spirit within thee free,*
> *My image,* not imparted to the brute,
> Whose *fellowship* therefore unmeet for thee
> Good reason was thou freely shouldst dislike,
> And be so minded still; I, ere thou spakest,
> Knew it not good for man to be alone,
> And no such company as then thou saw'st
> Intended thee, for trial only brought,
> To see how thou couldst judge of fit and meet:
> What next I bring shall please thee, be assured,
> Thy *likeness,* thy fit help, thy other self,
> Thy wish exactly to thy heart's desire.
>
> [8.434–51; italics added]

As with the other two examples of theodical dialectic that have been discussed, what emerges from this one is a realization of the harmony of the interests of creator and creature. Just as the Son's question turned out to have embodied the very thoughts of the Father (3.171), so, here, what may at first have looked like the creature's "arguing with God" is revealed to be an expression of what has been God's purpose from the start – an expression, indeed, of God's own image in man.

Moreover, as the dialectic progresses, there also emerges a further paradigm of theodicy, a model of theodicy as it ought to be conducted. Raphael, as we have already noted, gladly inquires into God's ways with man (8.226). He is well aware of God's love toward Adam, and he would simply like to hear how it has manifested itself. Adam, in answering Raphael as well as in questioning God, makes no proud assumptions about the sufficiency of creaturely reason to comprehend God. Rather, he admits before God: "To attain / The highth and depth of thy eternal ways / All human thoughts come short" (8.412). This is the attitude that was evidenced by Abdiel's refusal to answer Satan's question concerning how "in reason" the Son could "assume / Monarchy" over the inhabitants of heaven (5.794 ff.). Because God's purpose is not always apparent, an inquiry into his ways can be quite a legitimate and beneficial thing to engage in; but it must not be a matter of giving laws to God (5.822). Adam, accordingly, questioning God boldly and yet in a spirit of humility, is granted the privilege of learning personally about God's will for him. And as I have suggested, like the other examples of theodical dialectic we have examined, this one reveals in a dramatic way the consistency of God's will with the creature's genuine interests. God answers "thy wish exactly to thy heart's desire" (8.451). God justifies his ways by revealing his providence. Indeed, in this manner the dialogue between God and Adam presents a justification of God's ways, as does *Paradise Lost* as a whole, *through* an assertion of eternal providence, and in response to questions put both by Milton's characters and by his readers.

Now Milton's theodicy, to repeat a major premise, centers on the Free Will Defense. And a question the reader of *Paradise Lost* might well ask about the Free Will Defense is how Adam and Eve can truly be free given their unfallen relationship with God. What meaning could man's freedom have unless he lived in a state already like that of the postlapsarian world, in which, to echo Hick, "the divine reality is not unambiguously manifest to him"? In Eden, would man's life not be as meaningless and bored as that of a completely spoiled child? Part of this question I shall take up in Chapter 6, but for now it is enough to point out that Adam's conversation with God in book 8 of *Paradise Lost* exemplifies precisely the creative exercise of judgment and choice whose value is so vital an assumption of the Free Will Defense.[40] What may at first appear a needless game that God decided to play with Adam before giving him a wife can in retrospect be seen as something necessary for the function and realization, in more than one sense, of that which is God's image in man – his free spirit (8.440). And of course this requires of God a kind of self-limitation. He must not bombard man with knowledge of the truth, but allow him to discover and judge things for himself. For, as Davies says, "what is Man without a moving mind / Which hath a judging wit and choosing will?"[41] and how are such judgment and choice possible unless man exists at some sort of epistemic distance from the overwhelming radiance of God's truth? Milton does not avoid this issue. Rather, he constructs a model to show how the literal presence of God is consistent with – indeed, enhances – the cognitive freedom and trial of virtue that man requires: God himself, in person, tries Adam "to see how [he can] judge of fit and meet" (8.447–8).

Perhaps a word should be interjected here concerning what I have referred to as the epistemic distance from God at which man was created. Is it not, the skeptic might ask, really only a euphemism for ignorance? And how can one treat ignorance as a precondition of freedom when the state of the blessed – *non posse peccare* – is consistent with enjoyment of the Beatific Vision and traditionally has been looked on as freedom of the highest order? The answer to the first question is that the epistemic distance does imply a relative ignorance, though not in its loaded, postlapsarian sense; just as, in Augustinian ontology, privation of being is evil whereas limitation of being is not,[42] so the epistemic distance at which man is created from God implies limitation of knowledge but not privation. Thomas Goodwin, a seventeenth-century theologian and acquaintance of Milton's, describes it this way: The "Condition of Saints and Angels now in Glory" is such that "the manifestation of God to the Understanding . . . is so super-abundantly full" that "they cannot Sin . . . But, the law and measure both for Angels and Men by Creation, was that God should be so represented to them as to give them a power to cleave to God as their chiefest Good," or to turn in an idolatrous way to other "Objects."[43] And the answer to the second question, I think, is that the inability to sin of which Goodwin speaks is itself a consequence of the kinds of choice one has made while still in a state of *posse peccare*. As a present-day philosopher puts it, "The inability to do evil in heaven" is only a making permanent of that which one, by one's own "free choice here on earth, really desired to be achieved. That is, the Beatific Vision is, by God's irresistibly persuasive power, *not* a frustration but a fulfillment of what the godly have really chosen."[44]

The scene we have been considering shows godly choice in action. The fact that such choice is dramatically consistent with the presence of God and with sinless "debate" and learning would seem to undercut Hick's assumption that freedom can exist only if man is, as it were, created fallen.[45] For, even while God and a sinless Adam converse, there is a salutary epistemic distance between them. Moreover, God's allowing Adam to ask for a wife himself provides the kind of opportunity for self-discovery and exploration of the divine will that would never arise were all possible desires and all knowledge granted from the outset; and in showing us this process Milton also undercuts any simplistic or uncritical notion of Paradise as a kind of ultimate holiday resort where all one's needs and desires are catered to without one's having so much as to ring for room service. In this way the episode contributes to the poem's definition of innocence and provides both Adam and the reader with a demonstration of how providence seeks not only to meet man's genuine needs, but also to do so in a manner that ensures the integrity and scope of creaturely freedom. For the Free Will Defense, in short, it shows such freedom to be both possible and important.

Theodical parody: Adam and Eve

There is a final theodical model ancillary to the Free Will Defense that I would like to discuss in this chapter. It concerns Adam's and Eve's relationship with each other and the events leading up to their decision to separate and garden alone. As we recall, in his self-defense in book 3, God asks, "Not free, what proof could [men and angels] have given sincere / Of true allegiance, constant faith or love?" (103–4). Now what Milton does in book 9 is to show how this dictum applies to the allegiance, faith, and love of man to man, as well as of man to God, and by thus emphasizing freedom as a common criterion of meaningfulness in human beings' relationships both with God and with each other, to develop a parallel that has significance not only for his theodicy but also for the overall structure of his epic.

The fundamental issue in Adam and Eve's long discussion in book 9 leading up to their separation is the role of freedom in their relationship. That this freedom is a prerequisite to genuine allegiance, faith, and love, however, is not a claim that either contests; rather, what they disagree about is how that freedom ought to be exercised. Adam argues that the pleasures and responsibilities of marriage – such as the "sweet intercourse / Of looks and smiles" and mutual protection (9.238–9, 265 ff., 309 ff.) – are best enjoyed or fulfilled by their working together. Eve, on the other hand, suspects Adam of doubting her faith and love (9.286), "her faith sincere" (9.320), and replies by asking "what is faith, love, virtue unassayed / Alone, without exterior help sustained?" (9.335–6). Adam, in turn, does not deny that trial is necessary; but, apparently remembering Abdiel's response to Satan in book 6, he encourages a less superficial understanding of the nature of freedom. True freedom involves the obedience of will to reason, as God has ordained it (9.351–3, 344), as well as obedience of man to God. They must be on their guard not to do "what God expressly hath forbid"; and so, Adam gently urges, "Not . . . mistrust, but tender love enjoins, / That I should mind thee oft, and mind thou me" (9.356–8). For Adam's and Eve's mutual faith and love must both be seen in the context of their relationship to God, "whom to love is to obey, and keep His great command" (8.634–5), as Raphael has said. Therefore, just as man ought freely to obey God, so ought Eve to show allegiance to Adam. The parallel nature of the obligations is emphasized by Adam's invoking of that principle which we first heard enunciated by God himself, that allegiance is meaningless if compelled: "thy stay, not free, absents thee more" (9.372).

I shall return in Chapter 6 to the issue of who is to blame for Eve's improvident decision to work on her own; it is, of course, a further matter that vitally concerns the question of man's sufficiency to have stood. If for any reason he was not sufficient, then God's truth and justice might well be "without defence." At the moment, however, what one ought to notice is that God's expressly having forbidden something (9.356) by no means infringes on man's freedom with respect to that thing, because a command does not compel obedience.[46] Furthermore, to restate a major premise of the Free Will Defense, God has decreed

> that in the love and worship of [himself] . . . men should always use their free will. If we do not, whatever worship or love we men offer to God is worthless and of no account. The will which is threatened or overshadowed by any external decree cannot be free, and once force is imposed all esteem for services rendered grows faint and vanishes altogether. [CD, p. 189]

As this quotation from Milton's prose treatise suggests, Adam is right to claim that Eve's allegiance is worthless if compelled (9.372). But the point is that all Adam apparently need do in order to prevent Eve's wandering off by herself is to forbid it. And because it is constraint, not command, that negates freedom, he *can* forbid it. He would not thereby violate Eve's freedom to go if she so chose, any more than God's commanding them not to eat of the forbidden fruit prevents their freely doing so. Therefore, despite Adam's warning Eve, his failure to command her renders his parting words poignantly ironic: "God towards thee hath done his part, do thine" (9.375). For if Adam applied the advice to himself he would not hesitate to forbid Eve's going, and the Fall might never occur.

This, of course, is precisely one of Eve's points at the end of the book:

> Being as I am, why didst not thou the head
> Command me absolutely not to go,
> Going into such danger as thou saidst?
> Too facile then thou didst not much gainsay,
> Nay didst permit, approve, and fair dismiss,
> Hadst thou been firm and fixed in thy dissent,
> Neither had I transgressed, nor thou with me.
> [9.1155–61]

Although it can be argued here that Eve is exaggerating, her exaggeration is based on the truth. And Adam, in an effort to avoid that truth and so exculpate himself, recurs to the Free Will Defense:

> what could I more?
> I warned thee, I admonished thee, foretold
> The danger, and the lurking enemy
> That lay in wait; beyond this had been force,
> And force upon free will hath here no place.
>   [9.1170–4]

Yet regardless of how many critics and editors have been swayed by Adam's reasoning,[47] his claim is perfectly ludicrous. It is simply untrue that more than a mere warning would have forced Eve's obedience, and Adam knows it. He himself told Raphael about God's pronouncement of "The rigid interdiction, which resounds / Yet dreadful in mine ear, though in my choice / Not to incur" (8.333–6). How then can Adam imply that a rigid interdiction on his part would interfere with Eve's free will? He already has a model for the consistency of law with liberty. And so have we. Given the Free Will Defense as expressed by God in book 3 (lines 80–128) and again by Raphael in book 5 (lines 520–40), book 9's repeated and explicit appeal to free will as underlying the meaningfulness of Adam's and Eve's relationship with each other makes the parallel to man's relationship with God obvious. And the obvious contrast within that parallel is Adam's failure to be "firm and fixed" in his dissent.

The events of book 9 that I have been discussing have, I believe, three main functions that are relevant to theodicy. First of all, the manifest importance of freedom in Adam's and Eve's relationship with each other lends credence to the general claim God makes in connection with the Free Will Defense, that no true allegiance, faith, or love is possible unless human beings are free. We recall that, in *Areopagitica*, Milton fortified his argument with an appeal to the same principle's human application: "We our selves esteem not of that obedience, or love, or gift, which is of force."[48] He does the same thing in *Paradise Lost*.

Secondly, Adam's defense of himself at the end of book 9 is a kind of parody of the Free Will Defense as expressed by God in book 3. Of course the irony is that instead of displaying any sort of unfallen Godlikeness, instead of embodying the principle of reason, "by which to heavenly love thou mayst ascend" (8.592), postlapsarian Adam's argument indicates a perversion of his Godlikeness and so by its very similarity to God's argument makes the contrast between the states of sinlessness and sin the more poignant. Moreover, the paradigms of theodicy we have considered – the Son's and Adam's requests for justification of God's ways and Abdiel's presentation of such a justification – have been characterized by a lack of any adversarial "arguing with God" like that attempted by Satan in book 5, whereas in Adam's parody of theodicy at the end of book 9, argument and "mutual accusation" (9.1187) are precisely what predominate. And the result, of course, rather than being "fruits of joy and love," such as God beholds just prior to his self-defense in book 3, is "fruitless hours" (9.1188) palpably devoid of joy or love. In facilitating such contrasts, therefore, the Free Will Defense takes on a role of structural as well as theological and dramatic importance for *Paradise Lost*.

Finally, Adam's emphasizing free will in his conversations with Eve in book 9 draws our attention once again to the Free Will Defense, first by way of comparison and then, if we see through Adam's illogic, by way of contrast. And accompanying both God's and Raphael's presentations of this defense, as I have indicated, is a recognition that the freedom in question coexists with God's "rigid interdiction," to repeat Adam's own words (8.334; cf. 3.94 and 5.551–2). Thus God's simultaneously being "firm and fixed" in commanding abstinence from the forbidden fruit and himself refraining from any infringement of man's freedom provides a model, both in the logical sense of what policy Adam *could* have taken toward Eve and in the moral sense of what policy he *should* have taken.

Milton critics and Adam alike, therefore, are without excuse. It is true that if Adam genuinely faced the dilemma, in book 9,

of having either to abandon "hapless Eve" to the temptation of
Satan or else to compel her allegiance and so render meaningless something that ought, in God's good creation, to have been
of enormous intrinsic value, then God's self-defense in book 3
might well be undermined. However, by book 9, Milton has
already presented sufficient evidence *to prove* that being commanded is not inconsistent with being free, and therefore that
Adam faces no dilemma in this regard. Of course one might
have forgotten such evidence. But Milton is a poet who is particularly insistent on one's responsibility to remember what
one has learned and to apply it in making one's judgments.
Adam failed in that responsibility; and if the reader, in a similarly culpable lapse of memory, has accepted Adam's self-
defense, then he need only turn the page to the beginning of
book 10, where he will be told once again that Adam and Eve
were allowed to be tempted, but

> with strength entire, and *free will* armed,
> Complete to have discovered and repulsed
> Whatever wiles of foe or seeming friend.
> For still they knew, and *ought to have still remembered*
> The *high injunction* not to taste that fruit,
> Whoever tempted.
>
> [10.9–14; italics added]

Thus the reader, too, is prodded to remember God's high
injunction and its demonstrated consistency with free will. In
this way, Milton not only makes use of the Free Will Defense as
a philosophical model, but also, once again, transforms it into
a literary resource for facilitating his poetic justification of God
to men.

5

Theodicy, free will, and determinism

I have argued that Milton exploits the Free Will Defense as a literary and philosophical model. Now readers as well as writers employ models, consciously or unconsciously, and part of the purpose of this book is to make explicit some of the models Milton uses, in order to keep them from being shouldered aside by someone else's. My assumption in all of this is not that one must accept Milton's models before one can understand his poetry, but that no critical acceptance or rejection of them is possible at all unless one has some appreciation of what they are and mean. In Chapter 3 I argued that an orthodox Calvinist model of grace ought not to be allowed to displace the Arminian one that actually operates in *Paradise Lost*. In the present chapter I shall seek to show what model of free will functions in Milton's theodicy, first contrasting this version of free will with a major but little-recognized deterministic definition of it, secondly concentrating on the peculiar definition given to God's freedom and on its significance for the issue of divine justice, and thirdly turning to Milton's case against the better-known argument that human free will is inconsistent with divine foreknowledge. These topics constitute their own realm of philosophical debate, and I will not pretend to do more than merely introduce them as they pertain to the problem of evil; yet each is so important to theodicy that an account of Milton's justification of God would be seriously deficient if it lacked any acknowledgement of them.

"Compatibilism" and human freedom

Compatibilism is the position that free will does not preclude determinism and vice versa – or, as Peter Sterry put it in the seventeenth century, that

the *Freedom of all things* is *to act according to their natures;* and so is that of the will of man; and that in God and man, Necessity and Liberty concurr, and that whatever we do or will, we do or will it necessarily, as being moved to it by the first cause and a chained connexion of necessitating causes; by which all things in the world are carried on.[1]

If this position is correct, then the Free Will Defense – postulating as it does that God's decision to give man free will precludes divine interference with man's freedom to do wrong – is radically undermined, and the whole notion of free will is rendered theodically useless. In modern philosophical circles, accordingly, much of the debate about the Free Will Defense centers on the issue of compatibilism;[2] and so it did in the seventeenth century. Indeed, Richard Baxter, a year after Milton's death, looks back on the theological controversy of his age and declares that "the true life" of the difficulties "between the Synod of *Dort* and the *Arminians*"

is in this controversie between the defenders of *Necessary Predetermination,* and of *Free-will;* that is, . . . *Whether ever in Angels or Innocent man there was such a thing, as a will that can and ever did determine it self to a Volition or Nolition* in specie morali, *without the predetermining efficient necessitating premotion of God as the first Cause?* . . . or as *Hobbes* speaketh, Whether ever a created will, did act, without a necessitating premotion?[3]

As was noted in Chapter 3, Augustine, although seeking to base his theodicy on free will, tended to verge into compatibilism – at least with regard to postlapsarian matters – contending against the Pelagians "that God works in the hearts of men to incline their wills whithersoever He wills, whether to good deeds . . . or to evil."[4] Orthodox Calvinists and others in the seventeenth century followed this tendency of Augustinian theology and accordingly did indeed deny that a created will ever acted without a "necessitating premotion of God as the first Cause." Thomas Whitfield, for example, asserts "that though Gods will determine mans will, yet it determines to worke contingently and freely."[5] The principle is regularly applied to both prelapsarian and postlapsarian conditions. Since the Fall, man has required grace to perform any good action, so that without grace man necessarily sins. As William Pemble puts it, "When [divine] help is thus withdrawne, the creature . . . cannot chuse but fall and erre; yet inclines to that fall and error of its owne accord, and by its owne fault, not by enforcement and compulsion of Gods will."[6] With regard to the Fall itself, William Twisse asserts that "God not only so efficaciously administered the whole business that man should fall, but also that he should fall freely."[7] And similarly, as we have seen, the Westminster Confession declares that God's providence "extendeth itself even to the first fall, and all other sins, . . . and that not by a bare permission, but such as hath joined with it a most wise and powerful bounding; . . . yet so as the sinfulness thereof proceedeth only from the creature."[8]

This compatibilist position is more subtle than it may at first appear. It is not to be confused with hard determinism or fatalism, which would deny that things could be other than they are. The compatibilist recognizes that human choices are made and responsibilities thus incurred. However, the compatibilist will hold Jones responsible for a given action because Jones could have *acted otherwise,* had he so chosen; the incompatibilist (or libertarian) holds Jones responsible because he could have *chosen otherwise.* The compatibilist believes that one can ask, and in principle answer, the question *why* Jones chose as he did – believes, in other words, that there is a *sufficient cause* of Jones's choice. The libertarian sees that belief as begging the question, for given a sufficient cause of Jones's choice, it follows that Jones could not have chosen otherwise. The libertarian would contend, rather, that although there are *necessary* causes or conditions for Jones's, say, cheating on his income tax, nevertheless his choice is not sufficiently caused one way or the other, and he himself makes the determination. Asked why Jones does decide to cheat, the libertarian may point out that Jones would have to sell his car to pay the taxes he owes; but such reasons will not be treated as answering the question *why* in the sense of providing sufficient causation. And the compatibilist may therefore argue that a meaningful conception of free will *requires* determinism.[9]

Seventeenth-century orthodox Calvinists appear to have rejected the libertarian definition of free will because, put simplistically, it allows a person in a limited but crucial respect the capacity to be self-determining, an ability they ascribed to God alone. On a different level of consideration, the battle is essentially the one that was examined in Chapter 3. John Owen, tracing the history of "the old Pelagian Idol Free-will," sees the conception of a will not sufficiently caused as implying "an absolute independence of Gods providence . . . and of his grace":

Herein, saith Arminius, consisteth the libertie of the will: that all things required to enable it, to will any thing, being accomplished, it still remaines indifferent to will, or not . . . : There is, accompanying the will of man . . . libertie, . . . which, when all things prerequired as necessary to operation are fulfilled, may will anything, or not will it: that is, our free-wils have . . . an absolute, and uncontrollable power, in the territory of all humane actions.[10]

Arminians, of course, would deny this final inference, and point out that Owen is creating a false disjunction between God's absolute power and man's free will. They would protest that free will is not primordial, but rather a sort of delegated subsovereignty that God himself freely granted his creatures, for reasons we have already considered.

Nevertheless, Owen characterizes accurately the main difference between the compatibilist and libertarian models of free will. The latter involves a causal *indifference,* and I shall refer to this as the balance model, according to which, in a given moral choice, necessary conditions exist that allow the agent to choose one way or the other. As Charleton defines it, "The nature of this Liberty Elective seems radically to consist in that *Indifferency*, in respect whereof the Faculty called free, may or may not be carried on towards any particular object"; and he goes on to point out that this indifferency in general the "happy wit of *Cicero* . . . most conveniently compares . . . to a *Balance.*"[11] The other, primarily Calvinist model of freedom Charleton defines in the course of an attack on strict predestinarians, whom he accuses of "mincing, or extenuating the Elective Liberty of man into a meer *Libency* . . . and accordingly attempting to salve the *Repugnancy* thus; that the Elect are therefore Free, because they do their Good works *Libently,* or Willingly; and likewise, that the Reprobate are also Free, because they do their Evil works *Libently*" (p. 344). This "libency" is opposed not to necessity or predetermination, but to compulsion; and so long as one is not *compelled* to do evil, according to the compatibilist view, one is responsible for the evil one does, because it is done willingly, though necessarily.

In the mid-seventeenth century this view was very widespread,[12] and it had both prominent attackers and prominent defenders. The charge Milton mentions in *The Doctrine and Discipline of Divorce,* that the Calvinists make God "the author of sinne," was directly connected with the compatibilist component of their theology. Samuel Hoard attacks Calvin, Beza, and their followers for disingenuousness in their account of God's permission of sin. As he declares:

Permission, about whomsoever it is exercised, . . . is no more than a not hindring of them from falling, that are able to stand, and supposeth a possibility of sinning or not sinning, in the parties permitted: but with them it is a withdrawing or with-holding of grace needfull for the avoiding of sin, and so includeth an absolute necessity of sinning: for from the withdrawing of such grace sin must needs follow, as the fall of *Dagons* house followed *Sampsons* plucking away the Pillars that were necessary for the upholding of it.[13]

Developing further his case against the compatibilists, Hoard argues that "the Ancients made no distinction between those two words (*necessity*) and (*compulsion*) . . . : and did deny, that

God did necessitate men to sin, lest they should grant him hereby to be the Author of sin." He makes explicit the issue's theodical connection: The ancients "believed and contended, that the judgements of God on sinners could not be just, if they were held by the Adamantine chains of any absolute necessity under the power of their sins." And indeed, he charges that the notion of men's sinning *libently* is even more disastrous for theodicy than would be that of their being compelled to sin, for "if Gods decree do not only make men sin, but willingly too; not only cause that they shall *do evill*, but *will evill*, it hath the deeper hand in the sin" (p. 32).

Utterly unperturbed by compatibilism's theodically horrific consequences was its most famous seventeenth-century defender, Thomas Hobbes, whose debate with Bishop John Bramhall, published as *The Questions concerning Liberty, Necessity, and Chance,* explores at length all of the issues introduced so far in this chapter. Although scarcely a Calvinist, Hobbes acknowledges at the outset that the Arminian controversy is the occasion of his and Bramhall's dispute,[14] and throughout the debate he has no hesitation in drawing support from his decidedly more Christian compatibilist predecessors. Quoting the Synod of Dort to the effect that "liberty is not opposite to all kinds of necessity and determination," Hobbes adds that "all the famous Doctors of the Reformed Churches, and with them St. Augustine are of the same opinion" (p. 235).

Much of Bramhall's case against Hobbes consists in his drawing out the "inconveniences" of the compatibilist position,[15] including theodical inconveniences of the sort I have already touched on. For example, Bramhall claims that Hobbes's doctrine makes "second causes . . . to be the Rackets, and Men to be but the Tennis-Balls of destiny," and that therefore either "there is no such thing as sin in the world, because it proceeds naturally, necessarily, and essentially from God," or else "God is more guilty of it, and more the cause of evil than Man," because "the cause of the cause is alwaies the cause of the effect."[16] As Antony Flew has put it in our own day, the compatibilist position is perfectly consistent with divine manipulation and the "predestinarian nightmare."[17]

The philosophy of Hobbes, however, has a kind of built-in immunity to theodical objections by virtue of its voluntarism. According to Hobbes, power, efficacy of will – in God's case, omnipotence – is precisely what determines what shall be called good and just: "The power of God alone, without other help, is sufficient Justification of any action he doth"; and therefore "that which he does is made just by his doing" (p. 88). Bramhall does not deny "that old and true principle, that *the Will of God is the rule of Justice*" (p. 104), but he does deny that it licenses the kind of tautological theodicy that justifies whatever ways one imagines to be God's ways. As he declares:

It is the mode of these times to father their own fancies upon God, and when they cannot justifie them by reason, to plead his Omnipotence, or to cry, *O altitudo*, that the wayes of God are unsearchable. If they may justifie their drowsie dreams, because Gods power and dominion is absolute, much more may we reject such phantastical devises which are inconsistent with the truth, and goodness, and justice of God. [P. 99]

Nevertheless, despite the strength of Bramhall's case to the extent that it is based on theodicy, when it comes to specific questions of necessity and choice, which after all are the matter of his dispute with Hobbes, he seems on the whole to be overmatched. Part of this is a result of Hobbes's consistent refusal to accept any terms of Bramhall's argument that he considers scholastic or artificial, or to engage the bishop's charges when they are in the least rhetorically adorned. Hobbes's dismissals of scholastical discourse as "*Tohu* and *Bohu*, that is to say, Confusion and Emptiness," and of Bramhall's arguments as "filled up with wondering and railing" recur like a kind of leitmotiv throughout the work.

Bramhall, for his part, is less tactically astute and too readily accepts a rather simplistic faculty psychology. This allows Hobbes to charge that either the bishop's position involves, in spite of itself, a necessitation of the will as a result of the dictates of the reason, which in turn is determined by perception, or else it implies some notion of the will as a self-caused cause (p. 230). For the most part acquiescing to the latter half of this disjunction, Bramhall in effect facilitates Hobbes's attempts to caricature the libertarian position by speaking of the will as if it were some sort of disembodied, autonomous force. Summarizing Bramhall's position, Hobbes says in his preface, "To the Reader," that the bishop "maintaineth, That not onely the *Man* is Free to choose what he will Do, but the *Will* also to choose what it shall Will." Although I do not expect to settle the dispute between compatibilists and libertarians, I think that in the context of the present discussion it is important to recognize that the relatively unsophisticated notion of free choice as delegated subsovereignty – and the notion of a *person*, in this limited respect, as self-determining – at least promises to be more conducive to a coherent version of incompatibilism than does the mire of fragmentary faculties and incomprehensibly self-caused causes into which Hobbes, not without some success, seeks to drive Bishop Bramhall.

That the Hobbes–Bramhall debates are relevant to Milton and his theology has long been acknowledged. Samuel Mintz has pointed out that "some of Milton's arguments in *The Christian Doctrine* closely resemble Bramhall's, and sound as though they were directed against Hobbes."[18] Marjorie Nicolson has claimed that *Paradise Lost* was "the most magnificent of all replies to Hobbes," and she has explicitly linked this reply to the theodical nature of the epic.[19] However, unless we specifically recognize compatibilism as a central component of that which Milton opposes, we shall not appreciate the full theological and literary significance of his anti-Hobbesianism.

If we do recognize the terms of the compatibilist debate, Milton's position in the *Christian Doctrine* is unambiguous. Early in his chapter "Of Divine Decree," he asserts that "we must conclude that God made no absolute decrees about anything which he left in the power of men, for men have freedom of action."[20] He acknowledges only two types of necessity, "namely, when a given cause produces some single unalterable effect either as a result of its own inherent propensity, as when fire burns, which is called natural necessity [*necessitas naturae*],[21] or as the result of the compulsion of some external force, which is called compulsory necessity [*necessitas coactionis*]" (*CD*, p. 159; CM, XIV, 70-2). Free will is incompatible with either of these sorts of necessity, for they both involve what Bramhall calls "an Antecedent determination to one" (p. 30) – or *ad unum*, as it was usually expressed in Latin[22] – and both thereby preclude the option to do or not to do, which any genuine notion of choice requires. As Milton declares:

From the concept of freedom . . . all idea of necessity must be removed . . . If [necessity] restricts free agents to a single course [*ad hoc unum*], this makes man the natural cause of all his actions and therefore of his sins, just as if he were created with an inherent propensity towards committing sins. If it compels free agents against their will, this means that man is subject to the force of another's decree, and is thus the cause of sins only *per accidens*, God being the cause of sin *per se*. If it assists free agents when they are willing, this makes God either the principle or the joint cause of sins. Lastly, if it does nothing at all, no necessity exists. [*CD*, pp. 160-2; CM, XIV, 76-8]

As Milton recognizes in his *Artis Logicae*, "*causa causae, est etiam causa causati*" – "the cause of a cause is the cause of what is caused"[23] – so given that God is the first cause, compatibilism cannot avoid the charge that it makes God the author of sin. And therefore only incompatibilism is consistent with theodicy.

Milton emphasizes that he does "not deny that God's will is the first cause of everything. But . . . God's will is no less the first cause of everything if he decrees that certain things shall depend upon the will of man, than if he had decreed to make all things inevitable" (*CD*, pp. 163-4).

In fact, God made his decrees conditional in this way for the very purpose of allowing free causes [*causas liberas*] to put into effect that freedom which he himself gave them. It would be much more unworthy of God to announce that man is free but really deprive him of freedom; and freedom is destroyed or at least obscured if we admit any such sophistical concept of necessity as that which, we are asked to believe, results not from compulsion but from immutability or infallibility. This concept has misled and continues to mislead a lot of people. [CD, p. 160; CM, XIV, 74].

Although this last comment is undoubtedly directed against men such as Hobbes and his Calvinistic fellow compatibilists, we should not fail to notice the ways in which the tenor of Milton's anticompatibilist utterances also differs from that of Bramhall's argument. As I have indicated, part of Bramhall's vulnerability to Hobbes's critique stems from his reliance on the vocabulary of faculty psychology and from a tendency to speak of the will as if it were distinct from the person and somehow self-caused. Milton's discussion, although it does use terms such as reason and will, operates on a less theoretical level. Where Bramhall would use a term borrowed from scholastic philosophy, Milton is more likely to refer simply to a "man" or "free agent." Indeed, even where he does use a fairly technical term such as "free cause," it is clear that it refers to some human being, who can coherently be conceived of as actualizing the freedom he or she has been granted, rather than to a discrete, self-causing psychological entity.

Both this integrated approach to the psychology of choice and Milton's anticompatibilism are reflected in God's speech in book 3 of *Paradise Lost*. In "Of Predestination," in the *Christian Doctrine*, Milton disavows with specific reference to the Fall the compatibilist model of choice as libency – "for once it is granted that man fell, though not unwillingly, yet by necessity, it will always seem that that necessity either prevailed upon his will by some secret influence, or else guided his will in some way" (p. 174) – and it is precisely this subtle, compatibilist sort of necessity and influence that in *Paradise Lost* God is most concerned to dissociate himself from. Having identified will *and* reason with choice (3.108), he implies that man is an agent – his freedom is to be active, not passive (3.110) – and was made to serve God, not necessity (3.110–11).

> They therefore as to right belonged,
> So were created, nor can justly accuse
> Their maker, or their making, or their fate,
> As if predestination overruled
> Their will, disposed by absolute decree.
>
> [3.111–15]

No necessity imposed by God, no necessity in the scheme of things – indeed, no natural necessity inherent in man's own constitution ("their making") – causes man to stand or fall. God declares that the necessary conditions exist for *either* eventuality, and it is up to man to choose.

Later in *Paradise Lost,* when God again pronounces upon the nature of free will, Milton's acceptance of the balance model of choice is made explicit. This time, looking back rather than forward on the Fall, God denies that any divine decree concurred

> to necessitate [man's] fall,
> Or touch with lightest moment of impulse
> His free will, to her own inclining left
> In even scale.[24]

Whereas compatibilists reject this "indifferency" of the will (ἀδιάφορία),[25] Milton accepts the balance model as the one that is consonant with genuine human choice and divine justice.

In defense of the same model, Milton's Arminian contemporary Thomas Pierce takes on an opponent who implies that "if the first man were placed in aequilibria to do good and evil, he would not onely have been Gods, but Satans Image." This argument Pierce asserts to be "incomparably shallow," because, as he says, "the image of *Satan* consisteth in the *pressing motion to evil,* and not in an *Indifferency to good or evil.*"[26]

Milton, however, recognizes that the Fall in a way did bestow upon man Satan's image in this sense, and therefore he envisages grace as involving precisely the restoration of man to something like his original freedom and "aequilibrium." As God declares in *Paradise Lost:*

> once more I will renew
> His lapsed powers, though forfeit and enthralled

> By sin to foul exorbitant desires;
> Upheld by me, yet once more he shall stand
> On *even ground* against his mortal foe.
>
> [3.175–9; italics added]

In "Of Regeneration," in the *Christian Doctrine*, Milton asks, "What more could we ask of God . . . than that we should be . . . restored to the divine image and given the ability to obtain salvation if we desire it? . . . If anyone does not [desire it], he can blame nobody but himself. But if a regenerate will is not a freed will, then we are not renewed but forced into salvation" (*CD*, p. 463; CM, XIV, 370–2). In an irresistible bending of the will, compatibilists would see nothing inconsistent with freedom as they define it, for libency requires only that one be free to *do* as one wills. But for Milton, that original divine image in man, as Adam puts it in perhaps the pithiest statement of incompatibilism in *Paradise Lost*, involves his being *"both* will and deed created free."[27]

A failure to understand this position of Milton's has led critics to serious misjudgment of his theodicy, in particular his presentation of the Fall in *Paradise Lost*. For example, Marjorie Nicolson, in her article "Milton and Hobbes," although setting out to contrast the two men, ends up imposing on Milton a compatibilist model of freedom. Quoting Sumner's translation of the *Christian Doctrine*[28] – "Nothing happens of necessity because God has foreseen it; but he foresees the event of every action because he is acquainted with their natural causes" – Nicolson comments: "This idea Leibnitz . . . expressed . . . when he said that an individual who knew the nature of each of the atoms could foresee every possible event in the future" (pp. 429–30). Leibniz, however, is a compatibilist, and the idea of certain foreknowledge based on knowledge of natural causes is a deterministic conception quite foreign to the whole tenor of Milton's thought.

Indeed, if we examine what Milton actually wrote and refrain from cutting him off mid-sentence, the contrast with compatibilism is clear:

Neque enim quicquam evenit, quia Deus praevidit, sed unumquodque praevidit Deus, quia *ex causis propriis ipsius decreto libere
agentibus,* ipsique notissimis, ita est unumquodque eventurum. [CM,
XIV, 82; italics added]

(Similarly, nothing happens because God has foreseen it, but rather he
has foreseen each event because each is the result of particular causes
which, by his decree, work quite freely and with which he is thor-
oughly familiar. [CD, p. 164])

There is nothing of "natural" causes nor of anything smacking
of the natural necessity Nicolson apparently infers from Sumner's bad translation.[29] Yet this inference, coupled with a general unawareness of Milton's incompatibilism, permits her to
arrive at the theodically scandalous opinion that "the Supreme
Reason knew that, such was the *nature* of man and the *nature* of
Satan, ultimately the Fall must come" (p. 432).

A more recent critic, Dennis Burden, who also begins by
acknowledging the theodical intent of *Paradise Lost,*[30] similarly
employs a compatibilist model that results in an adverse mis-
representation of Milton's case. However, whereas Nicolson's
use of the model leads her to the conclusion that the Fall is
inevitable, Burden's supports the opinion that it ought to be
impossible.

Discussing the crucial episode in book 9 in which Adam and
Eve separate to garden alone, Burden charges that Adam's
"rationality is at fault since he is overcome by an argument and
not a passion. But if God in his providence made Adam wise,
it is hard to see how Adam's judgment could fail in any way at
all." Yet "for all his intelligence and shrewdness, he does let
her go. And that, in the light of what happened, was an unreasonable act" (p. 89). Now certainly one might agree that it was
an unreasonable act; but that entails no slur on divine providence unless one reads the phrase "made Adam wise" as
implying "made Adam such that he would necessarily always
judge and choose wisely" – unless, in other words, one imposes
on Adam's choices and actions a compatibilist model. Of course
one could always argue that Milton was mistaken in his incom-

patibilism; however, my point here is that if we are prepared to let *Paradise Lost* as much as possible be self-interpreting, then it is wrong to read it in compatibilist terms. If it is incorrect to claim that man's "making" caused the Fall (3.113), then we are likewise unjustified in claiming that it ought necessarily to have precluded the Fall.

It might be objected that Burden's analysis uses terms employed by Adam himself: God, he says, left "Nothing imperfect or deficient," and "left free the will, for what obeys / Reason, is free, and reason he made right" (9.345, 351–2). And as I pointed out in discussing Hobbes and Bramhall, a simple faculty psychology does lend itself to a deterministic interpretation. If reason is "perfect" in the sense of being "an infallible judge," which is how Nicolson describes it (p. 419), then it is hard to see how the will could ever be misinformed at all, unless reason were somehow oddly inarticulate. However, in *Paradise Lost* perfection does not preclude fallibility – God made man "perfect, not immutable" (5.524) – and the faculty psychology on which Milton briefly draws in book 9 is similarly tempered by the warning that reason, though "right," has, so to speak, a responsibility not to be falsely "appeared to" (9.352 ff.).

Furthermore, the faculty psychology that Adam outlines merely presents an analogy to the relationship between him and Eve; and to the extent that Adam himself neglects to heed the warning implicit in that analogy, we would more correctly say that Adam is at fault than merely that "his rationality is at fault." We should avoid the mistake of analyzing man's behavior, and the separation scene in particular, atomistically. Adam's reference to will and reason by no means leaves man carved up into discrete faculties; on the contrary, the very purpose of his speech is to emphasize the normative wholeness and integrity of man as God made him. Following his assertion to Eve that God created "Nothing imperfect or deficient," Adam adds, "much less man" – "his happy state" being "secure from outward force" (9.346–8). It is significant, I think, that Adam uses the generic "man" when he could have said "you" or "me." For he is answering a question that in effect restates God's account of freedom and sufficiency in book 3 (lines 99–106), but slips in an individualistic premise:

> what is faith, love, virtue unassayed
> Alone, without exterior help sustained?
> Let us not . . . suspect our happy state
> Left so imperfect by the maker wise,
> As not secure to single or combined.
>
> [9.335–9]

As we recall from Chapter 3, whereas Arminians see fallen man as being capable of accepting salvation *given the means* that God provides, namely, prevenient grace, Pelagians consider the unaided human will as sufficient for such an acceptance. Similarly, Eve's argument treats man's sufficiency as if it ought to be "Single" (9.325, 339), individual, and innate (9.336); and this leads her to exclude from consideration, and so to neglect, some of the very means integral to human sufficiency as God has ordained it. She espouses, in short, a kind of prelapsarian Pelagianism.[31]

We have already considered, by contrast, the case Adam presents to God in book 8, in which he argues his "single imperfection" and "unity defective" unless he is provided with someone with whom he can share "Collateral love" (8.423, 425–6); and we have heard God's reply that indeed it is "not good for man to be alone" (8.445). Of course in book 8 it is Eve herself who makes up this deficiency. Now, in book 9, Adam reiterates that it is best if he and Eve "sever not"; "tender love enjoins, / That I should mind thee oft, and mind thou me" (9.366, 357–8). One of the profound ironies of the poem is that this mutual minding, which ought to be a part of the collateral love Adam so fervently requests, is something that he himself neglects in his improvident decision to permit Eve to garden alone. He knows from experience that Eve makes up what, without her, would be a deficiency in himself. Recognizing as he does that that need is mutual, he is at fault in permitting her to sever from him.

Why, then, did Adam make this mistake? Indeed, why did the Fall occur if man truly was sufficient to have stood? As was pointed out early in this chapter, when the compatibilist asks such questions, he or she typically is seeking an answer in terms of sufficient causation – and that, where free will is concerned, begs the question. For as we have seen, the libertarian definition of free will postulates that a free choice is not, independently of the choice itself, sufficiently caused one way or the other. Therefore, on this level there is finally no answer to the question *why*, because it concerns "free causes."

Yet, of course, an incompatibilist such as Milton would answer the question, but in terms of necessary, not sufficient, causes or conditions. Let us be clear about this distinction, for it has confused many. The following definition is offered by the *Encyclopedia of Philosophy*: "A *necessary condition* is a circumstance in whose absence a given event could not occur or a given thing could not exist. A *sufficient condition* is a circumstance such that whenever it exists a given event occurs or a given thing exists."[32] Both categories are recognized by Milton, although he would call only the latter a *cause*. As he says in *Artis Logicae*, the former, "the cause *sine qua non*, as it is commonly called, is improperly . . . considered a cause" (CM, XI, 29). The terminology can be confusing, because a sufficient condition in some sense renders its effect necessary, whereas a necessary condition does not necessitate but, together with other necessary conditions, makes a thing possible. For example, we recall from Chapter 3 Augustine's analogy between physical nourishment and grace. As he says elsewhere, "Food does not . . . cause a man to live, and yet without it he cannot live."[33] Sufficient grace – "grace wherein thou mayst repent" – is likewise a necessary but, as we have seen, not a sufficient condition of repentance, at least not in *Paradise Lost*. Rather, given the existence of all other necessary conditions, it is the decision to believe that constitutes the sufficient condition. Accordingly, if an incompatibilist were asked why repentance took place, he or she would probably refer to the existence of various necessary conditions – which in ordinary language we usually call reasons. And similarly, if asked why man fell, an incompatibilist would talk about human mutability, the command not to eat of a certain tree in the garden, the temptations of the serpent, and so on. Indeed, what Milton does in *Paradise Lost* is to present perhaps the fullest account ever of such conditions, an account nevertheless qualified with what the compatibilist would consider the outrageous claim that all of those conditions put together fail to constitute sufficient cause for the Fall.[34]

I would like to mention two recent major articles that combine confusion of such terms with an uncritical imposition upon *Paradise Lost* of compatibilist categories. The first, by Mili N. Clark, is entitled "The Mechanics of Creation: Non-contradiction and Natural Necessity in *Paradise Lost*"; Clark asserts that " 'Sufficient to have stood, though free to fall' is a contradiction in concept . . . which the mythic structure of *Paradise Lost* repeatedly strives to overcome."[35] However, although this claim is repeated again and again throughout the article, usually in combination with an exceedingly fuzzy use of the term "contradiction," it appears simply to be based on a confusion of the senses of "sufficient." Clark reads "sufficient to have stood" as implying *sufficient conditions* for standing, which would indeed preclude any freedom to fall. Moreover, as if to sharpen the contradiction she has discovered, she goes on to contend that *Paradise Lost* presents humans not as free to fall, but as actually compelled to fall, being "creatures who must toil within the rounds of a natural necessity that impels them . . . into tragedy" (p. 242). I have already shown, I trust, how Milton would view the application of such compatibilist categories to the human choices connected with the Fall.

The second article, J. B. Savage's "Freedom and Necessity in *Paradise Lost*," involves an even more bald-faced squeezing of the poem into a compatibilist mold. Admittedly following A. J.

Ayer, a modern compatibilist, Savage chiefly presses the old compatibilist dilemma between necessity and randomness. In *Paradise Lost*, he says, to postulate free will

> requires . . . that we dismiss from mind any notion of cause as being applicable to the poem . . . However, if Adam's actions are not caused and are indeed free, then to the extent they are not caused they must occur by chance . . . To say there is no cause, no reason, for Adam behaving himself the way he does . . . is to imply that his actions are random, purposeless, wholly accidental.[36]

I think any incompatibilist would see this as a false disjunction: "Not wholly caused" simply does not entail "wholly uncaused." Nor, as I have indicated, would an incompatibilist accept the claim that one has no *reasons* for those decisions one freely arrives at.

Acknowledging no such objections, however, Savage proceeds to quarry *Paradise Lost* for further logical perplexities. By conflating the ordinary libertarian notion of freedom, as involving an ability to choose good or bad, with the traditional conviction, at times expressed by Milton, that "true liberty" involves choosing in accordance with right reason, Savage tries to show that "it can make no sense to say that the Fall is freely willed" (p. 259). Basing his case largely on references to Augustine, another compatibilist, Savage charges:

> The freedom appropriate to Adam in falling appears to amount to no more than a *nominal* freedom . . . If Adam is said to possess free will, it is only to the degree that he may be held accountable for what he wills, not that he may be considered free to have chosen otherwise, for such freedom is already agreed to be attainable only in willing the good.[37]

From his own univocal reading of freedom as invariably entailing right reason, Savage infers that if all the "conditions which Adam's freedom presupposes [were] actually satisfied, then it should be obvious that the Fall is a logical impossibility." Moreover, from a typically compatibilist argument he deduces that the mere fact "that the Fall is not . . . resisted is sufficient to concluding that it was in those circumstances irresistible and inevitable" (pp. 305, 307). And thus Savage, like Clark, claims to have generated from *Paradise Lost* a really knockdown contradiction.

Now my intention here is not to suggest that a theologian like Augustine is exempt from charges such as those Savage lays, or to prove that compatibilism is wrong or incoherent, or to deny that a compatibilist could present a useful analysis of the Fall in *Paradise Lost*. But what I would suggest is that one ought to respect incompatibilism as a viable position and recognize Milton's adherence to it. Compatibilist critics' failure to do either – indeed, their frequent failure so much as to acknowledge *any* position other than their own – can only result in judgments that are fundamentally uncritical. *Paradise Lost* and Milton's theodicy generally, as I have tried to show by considering briefly his engagement of some of the issues of his own day, are constructed around an incompatibilist model of freedom. And even if one does have charges to bring against that model, it must, I submit, at least be recognized and permitted to stand on "even ground," not condemned simply by being ignored or hooted out of court.

Divine freedom and divine justice

So far in this chapter I have been considering the implications of compatibilism and incompatibilism as they concern human choices and actions. I would like now to draw attention briefly to very similar issues as they relate to the choices and actions of God. Although Milton's position in this regard is not so fully spelled out as his view of human freedom, it is no less germane to his justification of God's ways.

In the course of discussing natural and compulsory necessity (*necessitas naturae et coactionis*) and insisting that neither can be accommodated to the concept of human freedom, Milton comments, as we have already noticed, that "in God a certain immutable internal necessity to do good, independent of all outside influence, can be consistent with absolute freedom of action."[38] In short, Milton accepts a *compatibilist* model of divine choice even though he rejects compatibilism as a view of human choice. My purpose in the next few pages is to sketch the context of this apparent anomaly and to indicate its significance for theodicy.

In his *Treatise on the Anger of God,* Lactantius attempts to answer a question posed by the Stoics: If God is so great, why is he not above caring about human sinfulness? Is not to be "excited, disturbed, and maddened . . . the part of human frailty"? Lactantius's answer is very simple:

> If God is not angry with the impious and the unrighteous, it is clear that He does not love the pious and the righteous . . . For in opposite matters it is necessary to be moved to both sides or to neither. Thus, he who loves the good also hates the wicked, and he who does not hate the wicked does not love the good.[39]

This argument represents an early attempt to explain in practical terms what God must do, given his own nature. Given that it is an aspect of that nature to love good, and given that love and hate, good and evil, are "opposite matters," one can logically conclude that God *must* hate evil.

Now much of theodicy, as we have already seen, involves just this kind of argument: God is justified, to put it crudely but not impiously, in doing or permitting what, in accordance with the logical limits of omnipotence, he cannot help but do or permit. The Free Will Defense, for example, postulates that given God's benevolent decision to create free creatures, he could not help but refrain from necessitating their choices. The assumption is that there must be consistency between what God does and either what he has already done, as in the case of the Free Will Defense, or else what he innately is, as in the case of Lactantius's answer to the Stoics. The assumption is eloquently exemplified by Milton's contemporary Nathaniel Homes with regard to Ps. 119:68:

> *Thou art good, AND dost good;* . . . which AND may according to the Hebrew, be meetly translated . . . *Therefore; vis. Thou art good, therefore thou dost good;* . . . But however we translate, these two are

chained together, as the *necessary cause,* and the *infallible effect* . . . ; that God doth good, because he is good; and upon both, as on a Foundation is built the knowledge, Faith and Hope of good *David,* what to think and expect of God.[40]

Whereas the character of earthly man, to whom the model of libertarian freedom applies, is not yet fully formed, the character of God is complete and changeless, so that his freedom is more like that of the saints in heaven, whose freedom has achieved its fulfillment in a state of *non posse peccare,* an inability to sin. Of course, as God says in *Paradise Lost,* his goodness is "free / To act or not" (7.171–2); but if it does act, it must act in a manner consistent with the divine attributes of goodness and justice.

This argument was very important to seventeenth-century Arminians. As we saw in Chapter 3, Arminianism was in part a response to voluntarism, which held that a thing is good *as a result* of its being willed by God. Clearly, if God's will is logically prior to goodness and justice, then the assumptions I have just outlined are rendered devoid of content, because in a voluntarist scheme what God wills is good merely by definition. Whereas a voluntarist might well argue, therefore, that God is essentially free, Arminians, precisely out of concern for the goodness and justice of God, are led to define his freedom in a more particular way.

Accordingly, Arminius himself asserts that "God is good by a natural and internal necessity, not *freely;* which last word is stupidly explained by the term [*incoacte*] 'unconstrainedly' and 'not slavishly.' "[41] Thus Arminius, like Milton, distinguishes two kinds of necessity, each of which is to be excluded from consideration where human freedom is concerned, but one of which, namely, natural necessity, is to be seen as functioning in the actions and choices of God. So clearly does Arminius summarize many of the issues I have been discussing in connection with compatibilism that I think it is worthwhile quoting him at some length. In his *Apology or Defence,* published in 1609, he gives the following account:

In a disputation, it was asked, "can necessity and liberty be so far reconciled to each other, that a person may be said *necessarily* or *freely* to produce one and the same effect?" . . . I declared, "that the two terms could not meet in one subject." Other persons said, "that they could," evidently for the purpose of confirming the dogma which asserts, "Adam sinned *freely* indeed, and yet *necessarily* . . ."

To disprove . . . my opinion, they brought forward an instance, or example, in which Necessity and Liberty met together; and that was God, who is both necessarily and freely good. This assertion of theirs displeased me . . . exceedingly, . . . and in a few words I thus prove its *falsity, absurdity,* and . . . *blasphemy* . . .

(1.) Its *falsity.* He who by *natural necessity,* and according to his very essence and the whole of his nature, is good, nay, who is Goodness itself, the Supreme Good, the First Good from whom all good proceeds, through whom every good comes, . . . He is not FREELY good . . .

(2.) Its *absurdity.* Liberty is an affection of the Divine Will; not of the Divine Essence, Understanding, or Power; and therefore it is not an affection of the Divine Nature, considered in its totality . . . But Goodness is an affection of the whole of the Divine Nature . . .

(3.) I prove that *blasphemy* is contained in this assertion: because, if God be freely good, (that is, not by nature and natural necessity,) he can be or can be made *not good.*[42]

Thus we see that what might be called "theological compatibilism," like "psychological *in*compatibilism," is maintained very largely out of a concern for theodicy.

In England, Arminius's position is followed by Thomas Pierce, as well as Milton. In his *Notes concerning Gods Decrees,* Pierce declares: "I conceive it *absurd* to say that God . . . *chooseth* to do *good,* (in opposition to evil) because he *is good,* and *doth good* by an *absolute necessity;* he cannot *choose to be,* or *to do,* any *otherwise*" (p. 63). However, one of the most significant and extensive seventeenth-century versions of essentially the same argument is produced by the famous Calvinist John Owen, in his *Diatriba de Justitia Divina,* which was mentioned very briefly in Chapter 3. As I indicated there, Owen seeks to oppose the voluntarism of fellow Calvinists, such as Twisse and Rutherford. Voluntarism, Owen recognizes, plays havoc with the doctrine of Christ's divine sacrifice for sins, for if God is absolutely free to do whatever he wills, then the work of the atonement was not really necessary, and comes to be viewed as just something else that God requires of his arbitrary "good pleasure." Mentioning Rutherford by name, Owen says that such men maintain all the "egresses," or outward actions, of God's justice

> to be so free and dependent on the mere free motion and good pleasure of the Divine will, that . . . *God might, by his nod, by his word, without any trouble*, by other modes and ways, besides the satisfaction of Christ, . . . take away, pardon, and make an end of sin, without inflicting any penalty for the transgression of his law . . . That punitive justice *necessarily* requires the punishment of all sins, according to the rule of God's right and wisdom, this is what they deny.[43]

Therefore, realizing that such a view is inimical to theodicy – especially because it implies not only arbitrary justification but also arbitrary damnation – Owen argues for theological compatibilism: "The Deity," he insists, is "both a *necessary* and *free agent*" (p. 32). God, in Owen's as in Milton's view, is absolutely free to exercise or refrain from exercising his creativity (p. 33; *PL*, 7.170 ff.); but this freedom is quite compatible with the necessity, given God's essential goodness, of acting in a good manner (pp. 33–4; *CD*, p. 159). Owen takes this "Arminian" argument concerning the divine goodness and extends it to include the whole matter of God's justice, and of his hatred of sin. "If God hate sin," reasons Owen, "he does it either from his *nature*, or because he so *wills it*: but it cannot be because he *wills* it, for in that case he might *not will it*" (p. 57). In short:

> If God punish sin, because, by virtue of his natural justice it is just that it should be punished, then it is unjust not to punish it. But is *God unjust? God forbid* . . . Away then with such speculations which teach that the mystery of the love of God the Father, of the blood of Jesus Christ, of the grace of the Holy Spirit are either indifferent, or at least were not necessary for procuring and bestowing salvation and eternal glory on miserable sinners. [P. 143]

In *Paradise Lost*, just before the Son offers himself for the redemption of mankind, God looks down from heaven upon the sin that mankind will commit, and declares:

> man disobeying,
> Disloyal breaks his fealty, and sins
> Against the high supremacy of heaven,
> Affecting Godhead, and so losing all,
> To expiate his treason hath nought left,
> But to destruction sacred and devote,
> He with his whole posterity must die,
> *Die he or justice must;* unless for him
> Some other able, and as willing, pay
> The *rigid satisfaction,* death for death.[44]

Readers of *Paradise Lost* have often asked themselves, I am sure: Why "must"? Why "rigid"? Does not such rigidity itself present a problem for theodicy? What I have been trying to suggest in this very short discussion of theological compatibilism is that the alternative to God's pronouncement is a position that itself runs absolutely counter to the aims of theodicy. Voluntarism, as indicated in Chapter 1, is a "heresy" that renders utterly vacuous the very assertion of divine goodness and justice that theodicy seeks to defend. Seventeenth-century Arminians and moderate Calvinists alike, therefore, Milton among them, affirm, as did Lactantius, that the necessity of God's hating and punishing sin is emphatically consistent with the divine attributes – indeed, is required by them. This recognition does not compel anyone, of course, to find God's utterances in book 3 pleasant; but I think it does enable us to see that there exists a positive relationship between God's judgment and the overall justice of his ways.

Human freedom and divine foreknowledge

"I confess," said Walter Charleton in 1652, "that the apparent discord betwixt the infallibility of Gods Prenotion, and the indetermination of mans Free Will . . . hath bin the rock, against which many of the greatest wits of all Ages and Religions have bin shipwrackt."[45] Neither considering myself a great wit nor wanting my own discussion to suffer "shipwrack," I nevertheless believe that an account of Milton's response to necessitarianism requires at least a brief recognition of the relationship between theodicy and divine foreknowledge. My contention, in short, will be that Milton steered a course past the rock, unsunk though not unscathed.

The critical passage, again, comes in book 3 of *Paradise Lost,* in God's self-defense. Having denied that the Fall is attributable to man's maker, making, or fate, God continues:

> As if predestination overruled
> Their will, disposed by absolute decree
> Or High foreknowledge; they themselves decreed
> Their own revolt, not I; if I foreknew,
> Foreknowledge had no influence on their fault,
> Which had no less proved certain unforeknown.
> So without least impulse or shadow of fate,
> Or aught by me immutably foreseen,
> They trespass, authors to themselves in all
> Both what they judge and what they choose.
>   [3.114–23]

C. A. Patrides has pronounced these lines, along with Milton's treatment of foreknowledge in *Christian Doctrine,* unconvincing and "unsatisfactory," but understandably so, "for no definitive solution is possible."[46] Such a curt dismissal, however, is itself unsatisfactory if one's aim is to understand the issues and Milton's treatment of them. The theodical stakes are simply too high for one not to seek some such understanding. As Milton himself puts it at the end of his attack on necessitarianism: One must conclude that "neither God's decree nor his foreknowledge can shackle free causes with any kind of necessity." For otherwise, God himself is made "the cause and author of sin"; and to refute this "would be like inventing a long argument to prove that God is not the Devil."[47]

If we examine contemporary seventeenth-century discussions of the matter, we discover that foreknowledge is another one of those issues for which Milton has to seek a "both/and" solution. Just as he aims to assert both grace and free will, both providence and divine justice, so he must affirm both the contingency of human actions and the omniscience of God. In the seventeenth century, the latter was in fact severely restricted by the Socinians, who argued that just as omnipotence can do only that which it is logically possible to do, so omniscience can know only that which it is logically possible to know; future free actions are intrinsically not knowable; and what is not knowable is therefore not *fore*knowable, even by God.[48] Orthodox Calvinists, on the other hand, saw God's foreknowledge as based on his decrees,[49] so that if anything is said to be divinely foreknown, it is to be inferred that it is also divinely decreed and thus predetermined. Arminians, in order to avoid both heterodoxy and necessitarianism, therefore had to steer a course between these positions, the mistakes, as Henry Hammond put it, being "very dangerous on either side."[50] Elsewhere Hammond offers as a model Augustine's position in the *City of God:* "We are by no means under compulsion to abandon free choice in favor of divine foreknowledge, nor need we deny – God forbid! – that God knows the future." Hammond's comment is that this opinion of Augustine's "is expressly contrary both to the *Calvinists* pretension on the one side, and the *Socinians* on the other."[51]

I do not think there is any question but that Milton's position as stated in the *Christian Doctrine* is the middle one that Hammond describes, and for the most part it is sufficiently well known that I need not discuss it in detail. Milton denies the Calvinist position that prescience is based on and posterior to the divine decrees: "For God's foreknowledge is simply . . . that idea of all things which, to speak in human terms, he had in mind before he decreed anything" (p. 154). This version of foreknowledge is also the one favored by Charleton, who calls it "precedent" or *"simple Praescience,"* and who, recognizing "the *Absurdities,* which . . . flow from the doctrine of *Decretory Praescience,"* accepts the former "as consistent to the *justice* of God, because consistent to the *Arbitrary freedome* of mans Will."[52] Milton similarly emphasizes the theodical motivation for his position: "We should feel certain that God has not decreed that everything must happen inevitably. Otherwise we should make him responsible for all the sins ever committed, and should make demons and wicked men blameless." Yet he immediately adds that "we should feel certain also that God really does foreknow everything that is going to happen,"[53] and in so saying he carefully separates himself from the Socinians as well as from the Calvinists.

For prescience as it is treated in *Paradise Lost* the claim of theodical safety is not so easy to establish. In the poem, for one thing, we are presented with an *experience* of foreknowledge as well as with a theoretical explanation, so the effects of speaking "in human terms" are felt more acutely and in a greater variety of ways. To that aspect of the problem, however, I shall return later. A more immediate difficulty is simply that the prose is in Latin and the poetry in English. Thus, even given the working assumption that the theology of each is similar – and this assumption itself should not be inflexible – it is hard, except in the case of exact cognates, to find specific linguistic clues in the treatise that will aid in determining meaning in the epic. What I would like to do, therefore, is briefly to show how some of the seventeenth-century discussions that are in English might illuminate a few of the more important terms and models relating to the issue of foreknowledge in *Paradise Lost,* and to correlate this illustration to discussion in the *Christian Doctrine* where appropriate.

One question on which the prose treatise is quite helpful is that which concerns the meaning of immutability, infallibility, and certainty. As we have already seen, in asserting free will Milton says that one must reject not only the notion of a compulsion imposed by absolute decrees, but also any "sophistical concept of necessity as that which . . . results . . . from immutability or infallibility [*immutabilitas aut infallibilitas*]" (CD, p. 160; CM, XIV, 74). It would seem that these two terms, along with "certainty," were used as synonyms in seventeenth-century discussions of foreknowledge, and that Arminian theologians carefully distinguished them from necessity. Charleton says that those who deny free will and assert a necessity flow-

ing from the divine decrees do so "lest the *Certitude* or Infallibility of the *Divine Praescience* be infirmed and staggered" (p.
274). Pierce reiterates that the orthodox Calvinists, "being *forgetful* . . . to distinguish *necessity* from *certainty of events*, . . .
call that *necessary* which is but *certain* and *infallible*."[54] He notes
elsewhere, moreover, that "the English of *Infallible* is *undeceiv-
able*, whereas [the enemies of *Arminius*] do use it to signifie *irresistible*." "Two short propositions," Pierce adds, "will *subdue*
their *error* . . . 1. What God decreed to *effect*, will come to pass
unavoidably, and by a *necessitation* . . . 2. But what he *onely*
decreed to *permit*, will *contingently* come to pass; yet . . . with
a *certainty* of *event*, because his *foreknowledge* is *infallible*."[55] In
short, those who ignore this distinction repudiate free will,
implying as they do that "the influence of [God's] *Decree*" in
one way or another necessitates all choices; whereas those who
assert prescience, but deny that it implies any necessity,
uphold "the *liberty* of mans *Will*" as being both "incoacted, and
without irrefragable impuls."[56] When, in his own defense, Milton's God uses words such as "influence," "impulse," "immu-
tably," and "certain," therefore, he is engaging the issue of foreknowledge in terms that have already been informed by
debates among Milton's contemporaries; and he thus becomes,
one might almost say, a seventeenth-century theodicist in his
own right.

God's use of the notion of certainty, however, raises a further
question: Even if foreknowledge does not itself necessitate or
influence events, does it not nevertheless imply a necessity?
Milton denies that God's foreknowledge causes sins, any "more
than if some human being possessed the same foresight" (*CD*,
p. 164); but, accepting the analogy, can we not infer from prescience, be it divine or human, the inevitability of the events
foreseen? Pierce, by means of a further analogy, between
knowledge of the present and knowledge of the past, seeks to
suggest that the question can be answered negatively. He bids
"the *obstinate* to consider, that *knowledge* is as properly of
things *past*, as *future*. But it implies a *contradiction*, for a *present*

act of *knowledge* to *necessitate* or *cause* a thing quite *past*. The Almighty knows at this instant that *Adam fell*, as well as he knew from *eternity* that *Adam would* fall."[57] Henry Hammond combines the analogies between knowledge human and divine, past and future, arguing thus:

As that which is present to me is certainly known by me, so are all things to come from all eternity, present to an *immense* Creator, be they contingent, or not . . . What is contingently come to pass, being done, is certain, and cannot be undone, and God sees it, as it is, therefore he sees it as done, and so certain, yet as done contingently, and so as that which might not have been.[58]

The past is in this sense certain and unchangeable, but no one infers from this fact that actions already performed were necessary or inevitable,[59] much less that present knowledge necessitates that which is known.

The difficulty about prescience arises, however, because in considering God's knowledge of possible future events we naturally treat events *as if* they were actual;[60] but to treat something in the future as a fait accompli obviously begs the question of its inevitability. In order to get a conceptual grip on future events we must suppose them to be as it were past, but must also remember, accordingly, that their certainty is a merely supposed certainty unless and until the event actually occurs. As Hammond puts it:

Here then is the errour, because God cannot err in his foresight, therefore you conclude from supposition of his prescience, that the thing, which you speak of, is certain, when yet it no way appears to you or me, that God ever foresaw it, but by our supposing that it comes to pass. Hence then comes all the supposed certainty, from supposing it to come to pass, which is the *certitudo ex hypothesi*, a certainty that it is, as long as it is supposed to be, and then Gods prescience hath nothing to do with it, but it would be as certain without supposing Gods prescience.[61]

As Milton's God says of mankind in *Paradise Lost*, their fault "had no less proved certain unforeknown" (3.119). In the view of both Hammond and Milton, the certainty that can be inferred from God's foreknowledge is thus no more indicative of any kind of determinism than is that certainty which an event proves to have once it is indeed an accomplished fact.

A final theoretical objection that needs to be considered here is based on scriptural passages such as Rom. 8:29, in which foreknowledge is linked very closely with predestination: "For whom [God] did foreknow, he also did predestinate to be conformed to the image of his Son." Does this not, one might ask, lend support to the orthodox Calvinist linking of foreknowledge with the divine decrees and so militate against a theory of simple, "uninfluential" foreknowledge? Milton's response is to distinguish between senses of knowing, and to claim that Rom. 8:29 uses the concept in a special way. This position is partly dictated by the logic of the text in question. For because not all are predestinated, not all are foreknown, and one must accordingly either deny that God foreknows everything in the comprehensive sense, or else define foreknowledge in a sense appropriate only to those who are predestinated. Very early in the history of biblical exegesis, Origen pointed out, in his commentary on Romans, that unless foreknowledge is considered in a restricted sense, we must conclude that the wicked, whom God surely foreknows in the comprehensive sense, are predestinated to be conformed to the image of his Son,[62] which of course is absurd. Judging by the usage of Scripture, however, Origen suggests that knowing often has a special sense, implying a particular affection or act of love toward someone, as when it is said that "Adam knew Eve his wife" (Gen. 4:1).[63] In his own discussion of Rom. 8:29, Milton similarly distinguishes God's "universal knowledge" from "knowledge which implies approval or grace, which is an Hebraic idiom"; and he concludes that "in our passage, the knowledge which implies approval can alone be intended."[64] Therefore, when it comes to simple prescience, Milton reiterates, we can say that "no man believes because God had prescience about it, but rather God had prescience about it because the man was going to believe" (*CD*, p. 183; CM, XIV, 124). In more general terms, as Origen says in discussing the same scriptural passage as Milton, "nothing is going to happen on account of God's knowing it will happen; but because it is going to happen, it is therefore known by God before it does happen."[65] And in this way, scriptural teaching is shown to comport with the denial of "influential" foreknowledge – a denial that theodicy and the doctrine of divine omniscience together require.

Now of course the best-known discussion of the issues I have been reviewing is in book 5 of Boethius's *Consolation of Philosophy*. Although Milton does not mention it, there is no question but that it was highly regarded by his contemporaries; Pierce, for example, in speaking of foreknowledge, refers to "the *Admirable Boethius* (to whom I ow my greatest *light* in this particular)."[66] And despite the fact that *Paradise Lost* does not embody the most distinctive characteristic of Boethius's treatment – namely, the concept that God's knowledge is actually *scientia*, rather than *praescientia*, because God dwells in an eternal present that transcends our categories of time and tense – Milton does present the model of knowledge as vision, which Boethius implies, and he does present God's vantage point as a high place. Boethius says that "divine knowledge . . . resides above all inferior things and looks out on all things from their summit."[67] In *Paradise Lost,* even Satan acknowledges the model of divine knowledge as "vision from the summit": Who, he asks, can "deceive [God's] mind, whose eye / Views all things at one view? He from heaven's highth / All these our motions vain, sees and derides" (2.189–91). And this conception is validated when, later, the poet himself tells us that God looks down on the world, "beholding from his prospect high, / Wherein past, present, future he beholds" (3.77–8). Thus Milton takes the model of *scientia visionis* and gives it a literal as well as a conceptual role in his epic.

Milton's presenting foreknowledge in this way is further indication, I think, of his rejection of "decretory prescience," together with the theodical difficulties it entails. However, it would seem that this presentation is one case in which theoretical considerations and literary demands do genuinely conflict.

As was suggested earlier, Milton in *Paradise Lost* gives us not only a theory but also an experience of foreknowledge. In thus allowing us to share God's prescience of the Fall he has no choice but to present the latter as a fait accompli. As Martin Evans rightly points out, "The abstract idea of an 'eternal present' is simply not translatable into narrative terms,"[68] and the result is that Milton is left with what *is* translatable, namely, a view of things as temporally present or past and hence already accomplished. In book 3, where we "see God foreseeing," God's speech very quickly shifts into the past tense. We are told that man "*will* fall" (3.95), but then that he *had* sufficient means to avoid falling (3.97), that "foreknowledge *had* no influence on their fault" (3.118), and so on. Hammond is right that "it no way appears to you or me, that God ever foreknew [anything], but by our supposing that it comes to pass." Even though we might be willing to accept the idea that something future to us is present to God, once God in the act of foreknowing is made narratively present to us we have no choice but to try to see what he sees as both present and future, and that we simply cannot do. As Hammond concedes, "No finite thing can be both present and future . . . in the *same respect*, present and future *to me*";[69] and this, it would seem, is a limitation that Milton did not adequately recognize.

The result, of course, is that the notion of free will upon which Milton's theodicy is based takes on an ambiguity that it would not have possessed had God uttered his judgment only after the Fall, epic time. If Milton's God creates a disagreeable impression it is not so much because he defends himself as because he does so while treating a future event as a fait accompli. As indicated by the arguments I have outlined, he could not help but do so. However, although Milton's God might be justified in creating an impression that he could not help but create, it is hard to see how Milton could be justified in placing him in such an awkward situation.

The perplexity that results from the human experience of foreknowledge is underlined but not resolved later, when, as so often happens in *Paradise Lost*, what has occurred on a heavenly level is repeated on an earthly level – when Adam, like God, beholds the future from a high place. Having ascended a hill, referred to in book 12 as "this top / Of speculation" (12.588–9), Adam, who is accompanied by Michael, is given a vision of the effects of his fall in which "future things" are represented "As present" (11.870–1). After viewing the Flood, Adam regretfully refers to such events as "by my foreknowledge gaining birth / Abortive, to torment me ere their being, / With thought that they must be" (11.768–71). Because God has asserted in book 3 that foreknowledge does not give birth to its object, and because Adam's responses to future history in books 11 and 12 often require correction, there is no reason to take his comment about foreknowledge as normative. Yet in being so bold as to give both his reader and Adam an experience of foreknowledge, Milton did risk their being tormented by the worry that what will be must be. And that, given the importance to his theodicy of denying any such necessity, was a mistake.

In this sense, therefore, Milton is not unscathed by the rock of foreknowledge; he sustains damage as a result of daring to sail as close to it as he does. But he does not "suffer shipwreck," partly because he is so careful to ward off notions of foreknowledge that are innately necessitarian. Even if the presentation of foreknowledge in *Paradise Lost* is ultimately unconvincing, that unconvincingness results from a literary intrepidity that more often than not in fact enhances the plausibility of Milton's theology. Furthermore, as the difficulty we encounter with foreknowledge in Milton is fundamentally literary and not philosophical, so it would require not a philosophical but a literary solution. Of course the issue is not finally solved in philosophical terms either; however, the case for the compatibility of foreknowledge and free will is strong enough in its own right that the position God enunciates in *Paradise Lost* is by no means radically undermined. Milton's presentation of divine prescience in *Paradise Lost* thus comports with, even if it does not positively support, the more general antinecessitarianism that was such an important part of his theodicy.

6

Eden and the "soul-making" theodicy

Having indicated ways in which Milton's literary handling of certain issues connected with the problem of evil creates difficulties, I would like in this chapter to present one of Milton's most original and successful theodical contributions. I argued generally in Chapter 1 that literature can impinge on theology; and what I shall seek to do now is to show how the particular literary act of presenting life in Eden informs and enriches Miltonic theodicy as a whole, as well as to suggest how theodicy in turn motivates and shapes Milton's presentation of the conditions – especially the prelapsarian conditions – "necessary to the constituting of human vertue."[1] I shall also examine briefly possible sources and analogues for his presentation and comment on its significance in the history of ideas.

"Soul-making" versus "Augustinian" theodicy

I would like to begin by making what is perhaps an obvious point: *The Fall* is largely a relative term; how it is conceived depends on what man fell *from* and what he fell *to*. Pre- and postlapsarian are, in turn, except in the purely literal, chronological sense, also relative notions, because the better the prelapsarian state is imagined to have been, the worse the postlapsarian state will appear; and the worse the postlapsarian state is believed to be, the greater will seem the benefits that man enjoyed before the Fall. Accordingly, seventeenth-century orthodox Calvinists, who believed in the total, or utter, depravity of man in his postlapsarian state, saw any challenge to that doctrine as also representing an attempt to minimize the Fall and to reduce the prelapsarian state to something less than the splendor they conceived it to have possessed. Arminians, therefore, believing that sufficient grace is bestowed on everyone in this fallen world so that all can choose to accept the offer of salvation or not, were routinely accused by orthodox Calvinists of impiously subverting the doctrines of total depravity and original righteousness. In *A Display of Arminianisme*, for example, John Owen begins his chapter entitled "Of the state of *Adam* before the fall" by referring to "the *Arminian* attempt, of readvancing the corrupted nature of man, into that state of innocency and holinesse, wherein it was at first, by God created"; and also to the Arminians' corresponding effort "to draw down our first parents . . . into the same condition wherein we are ingaged by reason of corrupted nature."[2]

The contrast implied by Owen's accusation is characterized by N. P. Williams as the contrast between "maximal" and "minimal" views of the Fall, the latter associated with some Greek fathers of the church, the former with mainly Latin fathers, particularly St. Augustine. "Augustine's beliefs as to the Paradisal state of unfallen man," Williams claims, "represent the culminating point of 'original righteousness and perfection.'"[3] The "minimal" view is defined simply by contrast to the "maximal" position of Augustine; according to the former, original perfection is less exalted, the results of the Fall are less serious, and the Fall itself therefore is less drastic than in the "maximal" view. Although, as will be indicated, "maximal" and "minimal" tend to be inadequate categories when it comes to classifying particular thinkers, they do provide a useful framework for discussions of the Fall and its related issues. In addition, Williams's categories serve to link theologians such as Owen and his Arminian opponents with contrasting tendencies within patristic thought. The Calvinists' debt to St. Augustine is well known; and as Carl Bangs has put it, a characteristic of seventeenth-century Arminians was "their rejection of Calvin in favor of the Greek fathers."[4] Finally, it is this contrast which provides the basis for John Hick's recent major reinterpretation of the history of the problem of evil in terms of what he refers to as "Augustinian" and "Irenaean" types of theodicy – a classification that in this chapter I should like both to exploit and to question.

I have already discussed Augustine's position on the metaphysical character of evil. His view concerning the historical origin of evil centers on the Fall and on the results of man's inexcusable disobedience to God. Augustine's presentation of life before the Fall emphasizes man's inexcusability by exalting, as Williams says, the perfection of that prelapsarian state. Augustine declares that

> Man in Eden lived in the enjoyment of God and he was good by a communication of the goodness of God. His life was free from want . . . There was not a sign or a seed of decay in man's body that could be a source of any physical pain. Not a sickness assailed him from within, and he feared no harm from without. His body was perfectly healthy and his soul completely at peace. And as in Eden itself there was never a day too hot or too cold, so in Adam, who lived there, no fear or desire was ever so passionate as to worry his will. Of sorrows there was none at all and of joys none that was vain, although a perpetual joy that was genuine flowed from the presence of God, because God was loved with a 'charity from a pure heart and a good conscience and faith unfeigned.' Family affection was insured by purity of love; body and mind worked in perfect accord; and there was an effortless observance of the law of God.[5]

Before the Fall, there was no such thing as a problem of evil. Both moral and natural evil are attributable to the Fall, and it is therefore man, not God, who needs justifying. As Williams points out, "The more glorious man's original state and endowments are made, the deeper, by contrast, became the criminality and guilt of the Fall" (p. 360). And yet, as we saw in Chapter 3, Augustine believes that such guilt can be expiated through the grace of God – a belief that serves to answer a further question that must arise, given the Augustinian view of the Fall: Why did God give man free will and the ability to disobey in the first place? As Augustine says:

Here we have an answer to the problem why God should have created men whom He foresaw would sin. It was because both *in them and by means of them* He could reveal how much was deserved by their guilt and condoned by His grace, and, also, because *the harmony of the whole* of reality which God has created and controls cannot be marred by the perverse discordancy of those who sin.[6]

This answer indicates some of the possible inadequacies of Augustine's theodicy. The reference to "the harmony of the whole" reflects his dependence on a Plotinian cosmology and its principle of plenitide. In such a system, to put it harshly, it is possible that human beings must be allowed to destroy themselves for the sake of cosmic variety. As Plotinus put it, if we criticize God's creation "we are like people ignorant of painting who complain that the colours are not beautiful everywhere in the picture: but the Artist has laid on the appropriate tint to every spot."[7] The whole is greater and more important than the part, and mankind is only a part. Augustine's reference to God's purpose being achieved "in them and by means of them," it seems clear, suggests that his justification of God rests ultimately on a view of man as a means, not as an end, and as someone whose interests can justifiably be sacrificed to a divine, cosmic, and fundamentally impersonal aesthetic.

I am, of course, generalizing. Among those who can be said to espouse an "Augustinian" type of theodicy, some have retained the Plotinian, aesthetic emphasis; others have simply concentrated on the doctrine of free will. However, we can by and large distinguish Augustine's approach to theodicy and the Fall, which has been the predominant one in the history of Christianity, from a view of the Fall expressed by some early Greek fathers, which emphasized not so much Adam's original righteousness and perfection as the potential with which he was endowed. As Hick interprets the view, Adam "had been created as a personal being in the 'image' of God, but had yet to be brought into the finite 'likeness' of God."[8] And in accordance with Williams's distinction between "minimal" and "maximal" views of the Fall, just as prelapsarian man is conceived of in the "Irenaean" view as being less perfect and God-like than in the writings of Augustine, so does the Fall appear less cataclysmic.

A corollary of the latter, "minimal" view is that the existence of evil, particularly natural evil, must be explained other than merely as a result of the Fall. The theodicy associated with this position accordingly tends to concentrate on an explanation in human terms of why it was good that evils should have been permitted. Irenaeus – who, as Hick's label suggests, developed the idea most fully – says that

> God permitted these things [such as tribulation] . . . for the benefit of that human nature which is saved, ripening for immortality that which is [possessed] of its own free will and its own power, and preparing and rendering it more adapted for eternal subjection to God. And therefore the creation is suited to [the wants of] man; for man was not made for its sake, but creation for the sake of man. [5.29.1]

Such a position thus includes a view of the instrumentality of evil and forms the basis for a theodicy that is largely teleological. Its focus is the likeness of God toward which the nature of man's earthly existence ought to conduce. It views the world, in the words of John Keats, as a "vale of soul-making."[9]

Whereas the "Augustinian" type of theodicy tends to emphasize the cosmic whole, rather than man, who is only a part of that whole, Irenaeus sees creation as being "for the sake of man"; and this is perhaps the chief difference of approach between the two types of theodicy. The "Irenaean" or "soul-making" theodicy begins not with a particular metaphysical system but with the assumption – backed up by the Christian teaching of God's love to mankind – that man, more than a means to some end, is in some sense an end in himself. This theodicy's version of the Free Will Defense is based not on what, given the principle of plenitude, God *must* create,[10] but on how the world, given the requisites of meaningful human existence, *ought* to be created. Tatian writes that man was created "free to act as [he] pleased, not having the nature of good, which . . . is with God alone, but is brought to perfection in men through their freedom of choice."[11] Theophilus says that God gave man a "starting-point for progress," and that if man had used it properly he "would have developed rapidly in the way of sanctification and intellectual perfection."[12] Origen, answering Celsus's question why God had not made man perfectly good in the first place, replies: "Where, then, is our free will? and what credit is there in assenting to the truth? or how is the rejection of what is false praiseworthy?"[13] Origen says elsewhere, moreover, that there must be a contrast of good and evil so that freedom can in fact be exercised: "If evil disappeared there would be nothing to stand over against goodness, and goodness, having no opposite, would not shine out with its greater brightness and proved superiority."[14] Irenaeus says, "It was necessary that man should in the first instance be created; and having been created, should receive growth" (4.28.3). "We cast blame upon Him, because we have not been made gods from the beginning, but at first merely men, then at length gods" (4.38.4). However if men had been created perfect, and "drawn by necessity and compulsion to what is good," argues Irenaeus, then

neither would what is good be grateful to them, nor communion with God precious, nor would the good be very much to be sought after, which would present itself without their proper endeavour, care, or study, but would be implanted of its own accord and without their concern. Thus it would come to pass, that their being good would be of no consequence, because they were so by nature rather than by will, and are possessors of good spontaneously, not by choice; and for this reason they would not understand this fact, that good is a comely thing, nor would they take pleasure in it. For how can those who are ignorant of good enjoy it? [4.37.6]

This view certainly overlaps that of Augustine, but it does reveal a significant difference in emphasis. Perhaps most importantly for a view of Paradise, the principles of the soul-making theodicy make it unnecessary to exclude from one's conception of prelapsarian existence every trace of natural and moral adversity, although the question just how much and what kind of evil was present in Eden is left open. In terms of

Epicurus's four-horned dilemma, which was considered in Chapter 1, God is in fact seen as able and unwilling to take away evils – unwilling because without the existence at least of evil *possibilities*, meaningful human existence is not conceivable. For example, if no pain were even to be possible in Eden, God would immediately have to intervene and change the laws of nature if Adam once looked as though he were about to stub his toe against a rock; and so no discipline or understanding would ever be required of man in his relationship with the natural world in which he lived. To some degree, it would seem, as Hick has put it, "that the 'rough edges' of the world – its challenges, dangers, tasks, difficulties, and possibilities of real failure and loss – constitute a necessary element in an environment which is to call forth man's finer qualities."[15] Furthermore, a similar requirement holds in the area of *moral* good and evil. As Irenaeus has said, the "good would be of no consequence" without "proper endeavour"; and moral endeavour requires, as in the natural realm, some possibility of real failure and loss. To quote Hick again, "The value-judgement that is implicitly being invoked here [in the soul-making theodicy] is that one who has attained to goodness by meeting and eventually mastering temptations, and thus by rightly making responsible choices in concrete situations, is good in a richer and more valuable sense than would be one created *ab initio* in a state . . . of virtue."[16]

Now the distinction between "Augustinian" and "soul-making" types of theodicy is, as I have already suggested, both useful and problematic. Williams's use of the terms "maximal" and "minimal" and Hick's presentation of the two theodical types can create the impression of a stricter contrast or polarity of positions than for the most part actually exists. Even Augustine's teaching, as Evans has shown, "is in fact a blend of minimal and maximal ideas."[17] The problem, no doubt, is that the view of fathers like Irenaeus, which is not very fully developed in any case, is attractive to modernistic theologians interested in adapting it to their own notions of evolutionary progress and the like. Without arguing the point here, I would simply like to propose that the early soul-making theodicists' view of the Fall was not really *minimizing* at all, but simply relied less exclusively on man's original disobedience as an explanation for the existence of evil than did the later view predominant amongst the Latin-speaking fathers.

A second, historical qualification of Hick's categories needs to be added. He suggests that the picture so far as the "Irenaean" theodicy is concerned is "one of unfulfilled beginnings in the first four centuries, and then an independent new start in the nineteenth century."[18] However, various forms of it were in fact known during Hick's gap. As Patrick Grant has shown, Thomas Traherne knew the writings of Irenaeus and followed him in significant ways in his own writings, not least in the association of prelapsarian life with childhood.[19] In accordance with his view that Adam was placed in the world to grow and mature, Irenaeus conceived of man as being created in a state of infancy (4.38.1–2). As Evans points out, this conception in the early fathers and their Hebrew predecessors immediately solves "the most difficult single problem of the [Genesis] story: how could Adam fall?"[20] And the tactic seems to have been clearly recognized in seventeenth-century theological circles as well. Francis Roberts mentions it in the course of denying that the tree of the knowledge of good and evil was so named "from any inward vertue in it, to confer the use of Reason to our first Parents, who are imagined to be created like Infants without the use of Reason, as some Hebrews think."[21] Furthermore, Anthony Burgess acknowledges, albeit disapprovingly, both this tactic and the problem it can be used to solve:

The Rabbins, who have as many foolish dreames about the Old Testament, as the Friars about the New, conceive *Adam* and *Eve* to be created without the use of reason, and that this tree was to accelerate it. And, indeed, the Socinians border upon this opinion, for they say, *Adam* and *Eve* were created very simple, and weak in understanding; and, say they, it's impossible to conceive, that if *Adams* soule were created so adorned with all knowledge and graces . . . how he should come to eate of the forbidden fruit, or to sin against God.[22]

It is the Augustinian theodicy's failure to answer this question concerning the intelligibility of the Fall that Hick most strongly criticizes:

> There is a basic and fatal incoherence at the heart of the mythically based 'solution'. The Creator . . . made men . . . as free and finitely perfect creatures, happy in the knowledge of Himself, and subject to no strains or temptations, but . . . they themselves inexplicably and inexcusably rebelled against Him. But this suggestion amounts to a sheer self-contradiction. It is impossible to conceive of wholly good beings in a wholly good world becoming sinful.[23]

Although one would agree with the latter claim, I would question Hick's assumption that the difficulty is essential to "the mythically based 'solution.' " The account of the prelapsarian state one finds in Augustine and many of his successors is only one interpretation of a story that Hick would like to rationalize, modernize, or do without altogether. If one is to maintain an orthodox view of the Fall, one need not be committed to seeing it as inexplicable, though neither must one render it wholly excusable. Milton, I would argue, presents the story of the Fall in such a way that man is still guilty on account of disobedience (even though the guilt is mitigated somewhat in view of the temptation by Satan),[24] and in such a way that the Fall *is* explicable, but not therefore decidedly less cataclysmic than it is for someone like Augustine. Milton, in short, working within the traditional Christian "myth," nevertheless produces a "soul-making" theodicy that both avoids Hick's criticisms and in turn provides a basis for criticizing some of the assumptions essential to Hick's own view.

Areopagitica, Lactantius, and the principle of contrariety

Probably the most striking single expression in Milton's works of the themes associated with a soul-making theodicy is the following passage from *Areopagitica*:

> Many there be that complain of divin Providence for suffering *Adam* to transgresse, foolish tongues! when God gave him reason, he gave him freedom to choose, for reason is but choosing; he had bin else a meer artificiall *Adam*, such an *Adam* as he is in the motions. We our selves

esteem not of that obedience, or love, or gift, which is of force: God therefore left him free, set before him a provoking object, ever almost in his eyes; herein consisted his merit, herein the right of his reward, the praise of his abstinence. Wherefore did he creat passions within us, pleasures round about us, but that these rightly temper'd are the very ingredients of vertu? They are not skilfull considerers of human things, who imagin to remove sin by removing the matter of sin . . . Banish all objects of lust, shut up all youth into the severest discipline that can be exercis'd in any hermitage, ye cannot make them chaste . . . Suppose we could expell sin by this means; look how much we thus expell of sin, so much we expell of vertue: for the matter of them both is the same; remove that, and ye remove them both alike. *This justifies the high providence of God,* who though he command us temperence, justice, continence, yet powrs out before us ev'n to a profuseness all desirable things, and gives us minds that can wander beyond all limit and satiety. Why should we then affect a rigor contrary to the manner of God and of nature, by abridging or scanting those means, which books freely permitted are, both to the *triall of vertue,* and the exercise of truth . . . Were I the chooser, a dram of well-doing should be preferr'd before many times as much the forcible hindrance of evill-doing. For God sure esteems the *growth and compleating* of one vertuous person, more then the restraint of ten vitious. [Pp. 527–8; italics added]

Milton in this passage begins with a version of the Free Will Defense that is based not on the requirements of the cosmos as a whole, after the fashion of those who assume the principle of plenitude, but on the requirements of meaningful human existence. Adam must not be a puppet. Secondly, if free will is to have adequate scope to exercise and authenticate itself, there will also inevitably be some possibility of sin – although Milton here does not distinguish as sharply as he might between the possibility and the actuality of sin, between "the matter of sin" and sin itself. And thirdly, the passage ends by reasserting the value judgment spelled out by Hick: The worth of human perfection achieved freely and in the face of some adversity is greater than that of any ready-made "virtue" implanted in man from the start.

Areopagitica, although written to justify freedom of the press rather than the ways of God, thus reveals that Milton has, in 1644, been considering the question of theodicy, and indicates what sort of answers to the problem he has envisaged. Can we say, however, whence Milton derives the answers he sketches in *Areopagitica?* Earlier in that work he expresses the "principle of contrariety," which the quotation just presented assumes and reasserts:

That which purifies us is triall, and triall is by what is contrary. That vertue which is but a youngling in the contemplation of evill, and knows not the utmost that vice promises to her followers, and rejects it, is but a blank vertue, not a pure . . . The knowledge and survay of vice is in this world . . . necessary to the constituting of human vertue, and the scanning of error to the confirmation of truth. [Pp. 515–16]

This principle was certainly not a novel one. Sir Thomas Browne, some two years before the publication of *Areopagitica,* declared, "They that endeavour to abolish vice destroy also vertue, for contraries, though they destroy one another, are yet the life of one another. Thus vertue (abolish vice) is an Idea."[25] In Milton's use of the principle there is also a hint of the Stoical theodicy. His reference to virtue's being achieved "not without dust and heat" (p. 515) recalls Seneca's view that "good men are shaken in order that they may grow strong," and that "all his adversities [the brave man] counts mere training."[26] However, there is evidence that Milton's own position was directly influenced by writings of the early church.

In an entry in his *Commonplace Book,* under the heading Moral Evil, Milton writes the following:

Why does God permit evil? So that the account can stand correct with goodness. For the good is made known, is made clear, and is exercised by evil. As Lactantius says, Book 5, c[hapter] 7, that reason and intelligence may have the opportunity to exercise themselves by choosing things that are good, by fleeing from the things that are evil. lactan de ira dei. c[hapter] 13. however much these things fail to satisfy.

(Cur permittit deus malum? ut ratio virtuti constare possit. virtus enim malo arguitur, illustratur, exercetur, quaemadmodum disserit Lactantius 1.5, c.7, ut haberet ratio et prudentia in quo se exerceret, eligendo bona, fugiendo mala. Lactan, de ira dei, c. 13, quamvis et haec non satisfaciunt.)[27]

The similarities between this entry (dated approximately 1639–41) and the passages I have quoted from *Areopagitica* are fairly obvious, and they have been competently discussed by Kathleen Hartwell and Ruth Mohl.[28] Yet so far as I am aware, Milton's use of Lactantius has not been specifically pointed out as relevant to a consideration of his theodicy. It is, of course, chapter thirteen of *De Ira Dei*, referred to here by Milton, that contains perhaps the most famous statement of the theological problem of evil – the one by Epicurus quoted at the beginning of Chapter 1. Moreover, although it is true that Lactantius was a Latin-speaking father, his views have been recognized as displaying a greater affinity with the Greek than with the Latin school. As Williams has put it, despite what he calls the father's "good share of the fanaticism characteristic of the African Church," Lactantius, "curiously enough, . . . represents . . . an abrupt reversion to an ultra-'Hellenic' and 'minimising' position."[29]

Indeed, in Lactantius we find clearly set forth the themes and attitudes typical of the soul-making type of theodicy. In reply to Epicurus, he opts for the second of the four possibilities, namely, that God

is able . . . to take away evils; but he does not wish to do so, and yet He is not on that account envious. For on this account He does not take them away, because He at the same time gives wisdom, as I have shown; and there is more of goodness and pleasure in wisdom than of annoyance in evils. For wisdom causes us even to know God, and by that knowledge to attain to immortality, which is the chief good. But Epicurus did not see this, . . . that if evils are taken away, wisdom is in like manner taken away; and that no traces of virtue remain in man, the nature of which consists in enduring and overcoming the bitterness of evils. And thus, for the sake of a slight gain in the taking away of evils, we should be deprived of a good, which is very great, and true, and peculiar to us. It is plain, therefore, that all things are proposed for the sake of man, as well evils as also goods.[30]

Again we see that man is treated as an end rather than a means, and is seen as having been placed in an environment conducive to soul making – a condition "peculiar" to man and a good that both presupposes and so justifies the adversity of evil.

Also, in the other section cited by Milton, Lactantius asserts the principle of contrariety:

Virtue can neither be discerned, unless it has vices opposed to it; nor be perfect, unless it is exercised by adversity. For God designed that there should be this distinction between good and evil things, that we may know from that which is evil the quality of the good; . . . nor can the nature of the one be understood if the other is taken away. God therefore did not exclude evil, that the nature of virtue might be evident.[31]

Thus it seems that there is at least prima facie evidence not only that Milton adhered to a soul-making type of theodicy but also that, in so doing, he was influenced directly by one of the foremost soul-making theodicists among the early church fathers.

Of course it might be objected that Milton concludes his entry "Why does God permit evil?" with the comment "quamvis et haec non satisfaciunt." However, although this remark does indicate that Milton is *less than wholly satisfied* with Lactantius's position, to translate *non satisfaciunt* as "fail to satisfy" (as does the Yale edition of Milton's works) or as "are not satisfactory" (as does the Columbia edition) seems to imply a more negative response than Milton probably intended.[32] Surely he would not have cited Lactantius only to disagree with him. Rather, Milton would in fact seem to approve of Lactantius's position in general, but to realize that more is needed if the question of God's permission of evil is to be answered fully. Perhaps the Lactantian view is limited by an over-concern with natural evils, opposing as it does the Epicurean norm of eliminating pain, and so furthering the stoical view, already glanced at in connection with Seneca, concerning the usefulness of the external, largely natural evils of pain and physical adversity. Or perhaps Milton sees that Lactantius's reference to the "slight gain" that would be achieved "in the taking away of evils" is a vast understatement, and that there is clearly more evil in the world than virtue requires. In *The Reason of Church Government*, for example, Milton identifies prelacy as "not such a kind of evil, as hath any good, or use in it, which many evils have, but a distill'd quintessence, a pure elixar of mischief, pestilent alike to all" (CM, III, 26). Indeed, his recognition of the existence of such completely dysteleological evil makes one suspect that Milton himself may have been exaggerating somewhat when in *Areopagitica* he suggests that "how much we . . . expell of sin, so much we expell of vertue." This – like Lactantius's claim that God "permitted the unjust . . . to be more numerous, that virtue might be precious, because it is rare"[33] – is well beyond what the principle of contrariety strictly requires, and Milton in his less polemical moments must have realized it. Nevertheless, he appears to have had no essential disagreement with the principle, for, its limitations notwithstanding, it recurs throughout his works.[34]

"Soul-making" theodicy: the logic of the literary

If *Paradise Lost* too can be shown to embody a soul-making type of theodicy, then a good deal of the major criticism that has been leveled at Milton's poetic justification of God's ways will have its assumptions undermined. C. S. Lewis, ironically a "pro-Miltonist," makes the claim that "Milton's version of the Fall story is substantially that of St. Augustine, which is that of the Church as a whole"; and he suggests that a recognition of this fact will help to avoid "various false emphases to which modern readers are liable." I think no one would want to deny Augustine's influence on the church, and so on Milton; nor would anyone disagree that, for both Augustine and Milton, "God made all creatures good" and "the Fall consisted in disobedience," which resulted from pride.[35] But as we have seen, there were in the early church differing views of the Fall and, accordingly, differing accounts of how evil could exist in a world created by a wholly good God. Augustine for the most part represents only one of the two distinctive (though again not necessarily antithetical) types of approach to the Fall and to theodicy, and it is therefore quite premature, even prejudicial, to assume that Milton must try to follow Augustine – or, what is worse, on this assumption to criticize *Paradise Lost* for some of the difficulties inherent in Augustine's position.

And yet this is precisely what happens when A. J. A. Waldock follows Lewis's lead. Milton appears, says Waldock,

> to be imagining his Adam and Eve as two fully developed and perfected people. This, as Mr Lewis reminds us, was the view of Augustine: Adam's mental powers, said Augustine, "surpassed those of the most brilliant philosopher as much as the speed of a bird surpasses that of a tortoise." In other words, Adam was a man *par excellence*, our own flawless type and model, man as he ought always to have been, if he had not fallen away.

Given these assumptions, Waldock goes on to suggest, quite logically, that "Adam as conceived by Augustine and (it would seem) by Milton is an Adam who simply cannot be shown."[36]

Waldock's discussion of the Fall is only one example of how a critic's own assumptions – or someone else's – can more powerfully direct his approach to a piece of literature than anything in the literature itself. Even apart from the prima facie evidence that has been presented for Milton's adherence to a soul-making type of theodicy, the text of *Paradise Lost* explicitly contradicts the assumption that, for Milton, Adam and Eve are "fully developed and perfected people." Raphael tells Adam in book 5 that the human race, by persisting in obedience, can be "improved by tract of time"; and in book 7, God himself points to the course of development mankind would ideally follow, "by degrees of merit raised . . . under long obedience tried" (5.498 ff.; 7.157 ff.). Man's being thus tried and raised simply cannot consist with any kind of original, static perfection.

However, are we really justified in declaring the theodicy of *Paradise Lost*, like that adumbrated in *Areopagitica*, to be substantially of the soul-making variety? I will argue that we can; but there is a major objection to our doing so that until now I have suppressed. In *Areopagitica* Milton conjectures that the principle of contrariety is a postlapsarian phenomenon: "Perhaps this is that doom which *Adam* fell into of knowing good and evil, that is to say of knowing good by evil. As therefore the state of man now is; what wisdome can there be to choose, what continence to forbeare without the knowledge of evill?"

(p. 514). The thought is reiterated in the *Christian Doctrine,* where Milton says that, because Adam tasted the forbidden fruit, "not only do we know evil, but also we do not even know good except through evil" (p. 352). Do such utterances not indicate that the principle of contrariety, and with it the soul-making type of theodicy, can operate only in the world as it "now is," and hence not in the Garden of Eden?

To answer this question adequately we must keep in mind two distinctions that have already been considered, namely, the distinctions between moral and natural and between possible and actual. The soul-making theodicy is often seen, as it appears to be in Lactantius, primarily as an explanation of natural evil. Moreover, modern philosophers such as Hick, given the "Augustinian" theodicy's difficulty in explaining all natural evil as a result of moral failings, see the alternative "stoical" valuation of suffering as justifying its presence even in the absence of sin.[37] However, there is no reason why the soul-making concept need be restricted to physical suffering. In *Areopagitica* Milton clearly sees it as justifying God in allowing *moral* adversity. Indeed, his vision of "the triall of vertue and the exercise of truth" can apply to either moral or natural evil.

But furthermore, as we noticed earlier, Milton does not in *Areopagitica* distinguish as sharply as he might between possible and actual evil; and it seems generally, in discussions of the soul-making theodicy, to be an easy assumption that actual evil is what personal growth and development require. Hick, for example, declares that "sin and natural evil are both inevitable aspects of the creative process."[38] However, it is at least conceivable, I would suggest, that soul making might require only *possible* evil, not actual; and I will argue that *Paradise Lost* provides a model of an environment in which both sin and natural evil are possible but in which neither is inevitable – in which, to make the distinction *Areopagitica* does not make, there is "matter of sin" without sin itself.

The shift or refinement in Milton's thinking might well have to do with the logical limitations of his literary subject. As Waldock rightly says, "Adam as conceived by Augustine . . . is an Adam who simply cannot be shown." Milton therefore needed to adopt some generally "soul-making" view of Eden and the Fall; and yet the traditional view of the goodness of creation and the sinlessness of the prelapsarian state required that Eden contain no actual sin or suffering.

Milton in his later writings developed a keen eye for the logical limitations and inadequacies of some traditional doctrines, and in accordance with the Ramist criterion of "naturalness" he did not hesitate to reject what he considered inconceivable. It was not conceivable that something should be made out of nothing, so Milton rejected the doctrine of *creatio ex nihilo* in favor of *creatio ex deo*. It was not conceivable, he thought, that there should be three distinct yet coessential persons in the Godhead, so he altered his own doctrine of God to conform to the requirements of natural logic. It was inconceivable that God should at once will a person's salvation and arbitrarily elect him to reprobation, so Milton rejected the orthodox Calvinist beliefs concerning double predestination and the twofold will of God. It was inconceivable that one's soul should exist independently of one's body, so Milton opted for the doctrine of thnetopsychism, teaching in *Paradise Lost* that spirit and body are not antithetical, but merely different in degree, "created all . . . [from] one first matter" (5.471–2); and to support his point he showed angels who both ate and had sex. It is also inconceivable that actions should take place in timelessness, so Milton assumed that time could apply even in eternity (5.580), and hinted that perhaps things earthly were "Each to other like, more than on earth is thought" (5.576). And likewise, it is inconceivable that life could be meaningful in an environment where there was no scope for human endeavor, where there were no "challenges, dangers, tasks, difficulties, and possibilities of real failure and loss" (as Hick puts it);[39] so Milton, in trying concretely and logically to imagine Eden in a way that agreed with the justice of God's ways, found it essential, with the necessary modifications, to extend to the prelapsarian world

as categories of natural thought the principles he had so eloquently outlined in *Areopagitica* back in 1644.

This of course is only a hypothesis, but I think that if we look
at the prelapsarian condition in *Paradise Lost* we shall see manifested there the theodical patterns suggested in *Areopagitica*.
To begin with a minor example in the area of natural evil, there
are in Milton's Eden the seeds of that which can cause real harm
to Adam and Eve. Apart from the assumption that if Adam
stubs his toe it will hurt, Milton makes the explicit point that
the midday sun's rays, in order to be "fervid" enough "to warm
/ Earth's inmost womb," must provide "more warmth than
Adam needs" (5.301; cf. 5.231, 369). Even in Eden, to avoid
heatstroke man must submit himself to nature's discipline. Milton makes no apology for this. And because Adam has a cool
bower to come home to, no apology is necessary. But what we
see here is not Augustine's tepid Eden, where there was "never
a day too hot or too cold."[40]

It is not surprising that Milton should present some kind of
discipline as a translapsarian necessity. In *The Reason of Church
Government* he has emphasized that nothing is more important
"throughout the whole life of man" than discipline, and that
"certainly discipline is not only the removall of disorder, but
. . . the very visible shape and image of vertue." He adds,
moreover, that even "the state of the blessed in Paradise . . . is
not . . . left without discipline."[41] It must have been but a small
step for him to go from ascribing it to the inhabitants of heaven
to ascribing it to the inhabitants of Eden.

In the view of Eden that Milton presents, discipline is
required not only by incidental matters such as the heat of the
sun at noonday, but also by the positive tasks that Adam and
Eve must perform in relation to their botanical environment.
Evans has convincingly countered the claim of critics such as
E. M. W. Tillyard that Adam and Eve, "reduced to the ridicu-
lous task of working in a garden which produces of its own
accord more than they will ever need, . . . are in the hopeless
position of Old Age pensioners enjoying perpetual youth."[42]

Evans recognizes that Milton's treatment of the state of innocence contains elements from the "mimimal" tradition: Adam,
says Evans, "is serving a kind of spiritual apprenticeship; he is
a novice learning to take his place in the order of perfection, not
a member of it already. He has first to undergo the preliminary
discipline of 'long obedience.' " Adam and Eve, as Evans
shows from a number of passages, have been commissioned to
tend a garden that is decidedly imperfect without their labors,
its plants displaying a propensity for "wanton growth," its
trees tending to become "overwoody."[43] Whereas Twisse, for
example, believes that the task of dressing the garden was insti-
tuted because "God would not have Adam to be idle in Paradise";[44] in Milton's view, "the garden will not remain perfect
of its own accord, and if Adam and Eve stopped working the
wilderness outside would soon engulf it."[45]

So the unfallen pair are not lotus-eaters; as Adam tells Eve,
"other creatures all day long / Rove idle unemployed . . . Man
hath his daily work of body or mind / Appointed, which
declares his dignity" (4.616–19). Of course, what this implies
for theodicy is that possibilities of natural evil such as we see
in Eden cannot be accounted for by the Fall, because they precede it; it is God, therefore, not man, who must take responsibility for them. However, God is also justified in permitting
them, for their existence conduces to the meaningfulness of
human life and serves to declare man's dignity. Thus evil possibilities such as sunstroke and an overgrown garden are in
accordance with a view that, as Irenaeus put it, "man was not
made for its sake, but creation for the sake of man"; they are
permitted "for the benefit of . . . human nature . . . , ripening
for immortality that which is possessed of its own power and
preparing and rendering it more adapted for eternal subjection
to God."[46]

In respect to Adam and Eve's natural environment in Eden,
therefore, it would seem simply incorrect to claim that Milton
"can find no adequate scope for their active natures."[47] Furthermore, it is not only in gardening that man is meaningfully

occupied. As Milton's contemporary Thomas Goodwin puts it, "As [man] was to till the Garden of *Eden,* so was he to till and manure his own Mind."[48] In Milton's Eden man has the opportunity of doing so in the process of developing socially and culturally as well. Adam, as we saw in Chapter 4, has a long and very challenging conversation with God before Eve is created; and in books 5 and 8 both Adam and Eve have the privilege, and experience the excitement, of entertaining an angelic guest. Although these episodes are part of the plot of *Paradise Lost* in a way that gardening is not, one ought not to treat them as merely incidental to what Milton is presenting generally as the conditions of meaningful prelapsarian existence.

In Milton's Eden, hospitality is an art and a challenge. When in book 5 Adam and Eve spy Raphael coming through the trees, they plunge themselves into a flurry of activity. Adam breathlessly asks Eve to "haste hither" and then "go with speed" (5.308, 313). He himself "will haste" and gather the meal's ingredients (5.326) while Eve "with dispatchful looks in haste" considers

> What choice to choose for delicacy best,
> What order, so contrive as not to mix
> Tastes, not well joined, inelegant, but bring
> Taste after taste upheld with kindliest change.
>
> [5.331–6]

Culinary arts, we see, are no postlapsarian invention. And even in Eden real skill and care are required to avoid flavor blur.

Moreover, during and after the meal there occurs what must have been one of the most intellectually stimulating conversations of all time; I need not analyze it here to suggest that the sort of prelapsarian social activities that *Paradise Lost* presents are anything but boring or lacking in scope. For Raphael's visit and Adam's talk with God represent not one-time things but the order of social contact that was intended to be a regular feature of man's unfallen existence. Raphael tells Adam,

> nor art thou such
> Created, or such place hast here to dwell,

> As may not oft invite, though spirits of heaven
> To visit thee.
>
> [5.372–5]

And Milton himself, in beginning book 9, implies that the particular social relations we have seen going on between heaven
and earth are only indicative of the larger pattern of prelapsarian life:

> No more to talk where God or angel guest
> With man, as with his friend, familiar used
> To sit indulgent, and with him partake
> Rural repast, permitting him the while
> Venial discourse.
>
> [9.1–5]

Adam and Eve's social life, of course, is complemented by
their relationship with each other. Their responsibilities
involve their own as well as the garden's fertility, and this too
engages them in sweet labor. Significantly, sex, like Adam and
Eve's other activities, exists both for their sakes and in accordance with God's plan; like everything else about creation it is
at once delightful and purposive. At dusk Adam and Eve pass
"hand in hand . . . to their blissful bower; it was a
place / Chosen by the sovereign planter, when he framed / All
things to man's delightful use" (4.689–92). We are reminded by
the couple's evening prayers, which immediately precede their
gentle lovemaking, that sex is not merely autotelic, but of significance to the rest of mankind as well as to the creator himself,
who has "promised from us two a race / To fill the earth, who
shall with us extol / [His] goodness infinite" (4.732–4). And
thus Milton's presentation of Adam and Eve as a couple whose
marriage includes a rich and happy sex life is another one of the
ways in which he makes prelapsarian life seem humanly real
and avoids creating "a meer artificiall *Adam.*"

There are three mistakes typical of much Milton criticism that
can be exemplified in regard to Edenic sex. The first one simply
involves the imposition of traditional categories on *Paradise
Lost* for the sake of establishing Milton's orthodoxy. Lewis, as

we have already seen, prescribes an "Augustinian" reading of the Fall. He goes on to quote Augustine's glowing description of Adam and claims that "we must assume . . . [that such a being existed] before we can read the poem." However, given Augustine's belief that there was in fact no prelapsarian sexual intercourse and Milton's presentation of sexuality, one must either reject Lewis's assumption or else deny the fact of the matter in *Paradise Lost*. Lewis would clearly prefer the latter alternative if it were open to him; as it is not, he can only squirm. "I do not mean," he adds, "that Milton's love passages are objectionable by normal human standards; but they are not consistent with what he himself believes about the world before the Fall."[49] And so Lewis escapes the alternatives just suggested by ascribing inconsistency to Milton himself.

Of course much more could be said about mistake number one, about the imposition on Milton of traditional views; but at the moment I want to fix on one detail of "Milton's love passages" and to indicate how it defines mistake number two. Lewis's difficulty with prelapsarian sexuality, he admits, "is raised in its acutest form when Milton's Eve exhibits sexual modesty. Her impulse on first meeting Adam is to turn back (*P.L.* VIII, 507); she is led to the bridal bower 'blushing like the morn' (*ibid.* 511)." Lewis says that Milton is in the "cleft stick" of having either to show Eve as exhibiting no modesty at all – something we could not accept – or else to make it look as if bodily shame predated the Fall. Although Lewis himself suggests a way out of the cleft stick – namely, to distinguish "bodily shame as we now know it from some kind of bashfulness or modesty which can be conceived as existing before the Fall"[50] – he nevertheless cannot shake off the impression he has of "shame as we know it," and so he is unable, as has just been indicated, to account for what he sees in *Paradise Lost* except by calling Milton inconsistent.

As a follower of Augustine's, it is not surprising that Lewis should associate a blush with bodily shame, because for Augustine, that which brings a blush is itself both a result and a mirror of man's fallenness. In *On Marriage and Concupiscience* he exclaims:

How significant is the fact that the eyes, and lips, and tongue, and hands, and feet, and the bending of back, and neck, and sides, are all placed within our power – to be applied to such operations as are suitable to them, when we have a body free from impediments and in a sound state of health; but when it must come to . . . the procreation of children, the members which were expressly created for this purpose will not obey the direction of the will, but lust has to be waited for to set these members in motion, as if it had legal right over them, and sometimes it refuses to act when the mind wills, while often it acts against the will! Must not this bring the blush of shame over the freedom of the human will, that by its contempt of God, its own Commander, it has lost all proper command for itself over its own members?[51]

Augustine also indicates elsewhere that "the connubial embrace . . . is by reason of this body of death . . . impracticable without a certain amount of bestial motion, which puts human nature to the blush."[52] And he castigates a Pelagian writer for holding a view that in fact is not greatly different from the one presented in *Paradise Lost*. Referring to the Pelagian, Augustine retorts:

Let him say, if his blushes permit him, that if no one had sinned, this vigour [of the members, or sexual desire] must have flourished like a flower in paradise; nor would there have been any need to cover that which would have been so moved that no one should have felt ashamed; rather, with a wife provided, it would have been ever exercised and never repressed, lest so great a pleasure should ever be denied so vast a happiness.[53]

Although Milton was no Pelagian, *Paradise Lost* clearly reveals him siding with Augustine's opponent here. Indeed, as Christopher Ricks puts it, "It is characteristic of Milton's courage and humanity that in insisting that sexual intercourse preceded the Fall he should also have asked us to imagine the full innocence of a prelapsarian blush."[54]

However, although blushing need not, in either the literary or the historical context, imply shame,[55] Lewis's being guilty of mistake number two – imposing postlapsarian categories on a poetic situation to which they do not apply – is no personal quirk; his interpretation is possible, perhaps even probable, given the combination of blushing's postlapsarian ambiguity and the reader's fallen perspective. As Ricks says of words like "wandering," blushing "is a reminder of the Fall, in that it takes us back to a time when there were no infected words because there were no infected actions."[56] And as Fish says, the reader's response "is bound up in the distinction he is repeatedly asked to make between Adam and Eve and himself. He is encouraged to compare his perceptions and reactions and linguistic habits with theirs . . . and to fashion from the comparisons a working definition of innocence."[57] I will not take time to go over Fish's argument, but his point here is of profound importance. For Lewis's difficulty results from a failure to do precisely what Fish specifies: to fashion a "working definition of innocence" that is not merely remote and mystifying.[58] The beauty of Milton's account of prelapsarian sexuality is that what he shows us is real and specific and recognizably human; the power of his account is that it establishes an explicit and educative contrast between what we see in Eden and what we know exists in our own experience as fallen creatures. Describing Adam and Eve's physical appearance, Milton says:

> Nor those mysterious parts were *then* concealed,
> *Then* was not guilty shame, dishonest shame
> Of nature's works, honour dishonourable,
> Sin-bred, how have ye troubled all mankind
> With shows instead, mere shows of seeming pure,
> And banished from man's life his happiest life,
> Simplicity and spotless innocence.
>
> [4.312–18; italics added]

But if one cannot get beyond one's guilty responses long enough to sense the innocent happiness of unfallen sexuality, the contrast between then and now will not work, and one will remain uneducated by it.

The third mistake, which I will mention only briefly and lay to the charge of no one in particular, is related by way of contrast to mistake number two. Lewis, as we have seen, recognizes certain similarities between prelapsarian and postlapsarian sexuality and believes that because of them we doubt the purity of what goes on between Adam and Eve before the Fall. However, for any contrast between pre- and postlapsarian existence to be very meaningful does require that some real, recognizable similarities obtain in the two things being contrasted. Lewis will accept similarities between pre- and postlapsarian sex only of a very remote sort; and to this extent he emasculates the contrast that Milton sets up. But the contrast can likewise be emasculated if one does nothing more than unreflectively enjoy the similarities between what Adam and Eve experience in Eden and life as we now know it. Mistake number three is merely to do this and to conclude that there is not such a great difference between pre- and postlapsarian existence after all, and that hence the Fall could not be so serious a matter as one had supposed. Although such a conclusion may appear attractive (especially if one would like to believe in a myth of progress), the existence of translapsarian categories, rather than mitigating the contrast between then and now, is in truth the very condition that allows Milton to develop the contrast in the first place.

What I am arguing, then, is that Milton's presentation of conjugal love in Eden is a major component of his working definition of innocence. Although he allows us to be perhaps painfully aware of the fallibility of this as well as of other aspects of life in the garden, he is insistent that sex at its most beautiful and meaningful did flourish in Eden. For if it did not, we should have to conclude that this profound dimension of human love was somehow occasioned by the Fall.[59] On the contrary, Milton would seem to say, what we must repent of is our fallenness, not our humanity; and sexuality, like fallibility generally, is part of being human. So there it is in Eden: the good gift of a good God.

However, even given all this scope for meaningful cultural, social, and conjugal activity, one might still wonder whether

Adam and Eve are truly moral beings, or whether theirs is but a "blank" and "cloister'd vertue" such as Milton in *Areopagitica* declares he "cannot praise" (p. 515). Was not Augustine right, that in Eden man encountered "no fear or desire . . . so passionate as to worry his will," and "of sorrows . . . none at all and of joys none that was vain"? Does not *Paradise Lost* confirm Thomas Goodwin's view that man before the Fall experienced "no contrary Passions to allay the Pleasures then enjoyed"?[60] The answer, it must be reasserted, is that such a view does not apply to *Paradise Lost*; and indeed, I would suggest, in rejecting the purely "maximal" position, Milton extended *Areopagitica*'s principle of contrariety to Eden because even there, he came to recognize, man could not be raised "by degrees of merit" without it.

In order to get a better idea why Milton had to avoid the sort of paradise described by Augustine and Goodwin, as well as to provide an analogue of how *Paradise Lost* might present an Eden with scope for "the constituting of human vertue," I think it is profitable to consider the literary figure Milton himself holds up as an example of "the true warfaring Christian": Spenser's Guyon, from book 2 of the *Faerie Queen*. In *Areopagitica*, after explaining how necessary it is that true virtue should contemplate evil and know "the utmost that vice promises to her followers," Milton goes on to say that it is for this reason that "Spencer, . . . describing true temperance under the person of *Guion*, brings him in with his palmer through the cave of Mammon, and the bowr of earthly blisse that he might see and know, and yet abstain" (pp. 515, 516).

We see from these comments that Milton, whether or not he realized it at the time of writing, has chosen a model which shows that the knowledge of evil is compatible with sinlessness. Guyon could not, of course, know and abstain in any morally significant way if there were no *possibility* of his sinning; yet his achieving virtue presupposes no actual sin. Similarly, in *Paradise Lost*, as Thomas Blackburn has pointed out, Adam and Eve before the Fall have a conceptual knowledge of evil and yet they are truly sinless: "Their innocence consists not of no acquaintance with evil but of no taint by it." Blackburn distinguishes the sort of knowledge of evil possessed after the Fall, "experiential knowledge of an actuality," from Adam and Eve's knowledge of it before the Fall, which was compatible with – and, I am arguing, conducive to – "intellectual enlightenment" and an "increase in moral acuteness."[61] As was demonstrated in the last chapter, in the *Christian Doctrine* Milton himself explicitly distinguishes *notitia approbationis* – "knowledge which implies approval" – from mere *scientia;* and in the state of innocence it is clearly the latter sort of knowledge of evil that man possessed. For as Adam tells Eve, "Evil into the mind of god or man / May come and go, so *unapproved,* and leave / No spot or blame behind."[62]

So Guyon knows, and yet abstains. But what is it he abstains from? Significantly for Milton, one of the temptations the Christian knight must overcome is that of giving himself over to sloth in Myrth's island paradise:

> It was a chosen plot of fertile land,
>   Emongst wide waues set, like a litle nest,
>   As if it had by Natures cunning hand
>   Bene choisely picked out from all the rest,
>   And laid forth for ensample of the best:
>   No daintie flowre or herbe, that growes on ground,
>   No arboret with painted blossomes drest,
>   And smelling sweet, but there it might be found
> To bud out faire, and her sweet smels throw all around.
>
> No tree, whose braunches did not brauely spring;
>   No braunch, whereon a fine bird did not sit:
>   No bird, but did her shrill notes sweetly sing;
>   No song but did containe a louely dit:
>   Trees, braunches, birds, and songs were framed fit,
>   For to allure fraile mind to carelesse ease.
>
>   [2.6.12–13]

"Carelesse ease": How near this comes to the conception of Eden that many have thought Milton obliged to present! Yet it is antithetical to his conception of real virtue and to Guyon's

Christian warfare and "knightly exercise" (2.6.25). This point is reemphasized late in book 2 of the *Faerie Queene* when we see Sir Verdant languishing in the Bowre of Blisse: "ne for honour cared hee, / Ne ought, that did to his aduauncement tend" (2.12.80). In Milton's paradise, by contrast, man has the God-given opportunity of advancement "under long obedience tried," and of honor through "daily work of body or mind . . . which declares his dignity."

In the *Faerie Queene* the principle of contrariety is expressed by Medina, who asks Guyon to tell the "doleful tale" of Mordant and Amavia on the grounds that "Ill by ensample good doth often gayne" (2.2.45). In *Paradise Lost,* in accordance with the same principle, Raphael relates the story of Satan's fall as an example of evil, of pride, of rebellion against God, so that Adam can "see and know, and yet abstain." It is necessary that he be thus educated, for he has not understood Raphael's caution, *"If ye be found / Obedient"* (5.513–14). Yet by means of the story Raphael recounts, Adam does learn what obedience is, in the steadfast character of Abdiel,[63] as well as its opposite in Satan. Adam very much needs, as later he admits, to be "warned, or by experience taught" (8.190); and significantly, it is literary experience that provides one such means of learning.

But what of other, more direct kinds of experience? Must not Adam and Eve, like Guyon, experience evil firsthand if they are truly to grow in the knowledge of good? The episode of Eve's satanically inspired dream (5.26–135) provides an example not only of just such an opportunity for soul making, but also of the way in which God's permission of evil actually operates. Satan has his own purposes in tempting Eve, and yet his very presence in Eden is something for which God himself bears ultimate responsibility, given the fact that he in his omnipotence permits it (1.210 ff.; 3.685). God does not, however, gratuitously create evil for the sake of its contrast with good; rather, "he directs a will which is already evil so that it may produce out of its own wickedness either good for others or punishment for itself, though it does so unknowingly," as Milton puts it in

Christian Doctrine. [64] In *Paradise Lost,* Eve's bad dream occasions
an exercise of compassion and trust by the unfallen couple and
thus provides positive testimony of how God's permitting evil
can produce good. It is surely one of the most touching
moments of the poem:

> [Adam] cheered . . . his fair spouse, and she was cheered,
> But silently a gentle tear let fall
> From either eye, and wiped them with her hair;
> Two other precious drops that ready stood,
> Each in their crystal sluice, he ere they fell
> Kissed as the gracious signs of sweet remorse
> And pious awe.
>
> [5.129–35]

So there are tears in Milton's Eden, whereas in Augustine's
there are "of sorrows . . . none at all." And yet the value and
goodness of Adam's response justify God's permitting the evil
dream to occur in the first place, and also ought to obviate the
persistent suspicion that such compassion and sharing of
"sweet remorse" were made possible only by the Fall. Even
Evans, who has done a great deal to show how meaningful Milton makes prelapsarian existence, suggests that "our feelings
about the state of innocence" are "ambiguous." To illustrate,
he quotes Edwin Muir's poem "One Foot in Eden," which is
spoken in the voice of Adam just after he has been expelled
from Paradise:

> . . . famished field and blackened tree
> Bear flowers in Eden never known.
> Blossoms of grief and charity
> Bloom in these darkened fields alone.
> What had Eden ever to say
> Of hope and faith and pity and love
> Until was buried all its day
> And memory found its treasure trove?
> Strange blessings never in Paradise
> Fall from these beclouded skies. [65]

In Milton's Eden there *are* "blossoms of grief and charity,"
which nevertheless presuppose no sin on man's part: The tears
that spring from Eve's eyes, just like the waters of that other

fountain that rises in Eden, serve to feed "Flowers worthy of Paradise" (4.241).

A second good purpose served by the dream is that it makes clear the sort of threat that Adam and Eve still face. They gain in knowledge of evil, though as I have stressed already it is not knowledge *approbationis*. Adam expresses to Eve the hope that "what in sleep thou didst abhor to dream, / Waking thou never wilt consent to do" (5.120–1); and it seems plausible that both of them, given this experience, would be better armed against temptation than they otherwise could be. They have in fact successfully undergone real spiritual warfare. Their virtue has been exercised in the "dust and heat" of "the race where that immortal garland is to be run for," as Milton says in *Areopagitica* (p. 515). In so saying, he echoes James 1:12, which declares: "Blessed is the man that endureth temptation: for when he is tried, he shall receive the crown of life which the Lord hath promised to them that love him." For such a blessing to be possible the inhabitants of the prelapsarian world, too, must be tempted. And so Milton gives us a glimpse of how they could indeed have been "Improved by tract of time" had they retained "Unalterably firm his love entire / Whose progeny" they were (5.498, 502–3).

For Milton the exercise of man's will thus requires an encounter with the "matter" of sin; and of course reason should direct one in making the right choice. Given the difficulty of portraying "inner states," this operation in a literary setting is often presented by means of an externalizing of reason, such that reason's voice comes from a figure of authority outside the person who must temper "passions within" and "pleasures round about."[66] In the *Faerie Queene* this process is accomplished in the person of the palmer, who guided Guyon

> ouer dale and hill,
> And with his steedie staffe did point his way:
> His race with reason, and with words his will,
> From foule intemperance he oft did stay,
> And suffred not in wrath his hastie steps to stray.
> [2.1.34]

It is interesting to note in this connection that Guyon's function as a knight presupposes warfaring, and that of his guide, the palmer, who represents reason, presupposes wayfaring. It is interesting too that, as Ernest Sirluck points out, where Spenser in fact has Guyon go through the Cave of Mammon without the Palmer to guide him, Milton seems to assume that the warfaring Christian always has need of reason; so he edits his memory of the *Faerie Queene* accordingly, and has the Palmer accompany Guyon throughout the journey.[67] In some key prelapsarian episodes of *Paradise Lost,* Milton uses the same technique of externalizing reason. Indeed, while Adam and Eve are at times apt "to rove / Unchecked," God himself makes sure that they are provided with reason's warning voice as well as with the sort of educative direct experience that has just been considered.

In these terms, Eve's description of her temptations to narcissism almost needs no comment. She oft remembers, she says, that day

> when from sleep
> I first awaked, and found myself reposed
> Under a shade of flowers, much wondering where
> And what I was, whence thither brought, and how.
> Not distant far from thence a murmuring sound
> Of waters issued from a cave and spread
> Into a liquid plain, then stood unmoved
> Pure as the expanse of heaven; I thither went
> *With unexperienced thought,* and laid me down
> On the green bank, to look into the clear
> Smooth lake, that to me seemed another sky.
> As I bent down to look, just opposite,
> A shape within the watery gleam appeared
> Bending to look on me, I started back,
> It started back, but pleased I soon returned,
> Pleased it returned as soon with answering looks
> Of sympathy and love; there I had fixed
> Mine eyes till now, and pined with vain desire,
> *Had not a voice thus warned me,* What thou seest,
> What there thou seest fair creature is thyself,
> With thee it came and goes: but follow me.
>   [4.449–69; italics added]

Of course, Adam too seems tempted to idolize Eve, to subordinate himself to "the charm of beauty's powerful glance" (8.533), as he admits to Raphael:

> when I approach
> Her loveliness, so absolute she seems
>
> . . . . .
>
> . . . that what she wills to do or say,
> Seems wisest.
>
> [8.546–50]

But Raphael warns him, "with contracted brow," not to be

> diffident
> Of wisdom, she deserts thee not, if thou
> Dismiss not her.
>
> . . . . .
>
> In loving thou dost well, in passion not,
> Wherein true love consists not; love refines
> The thoughts, and heart enlarges, hath his seat
> In reason, and is judicious, is the scale
> By which to heavenly love whou mayst ascend.
> Not sunk in carnal pleasure.
>
> [8.560–4, 588–93]

These temptations which arise from the "passions within" Adam and Eve have confused a number of prominent Milton critics. Waldock, having assumed that Milton was obliged to present a straightforward "maximal" view of the Fall, concludes that the transition "from sinlessness to sin" cannot be made "perfectly intelligible," and that Adam and Eve "must already be fallen (technically) before they can begin to fall."[68] Millicent Bell has suggested that the mind "cannot accept the fact that perfection was capable of corruption without denying [Adam and Eve's] absoluteness of perfection," which, according to "Milton's ancient material," they had to possess.[69] And Tillyard has claimed that Milton "anticipates the Fall by attributing to Eve and Adam feelings which though nominally felt in the state of innocence are actually not compatible with it."[70] However, there is simply no justification for assuming that Milton intended or had to present a simple "Augustinian" view of prelapsarian life; and indeed, what *Paradise Lost* itself reveals is something much more dynamic.[71]

Among Milton's contemporaries, moreover, the intelligibility of the Fall was a live issue, not something uncritically accepted. As we saw at the beginning of this chapter, Owen accuses the Arminians of trying "to draw down our first parents" into a corrupted state; and he goes on to charge that his opponents ascribe to unfallen man "a propensitie to sinne."[72] Without admitting the charge in quite such strong terms, Arminians were clearly willing to accept a view of man as obviously *fallible* rather than render the Fall unintelligible. As Milton himself says in *Christian Doctrine,* man's first sin resulted from the temptations of the devil and from "man's own inconstant nature."[73] Pierce quotes Andrew Rivet to the effect that the alleged *"inclination to sin"* would place "all the fault of the sin upon *God."* Pierce proceeds, however, to distinguish sharply between potential and actual sin – between fallibility and the Fall – and so undercuts the arguments not only of theologians such as Owen and Rivet, but of a good number of Milton critics as well:

If before [Eve] sinned, she was not *inclinable* to *sin,* how then did she *sin?* was it without or against her *inclination?* if her sin was voluntary, and not committed of necessity, . . . she had an *inclination* to which she *yielded,* and *thereby* sinned. And which if she had *resisted,* shee had not *falne,* but been *victorious.* Her *meere inclination* to sin was not her sin; for if it were, she sinned before she *sinned* . . . which would imply a contradiction.

Whereas Pierce's opponents saw this "minimal" sort of view as putting too much of the responsibility for sin on God, Pierce makes it clear that it is precisely in order to avoid impugning God's goodness that such a view is necessary: "Whence was the sin, if there was no *inclination?* not *from Eve her self,* who if she had *no inclination,* had no temptation from within; not from the *Devil,* whose *Temptations* have no force, if contrary to all our *inclinations."* Unless one admits these two necessary conditions – the ones, as we have just seen, also specified by Milton, namely, temptation and fallibility – one must conclude that "the sin of *Eve* was from *God alone.*"[74]

If we recognize Milton's vivid portrayal of Adam and Eve's unfallen fallibility for what it is, therefore, the Fall in *Paradise Lost* becomes much less perplexing, and Bell's claim concerning its "essential *causelessness*" (p. 863) is radically undermined. The Fall is uncaused only in the sense that apart from Adam and Eve's own final decisions it is not *sufficiently* caused; as was suggested in the last chapter, however, Milton presents a remarkably full and rich account of its *necessary* causes or conditions. In other words, he creates an elaborate situation in which, when the crucial temptation comes, things can go either way. For man *is* sufficient to stand, free to fall.

And once again, Milton allows both reader and character to experience those conditions. As well as being warned of evil by means of Raphael's account of the war in heaven, Adam and Eve acquire valuable knowledge about and victory over evil as it is manifested in Eve's dream; and both of them, as we have also seen, actively experience the possibilities of evil that exist within themselves. In Eden there was indeed desire "so passionate as to worry [man's] will" – again to contrast Augustine's position. Moreover, God, as the creator, was responsible for such evil possibilities.[75] Milton would not deny it. Yet God's ways are justifiable, first, in that the passions he created within us "rightly temper'd are the very ingredients of vertu": "Skilfull considerers of human things" will realize that an Adam created without such characteristics would be "a meer artificiall *Adam.*"[76] Secondly, God does not leave man to his own untried devices; in each case we have looked at in this discussion, God saw to it that either he or his messenger was there to provide the needed words of warning and reason.

And thirdly, just as Eve's evil dream forearms the unfallen couple by forewarning them exactly what Satan will tempt them to do – that is, to eat the forbidden fruit – so Adam and Eve's particular encounters with the unwholesome potential within themselves provide them with knowledge of the dangers that exist and with experience in dealing with what is to be probably Satan's most effective weapon when it comes to the Fall itself. Even in the dream, which the "Narcissus" episode naturally precedes, Satan begins with an appeal to Eve's vanity: She should get up, because "heaven wakes with all his eyes, / Whom to behold but thee, nature's desire" (5.44–5). When he actually encounters Eve in the garden he again begins with idolatrous flattery, calling her "sovereign mistress," "sole wonder," and again, "Sovereign of creatures, universal dame" (9.532–3, 612). He thus encourages her to commit the sin of aspiring to godhead: "what are gods that man may not become / As they, participating godlike food?" (9.716–17). Unlike Eve, of course, Adam is not deceived; but he is, we are told, "overcome with female charm" (9.999) – a phrase that echoes the word Adam used earlier in telling Raphael about his dangerous feelings for his wife, his weakness "Against the charm of beauty's powerful glance" (8.533). So God has vindicated his justice by rendering both Adam and Eve, like Guyon and his palmer in the *Faerie Queene*, "firmely armd for euery hard assay, / . . . gainst daunger and dismay." All that is required in addition is their own "constancy and care" (2.12.38).

Just what kind of constancy and care man must exercise in Eden is one of the main issues that comes up in Adam and Eve's crucial debate about whether to garden on their own. Eve, as we have seen, argues their safety:

> And what is faith, love, virtue unassayed
> Alone, without exterior help sustained?
> Let us not then suspect our happy state
> Left so imperfect by the maker wise,
> As not secure to single or combined;
> Frail is our happiness, if this be so,
> And Eden were no Eden thus exposed.
>   [9.335–41]

But here Eve is arguing on the basis of two incompatible premises – quite commonly also accepted by Milton critics. It is true that faith, love, and virtue are nothing unassayed. But given this requirement, and given that genuine assay presupposes some real possibility of failure and loss, man's "happy state" in one sense *must* be left "imperfect by the maker wise"; man's happiness *must* be frail; and, given the requirements for "the constituting of human vertue," Eden were no Eden *unless* "thus exposed." If Eden were to be completely secure, man could not be free; if man is to be free and not a puppet, there has to be an element of insecurity and imperfection. Eve (and Milton critics) cannot have it both ways.

Of course "security" is potentially very ambiguous. In book 5, Raphael has told Adam that he is "perfect, not immutable; / . . . but to persevere / He left it in thy power"; and now Adam recites the lesson by way of warning Eve: Man is "Secure from outward force; within himself / The danger lies, yet lies within his power" (5.524–6; 9.348–9). The "happy state" is perfect only *given* man's free and active participation. It is not a *sinecure,* which is the sense Eve seemingly wants to put on "secure." And of course her desire to be care*free* leads her to be care*less,* when in fact she should be remembering the dangers foreshadowed by her dream.[77]

Compare the situation in *Paradise Lost* once again with that of Spenser's Guyon. As we have seen, he is "firmely armd for euery hard assay, / . . . gainst daunger and dismay" only if his "constancy and care" are counted as part of his armor. His security results from his vigilance in the face of adversity, not from an absence of adversity altogether. In fact, if he had no temptations to overcome he would simply languish, like Verdant, with nothing that could conduce "to his aduancement" (2.12.80). Now in Eden, of course, as the heavenly chorus implies, man is "thrice happy," "whom God hath thus advanced, / Created in his image" (7.625–7). Yet further advancement is necessary: As we have seen, prelapsarian man was intended to undergo a process of soul making, to grow in the likeness of God, raised "by degrees of merit" and tried "under long obedience." The case is very similar with Guyon, Milton's example of the true warfaring Christian:

Thrise happy man, (said then the *Briton* knight)
Whom gracious lot, and thy great valiaunce
Haue made thee souldier of that Princesse bright,
Which with her bounty and glad countenance
Doth blesse her seruaunts, and them high aduance.
How may straunge knight hope euer to aspire,
By faithful seruice, and meet amenance,
Vnto such blisse?

[2.9.5]

Guyon is thrice happy by virtue of being a soldier of the princess, and yet his "aduancement" to that "blisse" depends on his own "faithfull seruice, and meet amenance." As the end of the heavenly song in *Paradise Lost* makes clear, Adam and Eve's bliss is likewise conditional: They are "thrice happy *if* they know / Their happiness, and persevere upright" (7.631–2).

In his footnote to this last line, Alastair Fowler suggests that Milton is "alluding to Virgil's exclamation over the happiness of simple peasants: 'O happy husbandmen! too happy, should they come to know their blessings! for whom, far from the clash of arms, most righteous Earth, unbidden, pours forth from her soil an easy sustenance' (*Georg.* ii 458–60)."[78] One of the things I have been trying to demonstrate in this chapter is that what Milton portrays in *Paradise Lost,* and I believe meant to portray, is quite the opposite of what Fowler's quotation from the *Georgics* suggests. Adam and Eve, unlike Virgil's peasants, ought to know their happiness; and given the manifold operation of the principle of contrariety in Eden, they *can* know it, and increase it. Moreover, this requires that they be not "far from the clash of arms" but rather in the very midst of spiritual warfare, as indeed they are. To Milton "an easy sustenance" would be anathema, and his amazing achievement has been to produce an epic, and a theodicy, which credibly present a picture of human life that is sinless and yet not slothful or without purpose.

I have already mentioned some of the implications this conclusion has for Milton criticism. I have also tried to show a historical link between the soul-making aspect of Milton's theodicy and one of the original proponents of this sort of justification of God among the early church fathers – namely, Lactantius. Of course Milton does not find Lactantius's position quite adequate: The principle of contrariety does not explain all the evil that exists in the world. In developing his own theodicy, therefore, Milton came also to emphasize free will and the evil possibilities that it entails. He agrees with Lactantius that "reason and intelligence" should "have the opportunity to exercise themselves by choosing things that are good" and "by fleeing from the things that are evil."[79] Yet he recognizes that this explanation accounts only for the evil that exists independently of reason and intelligence, not for that evil which arises as a result of a moral failure of that same reason and intelligence. In this sense, by giving man free will, God not only allowed him to choose evil, but also gave him power to create it. Hence, with regard to the evil that man creates, God is responsible for its possibility, man for its actuality. And this is why for Milton the Fall is still so important. He does not "minimize" its consequences. It did bring "death into the world, and all our woe" (*PL*, 1.3). But at the same time God could not logically have created a world in which it was the case both that man was free and that some kind of fall *could* not have occurred.

Milton's theodicy thus harmoniously combines soul making with the Free Will Defense, which was examined in Chapter 4. As I have argued, it was partly the requirements of literary coherence and concreteness that encouraged Milton to develop the soul-making aspect of theodicy in *Paradise Lost;* and in turn *Paradise Lost* can be seen as a demonstration that this aspect is by no means antithetical to many of the more traditional aspects of theodicy – the emphasis on free will being one of these. In this way, therefore, there may even be something about the concept of soul making that a poet can teach a philosopher, a theologian, or an intellectual historian. If they examine Milton's literary theodicy carefully, in any case, they will not find it to be superficial.

7

Paradise Lost and the Unfortunate Fall

In 1937, a year after making his remark about "the amazing superficiality of Milton's theodicy,"[1] Arthur Lovejoy published an article entitled "Milton and the Paradox of the Fortunate Fall," in which, as is now well known, he outlined a tradition within Christianity that views the sin of Adam as being a happy fault because "if it had never occurred, the Incarnation and Redemption could never have occurred"[2] – a tradition in which, Lovejoy also claimed, Milton participates. Now Lovejoy's hypothesis – it is not an argument – has become a kind of cliché of Milton criticism, and its uncritical acceptance has itself helped to create the illusion that Lovejoy's earlier claim about Milton's theodicy is true. For if Lovejoy's hypothesis is correct, then Milton's theodicy is superficial indeed. If God *needed* the Fall in order to reveal what Lovejoy calls "the plentitude of the divine goodness and power" (p. 164), then Milton's careful avoidance of absolute predestination, his assertion of free will and its reflection of the divine image, his defense of free will against different forms of determinism, his exquisite presentation of sinless paradisal human existence – virtually his whole justification of the ways of God – all turn out to be little more than a useless facade over the nightmare abyss of "divine" intentions. In short, if "the doctrine of the Fortunate Fall" and Milton's use of it really have been "splendidly taped down by Professor Lovejoy," as William Empson puts it, then Empson is almost surely justified in concluding that Milton's God must have been "working for the Fall all along" and that he is therefore deprived of "the last rag of excuse for his plot to corrupt the whole race of mankind."[3]

The aim of this chapter, however, will be to present an alternative hypothesis or "model" that, although itself not strictly demonstrative, is in literary, historical, and theological terms more coherent and satisfactory than Lovejoy's. The theory of the Fortunate Fall may in fact have been introduced to modern criticism by Lovejoy, but it has so vigorously outlived him and so continued to proliferate in scholarly essays on Milton (to say nothing of undergraduate papers) that a further attempt to deter its influence would seem to be justified. In making such an attempt, accordingly, I will take Lovejoy's presentation as typical of a general hypothesis that many others share, and will also recognize that my attempt to question the hypothesis and provide an alternative is itself only a continuation of the efforts of others.[4] That alternative – the hypothesis of the *Un*fortunate Fall – will be based, like the other arguments I have put forward in this book, on the issue of theodicy as a whole and on evidence drawn both from historical discussions relating to the problem of evil and from *Paradise Lost* itself.

Felix culpa: the paradox and the problem

One must begin by making clearer what the paradox of the Fortunate Fall actually is. The Fall, of course, represents mankind's fall into sin; and throughout historical orthodox Christianity, nothing is seen as being more serious and lamentable than sin: Once again, as Milton expresses it, it "Brought death into the world, and all our woe" (*PL*, 1.3). Nevertheless, it is also the case that Christ's Incarnation and Redemption, events standing at the very center of Christian belief, are cause for infinite rejoicing. In fact, to re-invoke a concept introduced in Chapter 4, these events are viewed as outweighing the evil of sin; as Anthony Burgess put it, on Augustine's authority, in 1646, God has "wrought greater good then sin was evill."[5] Now if this is true, and *if* the Fall was a necessary condition of that greater good, then the orthodox Christian must, as Lovejoy puts it, believe both that "the Fall [can] never be sufficiently con-

demned and lamented," and that "all its consequences . . . considered, it [can] never be sufficiently rejoiced over" (p. 164).
The paradox is given its most famous expression in the "Exultet" from the Roman Liturgy, which contains the exclamation:
*"O certe necessarium Adae peccatum, quod Christi morte deletum
est! O felix culpa, quae talem ac tantum meruit habere redemptorem!"* ("O inexorably necessary sin of Adam, which by Christ's
death is blotted out! O happy fault, which has merited so excellent and so great a Redeemer!")[6] And the claim is that the lines
spoken by Milton's Adam after Michael has given him a
glimpse of the Incarnation, Redemption, and Second Coming
reexpress the same paradox. Adam exclaims:

> O goodness infinite, goodness immense!
> That all this good of evil shall produce,
> And evil turn to good; more wonderful
> Than that which by creation first brought forth
> Light out of darkness! Full of doubt I stand
> Whether I should repent me now of sin
> By me done and occasioned, or rejoice
> Much more, that much more good thereof shall spring,
> To God more glory, more good will to men
> From God, and over wrath grace shall abound.
>   [12.469–78]

"Thus," declares Lovejoy, "Adam's sin – and also, indeed, the
sins of his posterity which it 'occasioned' – were the *conditio
sine qua non* both of a greater manifestation of the glory of God
and of immeasurably greater benefits for man than could conceivably have been otherwise obtained" (pp. 164–5).

Now before looking at this whole matter in specific terms, it
will be worthwhile to consider the general "unlikelihood" of
Milton's actually endorsing the *felix culpa*. Such a prima facie
case will not, of course, be conclusive, but it will at least serve
to raise critically the issue of "the Fortunate Fall in *Paradise
Lost*" – so often merely taken for granted, with the result being
an adverse view of Milton's poetic theodicy. Assuming (on the
basis of evidence presented in the preceding chapters) the gen-

eral coherence of that theodicy, I think there are some grounds for tentatively reversing the usual process, and allowing an understanding of Milton's justification of God to suggest the implausibility of Milton's accepting the paradox of the Fortunate Fall in the first place. For if the Fortunate Fall has negative implications for coherent theodicy, then it surely ought to be recognized that the reverse is also true. To put it somewhat tautologically, mutual repugnance can cut both ways.

Some of the Fortunate Fall's theodical repugnancies have already been indicated. As the quotation from Empson suggests, if the Fall is fortunate in the sense of being divinely dictated, then our old cardinal proposition number two – that God is wholly good – is seriously undermined, and Milton topples into theodical "heresy." Indeed, as was implied in Chapter 3, Empson's railings appear to be directed almost exclusively at a *voluntarist* deity; yet in fact, Milton strenuously rejects the notion that God issues a call of salvation to persons whom he actually plans to damn eternally. This being so, therefore, it would seem at least unlikely that Milton would fail to see the implications of parallels between that doctrine and one claiming that God both forbade the Fall *and* decreed it for his own ends.

Given the Fortunate Fall, theodical "heresy" would creep in from another direction as well. The doctrine of *felix culpa*, it seems clear, is a version of optimism, which denies ultimately that there is anything really evil in the world. If the Fall is fortunate, it is hard to conceive of anything to which that adjective might not apply. K. W. Grandsen, for one, has explicitly recognized the Fortunate Fall's "optimistic" implications: Even though, as he claims, in the universe Milton envisages "there can be no room for development or evolution," it is nevertheless "the best of all possible worlds."[7] If Milton espouses this form of optimism – if Adam's sin and the sins it "occasions" are all instrumental in achieving the greatest good – then it would appear that Milton has revised his opinion concerning the existence of sins that are "a distill'd quintessence, a pure elixar of mischief, pestilent alike to all."[8] For it is hard to imagine him conceiving something to be both fortunate in the sense of being necessary for the greatest good *and* quintessentially evil.[9]

The literary inconveniences that would follow from the Fortunate Fall are closely connected with those that are theological. One's reactions to the real or imagined doctrines implied in *Paradise Lost* – as Empson's discussion amply illustrates – are not wholly separable from one's reactions to the poem's tone, plot, characters, and so on. Indeed, many of the things about which Empson complains, such as what he considers to be the "police bullying" of Adam, although they have obvious theological consequences, do not represent the sort of difficulty that would very likely be alleged against a nonliterary doctrinal treatise. At the structural level, moreover, as W. H. Marshall has tried to demonstrate, the Fortunate Fall's theological clashing of gears would result in a conflict of the didactic and dramatic elements of *Paradise Lost;* "the explicit assertion in the final books of the Paradox of the Fortunate Fall," he claims, "involves repudiation, rather than subordination, of what we have felt during the first nine and a half books."[10] If book 12 does present the paradox, therefore, we as readers would seem to be left with a profound and irresolvable ambivalence about what has so far been presented as unequivocally "pestilent to all." And this ambivalence would reflect a flaw inherent in both the literary and the theological stuff of Milton's epic. At best, the latter would turn out to be much less "logical" than many have thought.

It would also turn out to be less tragic than Milton himself apparently intended. Proceeding on the premise that the tradition of seeing the Fall as "a 'happy' or 'fortunate' event" is "fully exploited in *Paradise Lost*," Grandsen asserts that its treatment of the Fall renders the poem comic: "Milton tried hard to make it tragic but failed."[11] Even if "tragic" is to be reinterpreted in light of the good that God will bring out of evil – even if tragedy is in some sense ultimately transformed into comedy – the Fall itself is not comic in the crucial sense unless it is *necessary* to the achievement of a greater good. And if it is thus necessary, as Grandsen and Lovejoy imply, then the tragedy of the Fall must be rejected, not only reinterpreted, and Milton would indeed appear to have failed in his intentions.

If Milton accepts the Fortunate Fall, furthermore, there also appear anomalies of a historical nature. One wonders, perhaps, in reading Lovejoy's article, how it is that such a preponderance of his sources are Roman Catholic. However, Milton would probably not have rejected a doctrine merely out of antipopery; and besides, Roman Catholicism has a longer history from which to draw examples of any tradition common to both it and Protestantism, as that of the Fortunate Fall no doubt is. But what of the main division among Protestants in Milton's time, that between Arminians and orthodox Calvinists? How do these two groups line up on the issue? The question would be irrelevant if it were not for the fact that the Fall's being fortunate and God's "working for it all along" are matters organically related to the central questions of predestination and the divine decrees, over which the Calvinists and Arminians split in the first place. As we saw in Chapter 3, most orthodox Calvinists, whose doctrine of predestination Milton rejects, do indeed believe that God positively decreed the Fall; and therefore, to the extent that this is a corollary of the *felix culpa,* Milton, if he truly accepted that paradox, would find himself in the Calvinist camp willy-nilly.

William Twisse declares that "all the question between . . . our Divines consists in this, Whether it were the will of God that *Adam* should fall by his permission, so to make way for God's glorious ends, to wit, the manifestation of his glory, in the incarnation of the Sonne of God, as also in the way of mercy, in the salvation of some; and in the way of justice, in the condemnation of others"; and he affirms that it was indeed the will of God, "least . . . way should be made for the manifestation of Gods glorious works by accident."[12] Samuel Hoard, whom Twisse is seeking to refute, agrees that God, to his own glory, turns evil to good, but denies that God's glory *requires* evil:

It is true, that God decreed to suffer sin; For otherwise there would be none. Who can bring forth that which God will absolutely hinder? He suffered *Adam* to sin, leaving him in the hand of his own counsell . . . This he doth, not because he stands in need of sin for the setting forth of his glory: for he hath no need of the sinfull man: . . . but . . . he . . . knoweth how to use that well which is ill done, and to bring good out of evill.[13]

John Goodwin, another prominent Arminian, puts it more forcefully:

God is not so poorly or meanely provided, in, and of himself, for the exaltation of his Name and Glory, as to stand in need of the dunghill of sin to make a foot-stoole for him whereby to ascend into his Throne. If the *goodnesse* and *righteousnesse* of man be nothing unto God, *profit* not him, much lesse can the sins of men claime *part and fellowship* in such a businesse. So then the sins of men [are] . . . contriveable to his glory, but no wayes requisite or necessary hereunto.[14]

And Thomas Pierce, a third Arminian contemporary of Milton's, sets forth a list of the orthodox Calvinists' "Horrible Affirmations," which include the claim, similar to the one made by Twisse, "that God made men with *this intent,* or *to this purpose,* that they might *really fall.* Because he *could not* attain his *principle ends* any *otherwise,* then by this *course.*"[15]

Although an extreme example of Calvinist teaching on the Fall, this quotation is no caricature. John Ball says that "God suffered [our first parents] to slip, that he might manifest the riches of his mercy in mans recovery."[16] Thomas Whitfield very explicitly draws out some of the themes attached to the doctrine of the Fortunate Fall: Not only is God "able to bring light out of darknesse," but "if there were no sin at all, he should loose a great part of his glory"; not only did God "draw forth a wonderful great good out of the fall of man," but he "is able to bring about the *best* ends by the worst meanes."[17] A thoroughgoing Arminian would of course agree that God turns evil to good and brings light out of darkness, but would deny that God needs sin and would stop short of Whitfield's "optimistic" implication that the best *requires* the worst. Thomas Goodwin, another Calvinist, is more careful to insist that "the *Sin* of *Adam* . . . was [not] a means, but at the utmost . . . an occasion" of grace and glory; but he also insists that if, in the Covenant of Grace "a Believers knowledge and enjoyment of God, were but compleated and filled up, . . . it would render us infinitely more happy, and more repleat with glorious contentment, than ever entred into *Adam's* heart; and would make this Estate of Grace below, a Heaven, in comparison of his Paradise."[18]

Alexander More, Milton's hated opponent, likewise asserts that Paradise pales beside the benefits of grace: "Who but a rank ingrate will say the gifts of Christ are not much to be preferred over the gifts of Adam? Whence therefore that cry, *O Felix culpa, quae talem meruit habere Redemptorem!*"[19] And Francis Roberts, with what he claims to be direct Augustinian authority, dilates rapturously on the glories occasioned by the Fall:

Who, but the most high God, could have extracted such a reviving Medicine, out of such a deadly Poyson: could have brought such clear light, out of such extream darkness? . . . If the First Covenant had not been marred; the second and more excellent Covenant had not been made. If the first earthly *Adam* had not been ruined; the second heavenly *Adam* Christ had not been promised. If One sin in *Adam* had not been so grievous Gods super-abounding grace in Christ had not appeared so glorious. *Oh my happy fault,* (said *Augustine*) *which while God is drawn by love to wipe away, that love of his also is opened unto me, desiring and Coveting it from my heart root! I could never so well have acknowledged his love, unless I had tried it in so great perils. Oh how happily did I fall, that after my fall did more happily rise again!*[20]

Clearer expressions of the doctrine of the Fortunate Fall one could not wish for. Both of these explicit endorsements of it, significantly, come – and could be expected to come – from the pens of orthodox Calvinists. If Milton, too, endorses the paradox, therefore, he does so at the cost of placing himself squarely in the midst of his own theological and personal opponents.

There are two further points to be drawn from the Calvinist – Arminian split over the Fortunate Fall. The first simply concerns the nature of that doctrine. One notices that an assertion of light's being created out of darkness or of men's sins' being "contriveable to [God's] glory" does not of itself imply the *felix culpa*. For often with that assertion goes the belief that God had other means, and did not need the Fall. As Twisse comments disapprovingly, his opponents simply think "that God could have brought forth other administrations of his providence in very great variety."[21]

The second point is a fairly obvious consequence of the first: If there were those who would deny that the Fall was fortunate, then the acceptance, tacit or otherwise, of the *felix culpa* cannot be assumed to have been universal or obligatory among seventeenth-century Christians. Merritt Hughes, for example, would thus appear to be mistaken in asserting that "all interpreters of Scripture . . . were agreed that the outcome of human history would be a proof of the 'Fortunate Fall.' "[22] And Lovejoy is wrong that this doctrine was "necessary – upon the premises of orthodox Christian theology."[23] Moreover, recognizing that all were not so agreed will help obviate the uncritical imposition upon a given Christian writer of what is merely *assumed* to be required by orthodoxy. Chapter 6 surveyed some of the damage caused by the assumption that there is only one way to view the paradisal state; and here similarly it must be acknowledged that a high view of the divine accomplishments in history entails no belief in the Fortunate Fall.

The unfallen image: prelapsarian process

Some of the issues related to Milton's soul-making theodicy are directly relevant, too, to the question of his acceptance of the *felix culpa*. So far I have presented admittedly circumstantial evidence to suggest the literary, theological, and historical improbability of Milton's accepting it; now I would like to address the problem more directly. There is a further important assumption of the Fortunate Fall theory that not only Milton's contemporaries but Milton himself undercuts. Lovejoy says that implicit in Adam's exclamation in book 12 is the view that "the final state of the redeemed, the consummation of human history, would far surpass in felicity and in moral excellence the pristine happiness and innocence of the first pair in Eden – that state in which, but for the Fall, man would presumably have remained."[24] Without the latter assumption, the deduction that man's final state is more glorious than anything man could have hoped for without the Fall is simply invalid; for as Virginia Mollenkott has put it, even though "God brings good out of evil by providing redemption, . . . the alternative might have been even *more* glorious."[25] Yet Lovejoy himself, albeit in a footnote, admits that "there were, in the early Fathers and later theologians, differing opinions: the view that the primeval state was not that in which man was intended to remain, but merely a phase of immaturity to be transcended, had ancient and respectable supporters."[26]

This view, in fact, was also in the seventeenth century widely acknowledged and, it would seem, widely held. Arminius said that if our first parents "had persisted in their obedience," it is "very probable that, at certain periods, men would have been translated from this [*animali*] natural life, by the intermediate change of the natural, mortal and corruptible body, into a body spiritual, immortal, and incorruptible, to pass a life of immortality and bliss in heaven."[27] John Goodwin similarly believed that man was intended to grow and develop: Unlike the devil, who "sinned in an estate of perfect Blessedness, . . . man, when he sinned, was but in his progress towards such a condition, and was not as yet possessed of it."[28] Anthony Burgess, a Calvinist who, as we saw in the last chapter, mentions disapprovingly the Socinian denial that Adam was "created . . . adorned with all knowledge and graces," also acknowledges that "it's made a question, Whether, if Adam had continued, he should have been translated into heaven, or confirmed onely in Paradise."[29] Richard Baxter first recognizes the same view and then, it seems, himself adopts it. In 1649 he writes that "*Calvin* and many more Interpreters think that if *Adam* had not fallen, he should after a season have been translated into Heaven without death, as *Enoch* and *Elias*. But I know of no Scripture that tells us so much."[30] In 1664 he is more definite about the sort of progression intended for Adam:

We deny not but as to *Degrees, Adam's Nature* was to grow up to more Perfection: And that his *Natural Holiness* contained not a *sufficient immediate aptitude* and *promptitude* to every Duty which might afterward be required of him; but this was to be obtained in the *Exercise* of that *Holiness* which he had: Even as a Vine or other Fruit-Tree, though it be *Natural* to it to bear its proper Fruit, yet hath it not an *immediate sufficient aptitude* hereto, whilst it is but appearing out of the Seed, before it be grown up to just Maturity.[31]

That Adam was in a "state of Heavenly hope" Baxter affirms in 1675.[32] And at the end of his life, in 1691, he explicitly brings together and endorses the ideas of Adam's translation to heaven and of his unfallen maturation:

Man's Nature being not made in its *utmost perfection,* but *in via,* with a desire of knowing God, loving him, pleasing him, and delighting in him yet more, according to his Capacity, we may gather, That obedient Man should have *attained that Perfection* . . .

But whether all this should have been given on *Earth* or in *Heaven,* is not so clear in Nature or Scripture: But . . . the matter is the less, because where-ever the place be, the same state of *Enjoyment* would make it a Heaven to such a person.[33]

Furthermore, not only Baxter but Milton too, as we noticed in the last chapter, must be counted among the proponents of that view which Lovejoy would leave buried in a footnote. The soul-making theodicy justifies the ways of God in part by describing what conditions are required for the constituting of human virtue, the assumption being that such virtue cannot in principle be infused into a person from the outset. Hence Milton, like Baxter, envisages an Adam and an Eve who are indeed *in via,* whose capacities are fitted to their relatively early stage of development, but whose exercise of holiness would lead them to a higher stage of perfection and enjoyment. As Raphael tells Adam:

> Your bodies may at last turn all to spirit,
> Improved by tract of time, and winged ascend

> Ethereal, as we, or may at choice
> Here or in heavenly paradises dwell;
> If ye be found obedient, and retain
> Unalterably firm his love entire
> Whose progeny you are. Mean while enjoy
> Your fill what happiness this happy state
> Can comprehend, incapable of more.
>
> [5.497–505]

And again, as the words of God make clear, the fruition of the process of soul making will result in a breaking down of the distinction between earth and heaven, such that man's translation will be as much an outgrowth of his own purification as its reward. Beholding earth from his heavenly throne, God says he will create

> out of one man a race
> Of men innumerable, there to dwell,
> Not here, till by degrees of merit raised
> They open to themselves at length the way
> Up hither, under long obedience tried,
> And earth be changed to heaven, and heaven to earth.
>
> [7.155–60]

As Dennis Burden acutely observes, one reason for the inclusion of such passages in *Paradise Lost* is that

Milton is worried about the idea of the Fortunate Fall. It is one thing to say that Adam is, as a result of the Atonement, better off than he was in Paradise, but something altogether different to suggest that he is better off than he would have been if he had stayed obedient. God's mercy cannot be allowed to make nonsense of his justice.[34]

Whether the teaching regarding man's improvement and eventual translation is sufficient to disconfirm the theory that *Paradise Lost* embodies the paradox of the Fortunate Fall is of course a question that needs to be considered further; but that teaching certainly does explode the common assumption that Adam and Eve were stuck in some static pristine state.

By contrast, however, those seventeenth-century Calvinists who hold that the Fall was both decreed and prerequisite for "the greater manifestation of the glory of God" have no interest in maintaining an alternative scenario for the growth and development of man had no fall occurred. Ball, for example, acknowledges the alternative only to assert its dubiousness: "Upon a supposition of *Adams* persisting in a state of obedience, to say that God would have translated him to the state of glory in Heaven, is more then any just ground will warrant."[35] Thomas Goodwin is even more emphatic in his denial of that which Milton so clearly envisages:

I think that *Adam*'s Covenant, and Obedience unto it, was not able to do so much as confirm him, and secure him in that Condition he was created in; so far was it from being able to have transplanted him into Heaven . . . I know no Promise for it, that after such a time, and so long Obedience performed, he should stand perpetually.[36]

If one believed that the Fall was fortunate and part of God's plan anyway, one simply did not need an "unfallen scenario." Milton, however, was insistent that man, not God, caused the Fall; that neither man nor God needed the Fall; that therefore neither sexual love, nor culinary arts, nor intellectual conversation, nor virtue itself presupposed the Fall. He believed, in short, that "it is . . . incredible that evil should be stronger" – or, we might add, more beneficial – "than good" (*CD*, p. 131). And thus he emphatically did need, and so did present, just such a vision of how things might have been had man persisted in the "long obedience" that the seventeenth-century Calvinist considered of so little avail.

The unfallen analogue: "more illustrious made"

Now of course the fact that Milton had plenty of incentive to deny the Fortunate Fall and that he *could* consistently have denied it even while asserting, as Lovejoy puts it, that "the final state of the redeemed . . . would far surpass in felicity and in moral excellence the pristine happiness and innocence of the first pair in Eden"[37] does not of itself prove that he *did* deny it. It simply makes it more likely that he would have done so. As was stated at the beginning of this chapter, my aim is not to establish a proof but to support a hypothesis which is more probable than that of the Fortunate Fall. And of course part of the process involves showing the latter hypothesis to be *im*probable. Accordingly, I have tried to demonstrate that some of its key assumptions are unwarranted or downright mistaken: The doctrine of the Fortunate Fall is not required by Christian orthodoxy, the Fall was not a *conditio sine qua non* of dramatic human development, and the *felix culpa* therefore cannot be inferred from such development and final felicity given the Fall.

There is, however, a further assumption made by Lovejoy and others who have written on the Fortunate Fall that at first sight seems undeniable: namely, that without the Fall, "the Incarnation and Redemption could never have occurred."[38] Yet this too is a claim that, in a crucial sense, is incorrect. That the *Redemption* presupposes the Fall is of course true; in fact, it is a tautology. One cannot ransom that which is not held captive. But it is certainly questionable whether the Redemption per se would be sufficient to render the Fall fortunate. By definition, redemption simply involves something's being restored to an original state, and therefore would not of itself seem to entail the superadded goodness that the notion of the *felix culpa* requires.[39] Only when the Redemption is considered together with the Incarnation do there appear to be sufficient grounds for maintaining that the result is *more* wonderful than what the first creation brought forth. The critical question thus becomes whether that which is achieved by the Incarnation itself presupposes the Fall.

Within the history of Christian theology perhaps the most startling view in this regard is that of Duns Scotus, who makes the emphatic though relatively little-known claim that the Incarnation would indeed have occurred even if there had been no Fall. As Fr. Allan B. Wolter says, that claim is a corollary of the doctrine of "the Absolute Primacy of Christ," which "proclaims that humanly speaking God first intended Christ as King and center of the universe. Only secondarily, so to speak, did God conceive Christ as redeemer of fallen man."[40] As Peter A. Fiore puts it, proponents of this view maintain "that God's principal motive in decreeing the Incarnation was the dignity and glorification of Christ."[41] Scotus himself, under the heading "Whether Christ be predestined to be the Son of God," presents the following question and response:

> What is the order of this predestination [i.e., of Christ's glorification and incarnation] with respect to the other things that are predestinated? It is said that the Fall of Man is the necessary grounds for this predestination. According to this view, God saw that Adam was going to fall, saw that Christ in this manner would redeem him, and therefore foresaw Christ's taking on himself human nature and glorifying it with such a glory.
>
> However, I say that the Fall was not the cause of the predestination of Christ; on the contrary, if there had been neither an angelic nor a human fall, still would Christ have been thus predestinated.[42]

One could hardly wish for a more unequivocal statement of the issue. Certainly, whatever else it does, it renders indefensible any claim that in Christian orthodoxy the Fall is necessarily a precondition of the Incarnation or of that centering of the universe in Christ which the Incarnation consummates.

Scotus admits, of course, that "Christ would not have come as a redeemer, if man had not sinned . . . If man had not sinned . . . there would have been no need of a redemption." However – and this is the essence of the matter – "neither is it likely that the highest good in the whole creation is something that merely chanced to take place, and that only because of some lesser good."[43] "For Scotus . . . the crux of the problem," as Wolter says, is whether "the universe [is] sin-centric or Christocentric" (p. 368). If it is affirmed that a Christocentric universe is conditional on the Fall, and if the Fall is thereby conceded to be fortunate, then one has no choice, Scotus recognizes, but to see the good purpose of God as being dependent on the sin of his creatures. And that, given a high view of the divine goodness, would be intolerable.

Now I am not about to suggest that Scotus's position was taken over in its entirety by Milton; in fact, it does not appear to receive any explicit acknowledgement from either him or his

English contemporaries. Despite what would be its usefulness in undermining the claim that God needed the Fall, as keen an Arminian theodicist as Pierce apparently was unaware of the view that distinguished between the Incarnation and the Redemption and declared the former to be decreed absolutely, without regard to the Fall; and he thus had to explain matters differently: "The *permission of sin* is not designed by God as a *means* of bringing in any *former decree* of *giving Christ.*" Rather, God, foreseeing that man will sin, "doth also foresee an opportunity of magnifying his *mercy* in giving *Christ,* and accordingly *decrees* to *give* him."[44]

Nevertheless, there are very significant implicit parallels with Scotus's view in the writings of some of Milton's contemporaries and indeed, I will argue shortly, in *Paradise Lost* itself. Thomas Goodwin, for example, distinguishes very clearly between that which presupposes the Fall – namely, the Redemption – and that which does not.[45] In writing on "the Order of Christ's Election," Goodwin asserts that Christ was predestined

for these higher ends than our Salvation is; 1. For God's own self to delight in . . . 2. To behold the Image of himself in a Creature . . . 3. By that Union with that Man, to communicate the God-head unto that one Creature . . . All which are Ends that stand out of his Being Mediator for us; and are far higher ends than the Glory thereof.[46]

Moreover, Goodwin teaches, "having thus absolutely chosen [Christ], and therewith endowed him with the Royalty to be the Soveraign end of all," God ordained "a double Relation of Christ unto us for his Glory . . . 1. The Relation of an Head; wherein we were given as Members to him . . . 2. The Relation of a *Saviour,* and *Redeemer;* which is a superaddition to that of Head-ship." Goodwin, like Scotus, makes it very clear that the goodness of God in predestinating Christ must not be seen as "beholding to mans sin"; and he accordingly emphasizes and exalts those blessings, such as the conferring of holiness, the adoption of believers as sons of God, and their communion with God, which the anointing of Christ conduces to, but which are "distinct from and antecedaneous to those that necessarily suppose the fall." Declares Goodwin:

I shall end only in this, That as all those first Benefits do not depend upon Mans having sinned first, so . . . this Foundation of Christ, considered as an *Head* to us, might be, and was a sufficient ground to bestow them upon us in Election, upon our relation to him, as given of God, as he is Christ, and as he is an Head and Husband to us.[47]

Once again, the universe, God's glory, and his good will to men must be centered in Christ, not in sin; and the best must not need the worst.

Probably the most important scriptural basis for this expounding of the headship of Christ is Eph. 1:9–10, which speaks of the mystery of God's will and his purpose "that in the dispensation of the fullness of times he might gather together in one all things in Christ, both which are in heaven, and which are on earth." Commenting on this verse in 1651, John Goodwin (the Arminian) notes that "by *All things* . . . , by the joynt consent of all Interpreters, [is meant], Angels . . . and Men"; and he adds that "when the Apostle saith, that Gods Project or Design was, to recapitulate, or recollect, or *gather all things into,* or unto, *an Head, by Christ,* both Angels and Men, He supposeth, . . . That both stood in need of an *Head, i.e.* of one set in place of Power and Authority over them."[48] And Thomas Goodwin, who has an entire series of sermons on Eph. 1:10, not only reemphasizes the parallel between men and angels under the headship of Christ, but also, on the basis of textual evidence, asserts that there is not one but two gatherings of all things in Christ. For the word translated "gather together in one" is ἀνακεφαλαιώσασθαι. The prefix *ana,* of course, implies a repetition; and so Goodwin declares

that God, to illustrate the glory of his grace, and of his Christ, purposed a second gathering after a first, both of men and Angels . . . The first serves to magnifie his Grace in Christ, the Head, to Angels, who are *All things* in Heaven. And the second to magnifie his Grace to the Sons of Men, the *All things* in Earth, both as Head and Redeemer.[49]

Now one need posit no simple identity between this position and that of Milton in order to recognize that views of Christ's headship such as those expressed by Goodwin have great importance for an interpretation of the exaltation of the Son in *Paradise Lost*. First, as has already been indicated, sharply distinguishing the role of Redeemer from that of Head allows one to appreciate that the manifestation of God in Christ, and with it the communication of benefits to his creatures, is not dependent upon those creatures' having sinned. In his *Christian Doctrine* Milton does not speculate concerning what depended on the Fall and what did not, although he does take the "all things in Heaven" of Eph. 1:10 as meaning the angels; and, having quoted that verse, he points out that the angels "are reckoned as being under Christ because he is their head, not their Redeemer."[50] In *Paradise Lost*, however, this theoretical-sounding distinction is made to play a vital role in a poetic and narrative model that, for the purposes of theodicy, blasts an assumption without whose support the whole theory of the Fortunate Fall is in grave danger of collapsing. The giving of the Son as Messiah, the uniting of all things under him as their Head, the "epiphany" that the creatures can experience by no other means – the Son being *the* divine similitude, "In whose conspicuous countenance . . . the almighty Father shines, / Whom else no creature can behold" (3.384–7) – all of these benefits are in *Paradise Lost* conferred in a wholly sinless universe. Milton thus presents once more by means of angelic analogy a picture of how things could have been for mankind. In *Paradise Lost* there is indeed, again to borrow from Goodwin's exposition of Eph. 1:10, "a *Vision of God*, which the Angels were not created unto, which in Christ they are raised up unto."[51] Therefore, just as Abdiel provides a model of how Adam could have stood rather than fallen, so the anointing of Christ as Head and Messiah at the beginning of time demonstrates the accomplishment in an unfallen world of that which the Bible explicitly envisages as occurring in the fullness of time, and of that of which so many have considered a fallen world to be a precondition. And to this extent, clearly, it can be denied that Adam's sin was *certe necessarium*.

Furthermore, however, recognizing that the eschatological exaltation of the Son as biblically envisaged entails a *recapitu-lating* or *reuniting* dispels any suspicion that Milton did not quite know what he was doing – or was merely fudging – when he included two exaltations of Christ in *Paradise Lost*. It is surely not the case, as Allan H. Gilbert seems to imply, that the "duplication . . . resulted from the late composition of Book III,"[52] nor, as some believe, that the exaltation in book 5 is nothing but a narrative expedient for motivating Satan's rebellion. Such opinions merely trivialize what in fact is the depth and complexity of Milton's theological purpose. For as W. B. Hunter rightly says, "When Milton writes any Christian dogma into *Paradise Lost,* he really means it."[53] I would add only that Milton's narrative ingenuity not merely accommodates itself to theology but actually informs and enriches it.

What, then, does Milton in fact accomplish, narratively and theologically, by presenting the exaltation of Christ in *Paradise Lost?* The very first words, chronologically, of the poem are those uttered by God to the assembled hosts of angels one day in eternity when "As yet this world was not":

> Hear all ye angels, progeny of light,
> Thrones, dominations, princedoms, virtues, powers,
> Hear my decree, which unrevoked shall stand.
> This day I have begot whom I declare
> My only Son, and on this holy hill
> Him have anointed, whom ye now behold
> At my right hand; your head I him appoint;
> And by my self have sworn to him shall bow
> All knees in heaven, and shall confess him Lord:
> Under his great vicegerent reign abide
> United as one individual soul
> For ever happy.
>
> [5.600–11]

Here we have a peculiar literary situation in which one speech echoes another that is earlier in the poem but later absolutely.

In book 3, in his synopsis of salvation history, God tells the Son that the latter will sit in God's throne

> incarnate, here shalt reign
> Both God and man, Son both of God and man,
> Anointed universal king, all power
> I give thee, reign for ever, and assume
> Thy merits; under thee as head supreme
> Thrones, princedoms, powers, dominions I reduce:
> All knees to thee shall bow, of them that bide
> In heaven, or earth, or under earth in hell.
>
> [3.315–22]

The parallels between these passages hardly need to be elaborated. Both clearly present a vision of thrones, princedoms, and powers doing obeisance to and being united under the headship of Christ the anointed king. In each, furthermore, the echo of Phil. 2:9–10 is unmistakable: "God . . . hath highly exalted him, and given him a name which is above every name: That at the name of Jesus every knee should bow, of things in heaven, and things in earth, and things under the earth." However, in the passage from book 5 this echo is truncated: On reading "knees in heaven," anyone who remembers either Philippians or its echo two books earlier in the epic wants to add "and in earth," and yet immediately realizes the inappropriateness of doing so because he has just been told that the earth is not yet created. Moreover, if one stops to consider further the differences that the parallels between the passages thus serve to frame, one notices at the original "begetting" of the Son that just as there was a heaven but no earth, so too was the Son anointed Messiah and Head but not Redeemer. For of course there was no fall from which anyone or anything needed redeeming. And by thus presenting the Son's exaltation and headship in the absence of human or angelic sin, Milton subtly but decisively demonstrates that a Christocentric universe presupposes neither.

The point is especially significant, given that nothing in Milton's materials dictated the placing of Christ's anointing before any human or angelic fall. John Goodwin, despite the parallels between his and Milton's presentations of the headship of Christ, clearly assumes the Fall and its results to be part of the context of the gathering together which that headship effects. Accordingly, he declares that "the Death of *Christ* was necessary for the bringing about the glorious Projection of God, I mean, the *gathering of all things, whether in Heaven,* or on Earth, under . . . the same *Head, Christ.*"[54] The headship of Christ could thus, like the Redemption, be conceived to be both temporally and logically *post*lapsarian.

But Milton leaves neither the reader nor, it must be remembered, unfallen Adam in any doubt that the Son's being "proclaimed / Messiah king anointed" in every sense *precedes* the Fall (5.663–4). Even after the Fall, when Michael is presenting the history of salvation to Adam, clearly it is he who *already* is "the true / Anointed king Messiah" who will be born of a virgin, destroy Satan's works in his deeds and in his death, and rise again for the redemption of mankind (12.359 ff.). If either Adam or Milton's reader hears the echo of those words spoken in book 5, he will have cause to recall also that that anointing of the Messiah was an accomplished fact before the Fall, indeed, before the foundation of the world.

The title "Messiah" is emphasized repeatedly in books 5 and 6;[55] and Abdiel, whom Milton apparently considers the first Christian commentator and apologist, in countering the jealous arguments of Satan further explicates the Son's newly announced role. As we saw in Chapter 4, Satan views the Son's anointing as a divine power play that does nothing but abuse the angels and their "imperial titles" (5.800–1). Abdiel replies by stressing the angels' experience of God's goodness as well as his purpose "to exalt / Our happy state under one head more near / United" (826–31). Abdiel in no way denies God's power, but he shows that there is more to the divine decree than power alone.[56] Fowler remarks that "Abdiel appears to regard the Messiah's kingship over the angels as a kind of incarnation,"[57] and this suggestion is by no means as farfetched as it may at first appear. For just as the "humiliation" of the Son's human incarnation, foretold by God in book 3, will "exalt / With [him his] manhood" (3.313–14), so the angels, as Abdiel asserts, are not "obscured" by the Son's reign but rather "more illustrious made, since he the head / One of our number thus reduced becomes" (5.841–3). In this way the angelic analogy again demonstrates that not only the Son's anointing but also the creatures' participation in his divine exaltation could have been a prelapsarian reality.[58]

Let me press one step further the suggestion that Milton presents a kind of prelapsarian Incarnation.[59] There is certainly precedent for asserting that the angels had a revelation of the incarnate Christ. Aquinas affirms that "among the mysteries of grace the most outstanding is that of the Incarnation of Christ, and this the angels knew from the beginning."[60] Moreover, Calvin refers (albeit scathingly) to the opinion that Satan was "moued . . . to worke mans destruction" on account of jealousy, "because he foresawe that the sonne of God was to take vpon him humane fleshe."[61] As has already been pointed out, Milton accepts that Eph. 1:10 refers to men and angels; and in *Christian Doctrine,* in connection with the same verse, he also explicitly identifies headship with the Incarnation.[62] Now in *Paradise Lost* there is no question that the exaltation of the Son occasions Satan's revolt itself. And what I am suggesting is that by investing that exaltation with much of the character of the Incarnation, Milton builds not only on the poem's own parallel between things human and angelic, but also on the tradition that Satan envies the Son his special role – the difference being, of course, that in *Paradise Lost* what occasions the envy is not something vaguely *fore*known but rather an event known and experienced firsthand, on that day (5.662) which stands at the very beginning of Milton's heavenly "history."

The dramatic brilliance of having Satan thus react to something that has, as it were, taken place right on stage scarcely needs comment, although it has been less widely recognized than has the dramatic weakness of God's reacting, in book 3, to events that he merely foresees. Yet the exaltation of Christ in

Paradise Lost is an accomplishment of profound theological as well as narrative significance. For it also provides, as has already been indicated, an analogy or model that seriously undermines the assumption that but for the Fall, the Incarnation *could* never have occurred, or that it would have no occasion or meaning.[63] Indeed, to the extent that the meaning of the Incarnation consists in the establishing of a Christocentric universe, in a greater manifestation of the glory of God, in a gracious condescension of the Son toward God's creatures, in those creatures being united under the headship of the Messiah and thereby receiving greater benefits than could otherwise be obtained, this mystery does in *Paradise Lost* have prelapsarian occasion, meaning, and prominence, all revealed to fallen reader and unfallen Adam alike. There is historical precedent as well as internal, literary support, moreover, for both this claim and the claim that, without the Fall, mankind's destiny would have been one not of static innocence but of cultural, moral, and spiritual development. Sin is no *conditio sine qua non* of soul making, and Adam is shown that, too. It may well be that in some sense the Fall occasions more glory to God than there would otherwise be; but as John Goodwin says, even though sin is "contriveable to [God's] glory," it is "no wayes requisite or necessary hereunto."[64] And likewise for Milton, the Fall was no *felix culpa*.

The hypothesis of the Unfortunate Fall

How, then, does this whole hypothesis of the Unfortunate Fall in *Paradise Lost* stand up when it comes to the crucial, exclamatory passage in book 12? The hypothesis of the Fortunate Fall, even given its wrong assumptions, could still be correct. Indeed, it would seem that if we take Adam's speech (quoted on p. 204) out of context, the decision could go either way. Lined up with Lovejoy's "analogues," it certainly can sound like a version of the *felix culpa*. Lovejoy admits, of course, that Adam expresses "merely a doubt whether he

should repent his sin or 'rejoice much more' over its consequences. Yet," he goes on, "Adam could have had no reason
for his doubt except upon the assumption that the sin was truly
prerequisite to the 'much more good' that was . . . to 'spring'
from it; and an intelligent reader could hardly have failed to
conclude that the doubt was to be resolved in favor of the second alternative."[65] This conclusion is overly hasty. For if Milton's "intelligent reader" is at least as familiar with Scripture as
with the "Exultet" from the Roman Liturgy, he or she can hear
at the end of Adam's exclamation, as Mollenkott has already
pointed out,[66] an echo from the book of Romans: "But where
sin abounded, grace did much more abound" (5:20) – as Adam
says, "over wrath grace shall abound." And in Romans, the
Apostle adds, two verses later: "What shall we say then? Shall
we continue in sin, that grace may abound? God forbid" (6:1–
2). It is hard to imagine that any reader of *Paradise Lost* who
remembers that context would elect the alternative favored by
Lovejoy.

A more immediate context is provided by the poem itself.
First, it is worth noting that Adam's reference to the "much
more good" *springing* from his sin is in grim contrast to
Michael's use of the same word when introducing that series of
visions to which Adam in books 11 and 12 is responding:
"Adam, now ope thine eyes, and first behold / The effects
which thy original crime hath wrought / In some to spring from
thee" (11.423–5). In what follows, of course, Adam is given
plenty of cause for repenting "of sin / By [him] done and occasioned" (12.474–5).

Furthermore, Adam's responses to what he is shown generally require correction or modification. For example, on beholding the degradation that ensues from the Fall, Adam exclaims,
"O miserable mankind . . . ! Better end here unborn"; and he
goes on to ask querulously why life is "Obtruded on us thus"
(11.500–4). Michael replies by explaining the justice of the situation, and Adam then "submits" (11.526). Later, having
learned that Messiah is going to come, Adam, again getting

excited, asks where and when the fight between Christ and Satan will take place (12.384–5). And again Michael must temper Adam's response, this time by telling him that the battle will not be military in nature, and in fact will involve the victor's "temporal death" (12.386 ff., 433).

Adam's immediate reactions to what he sees are of course very human. They are poetically valid in the sense that they are part of the overall drama of his response to the Fall and its consequences as well as typical of subsequent human attitudes and "solutions," be they "abortionist" ("Better end here unborn"), "militarist," or, in the case in question, "optimistic." But they are not normative. The attentive reader learns to expect them to be tempered or significantly reconsidered. And indeed, in Adam's next speech after exclaiming about the "much more good" that will take place, he himself concludes:

> Henceforth I learn, that to obey is best,
> And love with fear the only God, to walk
> As in his presence, ever to observe
> His providence, and on him sole depend,
> Merciful over all his works, with good
> Still overcoming evil.
>
> [12.561–6]

God brings more good out of evil than there was to start with. He creates a "far happier place" at the end of time than Paradise was at the beginning (12.464). Adam truly does become a *felix peccator*.[67] Yet he also learns that, the greater good notwithstanding, obedience is *best*. And in this way he arrives at the conclusion the reader ought already to have reached; for as God himself decisively affirms, man would have been even "Happier, had it sufficed him to have known / Good by it self, and evil not at all" (11.88–9).

Thus the hypothesis of the Unfortunate Fall. It is, to be sure, as Barbour says of models generally, only "partial and inadequate."[68] I am not pretending that it solves all the critical problems related to the Fall that one might encounter in Milton's poetry. However, it is hard to conceive of a more important question in the study of Milton than whether the Fall is fortunate or unfortunate: It is absolutely crucial to both the subject and the "object" of *Paradise Lost* – to the Fall of Man itself and to the justification of the ways of God. And I submit that what has been offered in this chapter, even if "partial and inadequate," *more* adequately "saves the appearances," be they literary, historical, or theological, than does the alternative hypothesis – the fallacy of the Fortunate Fall – which has for almost half a century hung like a pall over Milton's epic and over his theodicy. To be quite rid of its influence is probably more than one can now reasonably hope. But it is certainly time for Milton's "intelligent reader" to recognize how torn and insubstantial its fabric really is.

Epilogue

It has become almost a cliché that Milton sets out to justify the ways of God to men. Yet especially in an age in which belief in God is unfashionable (unless one finds oneself running for public office or facing sudden death), the whole notion of justifying God can appear dusty and academic, or simply banal – this in spite of the genuine triviality of so much of life in our Western society.

In the face of these discouragements, however, and mindful too of the meager number to which this book will probably speak (perhaps one-thousandth of 1 percent as many as have watched television's most popular soap opera), I have attempted here to make a case for reconsidering the importance for literature of the problem of evil, the importance of Milton's literary contribution to theodicy, even the importance of the whole issue of evil and of a possible human reconciliation of it with the existence of an omnipotent good God. I have tried, furthermore, to put my case critically but in a way that does not ignore the motivations, assumptions, and commitments without which Milton would not have written *Paradise Lost,* without which I would not have written this book, and without which you would probably not be reading Milton or this book. We are all human beings inhabiting the same world and with a similar longing – or am I mistaken? – to understand where we came from and what life is all about.

Milton believed that such elemental questions about genesis and meaning could not be answered without reference to the God from whom, in whom, and to whom are all things. And they could not be answered in a way supportive of faith, hope, or love unless that God were believed to be a good God. As Nathaniel Homes pointed out in 1653, when the Psalmist prays, "Thou art good, and doest good; teach me thy statutes" (Ps. 119:68), we can read his *and* as a *therefore*: "*Viz. Thou art good, therefore thou dost good; therefore teach me thy Statutes;* But however we translate, these two are chained together, . . . that God doth good, because he is good; and upon both, as on a Foundation is built the knowledge, Faith and Hope of good *David*, what to think and expect of God."[1]

The goodness of God is a foundation, and in this sense theodicy's conclusion is also its starting point. That is not to say that the quest of theodicy leads nowhere. It led Milton through profound depths of thought and meaning to incomparable spiritual and poetic heights; without it we should not have had *Paradise Lost.* Yet in the end, the end is the beginning. And even in the first poetry that Milton ever wrote in English, he joins with the Psalmist in confessing that the goodness of God is the basis of his worship. To be sure, the work of the fifteen-year-old is not great poetry, but it stands as a fitting prolepsis of the theodical quest's epic consummation, of that combined greatness of poetry and argument which remains unparalleled in English. For Milton, indeed, theodicy begins and ends with the same word which is the beginning, and the fulfillment, of the very image of God in man:

> Let us with a gladsome mind
> Praise the Lord, for he is kind,
>   For his mercies ay endure,
>   Ever faithful, ever sure.[2]

Appendix: The unfortunate fall of Satan

Having considered the case against the theory of the Fortunate Fall as applied to Adam and Eve, the alert reader might well respond by asking about Satan. Was not his fall, and that of his cohorts, a precondition for the very creation of mankind? If man was created to fill the gap that occurred as a result of the angelic revolt, then must not the entire human race rejoice in that fall: "O happy fault that merited our *creation*"?[1]

The simple answer is yes – *if*, that is, man was created merely to fill the gap. Such a supposition, however, is not entailed by anything that Milton says; and it would therefore be incorrect to impose the hypothesis of a fortunate angelic fall upon *Paradise Lost*.

Perhaps the clearest model of the *un*fortunate fall of Satan is that outlined by St. Anselm in his *Cur Deus Homo*, where he refers to that "part of our belief" according to which God designed "to make up for the number of angels that fell, from human nature which he created without sin."[2] Anselm, assuming that God ordained a "reasonable and complete number" of rational beings and that "man was created after the fall of the evil angels,"[3] recognizes two possible interpretations: Either (1) the angels were "created perfect in number and . . . afterwards man was created to complete their number when it had been lessened"; or else (2) "they were not perfect in number, because God deferred completing the number, . . . determining in his own time to create man" (p. 213). However, because it would be wrong to treat any "nature" created by God as if it were superfluous, the second interpretation is the only one acceptable. Thus Anselm concludes that mankind "was made for itself, and not merely to restore the number of beings possessing another nature. From which it is plain that, even had no angel fallen, men would yet have had their place in the celestial kingdom. And hence . . . there was not a perfect number of angels, even before a part fell" (pp. 214–15).

Anselm's motivation for taking such a position, as he himself admits, is partly theodical. For "had a perfect number of angels been created, and had man been made only to fill the place of the lost angels, it is plain that, had not some angels fallen from their happiness, man would never have been exalted to it." And of course such a supposition would lead, given the fall of the angels and the creation and exaltation of men, to what Anselm refers to as an "unholy joy" ("perversa gratulatio") among those so exalted (p. 215). Again, therefore, one must adopt the second interpretation. Although it may be true in some sense that the gap created by the fall of the angels is filled by mankind, one must affirm that the gap was *more* than filled, that mankind would have been created regardless of the angelic fall. For the goodness of God and of his creation ought not to be seen as depending upon evil. Anselm's second model, indeed, demonstrates that Satan's fall need not thus be seen as fortunate.

Now which of Anselm's two models do we find presented in *Paradise Lost?* We in fact find both. As he so often does, Milton gives us a choice: We can either adopt an interpretation that is consistent with the glory and goodness of God, or we can follow Satan. And in *Paradise Lost* it is Satan alone who fastens upon and promulgates the interpretation that Anselm rejects. Four times Satan mentions the "ancient and prophetic fame in heaven" that foretold the creation of man (2.346). The first time he mentions it he refers to mankind as "A generation, whom [God's] choice regard / Should favour *equal* to the sons of heaven" (1.653–4; italics added). The next time, however, he says that man is to be "favoured *more* / Of him who rules above" (2.350–1; italics added). And then, for the benefit of Sin and Death, Satan insinuates the "gap" theory for the first time: God has created "A race of upstart creatures, to supply / Perhaps our vacant room" (2.834–5). Finally, of course, Satan believes his own propaganda. For how much easier it is to destroy a victim if one can fuel one's malevolence with envy. On returning to hell after his infamous journey, Satan boasts to his fallen comrades how he

> found
> The new created world, which fame in heaven
> Long had foretold, a fabric wonderful
> Of absolute perfection, therein man
> Placed in paradise, *by our exile*
> *Made happy:* him by fraud I have seduced.
>   [10.480–5; italics added]

No longer is there any "perhaps." Satan has achieved the certainty of the tyrant, unruffled by the illogicality of his assumption that that which was long foretold came about merely as the splenetic reaction of an offended deity.

If one already holds this Satanic view of the relationship between the creation of man and the fall of the angels, or if one is simply unaware of any alternative model, then what God says in book 7 of *Paradise Lost* does not obviously clash with Satan's position. For, the angels having fallen, God declares that

> heaven yet populous retains
> Number sufficient to possess her realms . . .
>
>   .   .   .
>
> But lest [Satan's] heart exalt him in the harm
> Already done, to have dispeopled heaven
> My damage fondly deemed, I can repair
> That detriment, if such it be to lose
> Self-lost, and in a moment will create
> Another world, out of one man a race
> Of men innumerable.[4]

However, as Anselm makes clear, it is not the idea of mankind's compensating the loss of the angels that makes the difference between a model consistent with theodicy and one that is not; the decisive issue is whether the creation of mankind does anything more than compensate in this way. And God's words here imply no mere replacing of a certain number of angels with the same number of human beings; rather, what is envisaged is the angels' loss being more than compensated – the numerable by the *innumerable* (line 156).

For Milton, as for St. Augustine, "out of this mortal race of men . . . God gathers, by his grace, so numerous a people that out of them He fills the places and restores the ranks emptied by the fallen angels." And yet this does not imply that the fall of the angels was necessary for the creation of mankind and was therefore (from mankind's point of view) fortunate. For what God does is to produce more good than there was evil, not merely to "repair / That detriment" but to do more than repair it. As Augustine continues, "Thus it is that the beloved City . . . is not deprived of the full complement of its citizens and, in fact, may even rejoice in a fuller complement than it had before the angels' fall."[5] If heaven has room for this fuller complement, therefore, one cannot assume that the inclusion of men required the exclusion of angels. And indeed, unless the creation or the heavenly bliss of mankind thus presupposes the angelic fall, one is humanly and Miltonically unjustified in concluding that that fall is fortunate.

Notes

All quotations of Milton's poetry are taken from *The Poems of John Milton*, ed. John Carey and Alastair Fowler (London: Longmans, 1968).

Abbreviations

CD	Milton, *Christian Doctrine*, ed. Maurice Kelley, trans. John Carey, in *Complete Prose Works of John Milton*, ed. Don M. Wolfe et al., Vol. VI (New Haven: Yale Univ. Press, 1973)
CM	*The Works of John Milton*, ed. Frank Allen Patterson et al., 18 vols. (New York: Columbia Univ. Press, 1931–8)
Evans, *PLGT*	J. Martin Evans, *"Paradise Lost" and the Genesis Tradition* (Oxford: Oxford Univ. Press, Clarendon Press, 1968)
Hick, *EGL*	John Hick, *Evil and the God of Love* (London: Macmillan, 1966)
Lovejoy, "MPFF"	Arthur O. Lovejoy, "Milton and the Paradox of the Fortunate Fall," *ELH*, 4, No. 3 (1937), 161–79, rpt. in *Critical Essays on Milton from ELH*. (Baltimore: Johns Hopkins Univ. Press, 1969), pp. 163–81 (references are to the reprint)
PL	Milton, *Paradise Lost*, in *The Poems of John Milton*, ed. John Carey and Alastair Fowler (London: Longmans, 1968)

Chapter 1. The contexts of Milton's theodicy

1. Coleridge, Lecture X, "Milton," February 27, 1818, in Coleridge, *The Complete Works*, ed. W. G. T. Shedd (New York, 1853–), IV, 303.

2. The term was coined by G. W. Leibniz in his work of 1710 entitled *Theodicée*. The best English edition is Leibniz, *Theodicy*, ed. Austin Farrer, trans. E. M. Huggard (London: Routledge and Kegan Paul, 1951).

3. Lactantius, *A Treatise on the Anger of God*, chap. 13, trans. William Fletcher, in *The Ante-Nicene Fathers*, ed. Alexander Roberts and James Donaldson (rpt. Grand Rapids: Eerdmans, 1975), VII, 271.

4. John Hick says that the term "metaphysical evil" seems to have been coined by Leibniz (*Evil and the God of Love* [London: Macmillan, 1966], p. 19; cited hereafter as Hick, *EGL*). However, see Thomas Hobbes, *The Questions concerning Liberty, Necessity, and Chance . . . Debated between Dr. Bramhall . . . and Thomas Hobbes* (London, 1656), pp. 145–6. Bramhall distinguishes moral, natural, and metaphysical *goodness*. Hobbes traces Bramhall's doctrine that "whatsoever hath a being is good" to "the Schooles" and ultimately to Aristotle. Predictably, Hobbes retorts that Bramhall's "*Metaphysical goodness* is but an idle tearm." To some extent my discussion in these paragraphs is based on Hick, as well as on Norman L. Geisler, *Philosophy of Religion* (Grand Rapids: Zondervan, 1974), pp. 311–403.

5. Plotinus, *The Enneads*, trans. Stephen MacKenna, 2nd ed. (London: Faber, 1956), 2.9, 13; 3.3, 7.

6. Augustine, *Enchiridion*, chap. 12, in *The Works of Aurelius Augustine*, ed. Marcus Dods (Edinburgh: T. and T. Clark, 1871–), Vol. IX.

7. The thesis that Plotinus (particularly his *Enneads*) influenced Augustine is defended by Paul Henry, "Augustine and Plotinus," *Journal of Theological Studies*, 38 (1937), 1–23.

8. *The Confessions of St. Augustine*, trans. Rex Warner (New York: New American Library, 1963), 7.12.

9. Aquinas, *Commentary on Dionysius' "On the Divine Names,"* chap. 4, lect. 14a., in *An Aquinas Reader*, ed. Mary T. Clark (New York: Image Books, 1972), p. 54.

10. See Alvin Plantinga, *God, Freedom and Evil* (London: George Allen and Unwin, 1975), p. 28, as well as pp. 7–64 passim.

11. For discussion of a famous example of this approach, see H. B. McCullough, "Theodicy and Mary Baker Eddy," *Sophia*, 14, No. 1 (1975), 12–18.

12. Voltaire, *Candide; or, Optimism* (Harmondsworth: Penguin, 1947), passim; Barth, *Church Dogmatics* (Edinburgh: T. and T. Clark, 1956–69), Vol. III, pt. 3, p. 318.

13. Fish, *Surprised by Sin* (Berkeley and Los Angeles: Univ. of California Press, 1971), p. 1; cf. p. 354.

14. *PL*, 7.31, 1.26. Cf. *Samson Agonistes*, lines 293–4: "Just are the ways

of God, / And justifiable to men." Of course *PL*, 8.226 ("the ways of God with man"), can be cited in support of the more usual, less interesting reading of 1.26.

15. C. Hill, *Milton and the English Revolution* (New York: Viking Press, 1977), pp. 5, 97–8.

16. Ibid., p. 9.

17. Ibid., p. 3.

18. Drummond, "An Anti-Miltonist Reprise: I. The Milton Controversy," and "II. Antagonistic Styles and Contradictory Demands," *The Compass*, No. 2 (Dec. 1977), pp. 28–45, No. 3 (Apr. 1978), pp. 39–59 (pt. I, p. 39).

19. Ibid., p. 33. Drummond borrows heavily here on suggestions made by Bernard Bergonzi, "Criticism and the Milton Controversy," in *The Living Milton*, ed. Frank Kermode (London: Routledge and Kegan Paul, 1960), pp. 162–80. See F. R. Leavis's chapter entitled "Milton's Verse" in *Revaluation* (London: Chatto and Windus, 1956), pp. 42–67; and A. J. A. Waldock, *"Paradise Lost" and Its Critics* (Cambridge: Cambridge Univ. Press, 1947), passim.

20. Auerbach, *Mimesis*, trans. Willard R. Trask (1953; rpt. Princeton: Princeton Univ. Press, 1973), p. 23; cf. pp. 11–12. J. Martin Evans has made the same point regarding the applicability of Auerbach's analysis; see Evans, *PLGT*, pp. 21–2.

21. Drummond, "An Anti-Miltonist Reprise," pt. II, p. 51.

22. See Evans's discussion of the interpretative, narrative, and metaphysical questions that the poet as well as the theologian must answer (*PLGT*, pp. 23–5).

23. Patrides, *"Paradise Lost"* and the Language of Theology," in W. B. Hunter, C. A. Patrides, and J. H. Adamson, *Bright Essence* (Salt Lake City: Univ. of Utah Press, 1971), p. 168. Patrides is attacking, of course, Maurice Kelley's *This Great Argument* (Princeton: Princeton Univ. Press, 1941). Patrides restates his case for Miltonic dualism in "Milton and the Arian Controversy," *Proceedings of the American Philosophical Society*, 120, No. 4 (1976), 245–52, and has it rehearsed for him by his doctoral supervisee Gordon Campbell, who declares that the nature of *Paradise Lost* is "not theological," even "anti-theological" ("The Intellect and the Imagination," D.Phil. Thesis York Univ. [England] 1973, p. 356). See also Campbell's recent introduction to *John Milton: The Complete Poems*, ed. B. A. Wright (London: J. M. Dent, 1980), p. xxiii.

24. Arnold, *The Complete Prose Works* (Ann Arbor: Univ. of Michigan Press, 1960–), IX, 48–9.

25. I echo, of course, *Areopagitica*, in *The Complete Prose Works of John*

Milton, ed. Don M. Wolfe et al. (New Haven: Yale Univ. Press, 1953–), II, 550–1. It should also be remembered that the work Patrides would critically proscribe was introduced by Milton as "my dearest and best possession" (*Complete Prose Works*, VI, 121).

26. Lewis, *The Discarded Image* (Cambridge: Cambridge Univ. Press, 1964), p. 14. Patrides points out the relevance of models for Milton in *"Paradise Lost* and the Language of Theology," p. 172.

27. See Richard H. Bube, *The Human Quest* (Waco: Word Books, 1971), pp. 174–6.

28. Barbour, *Myths, Models and Paradigms* (London: SCM Press, 1974), p. 69.

29. MacCaffrey, *Paradise Lost as "Myth"* (Cambridge, Mass.: Harvard Univ. Press, 1959), p. 21.

30. Barbour, *Myths*, p. 24.

31. Quoted in ibid., p. 24.

Chapter 2. God and Chaos

1. Unless otherwise noted, all quotations of Scripture will be from the Authorized (King James) Version.

2. What Herman Dooyeweerd would call the biblical "ground motive"; see L. Kalsbeek, *Contours of a Christian Philosophy* (Toronto: Wedge Publishing, 1975), pp. 62–6.

3. *The Geneva Bible: A Facsimile of the 1560 Edition* (Madison: Univ. of Wisconsin Press, 1969), p. 1; abbreviations expanded.

4. See Gaspar Olevian's "Epitome" of John Calvin's *Institutes of the Christian Religion,* trans. Henry Beveridge (rpt. Grand Rapids: Eerdmans, 1975), I, 27: "The first article of the Apostles' Creed is concerning *God the Father,* the creation, preservation, and government of the universe, as implied in his omnipotence. Accordingly, the First Book of the Institutes treats of the knowledge of God, considered as the Creator, Preserver, and Governor of the world, and of everything contained in it."

5. Plato, *Timaeus,* trans. Desmond Lee (Harmondsworth: Penguin, 1965), 30 (p. 42).

6. Ibid., 48 (p. 65); see 52–3 (pp. 70–2) for a more detailed description of the chaos God found. See also Hick's discussion of the *Timaeus* and dualism, in which he suggests that Plato's "necessity" signifies not "rigid determination . . . but something more like chaos and randomness . . . In other and earlier dialogues this Necessity, which is the source of evil, is virtually identical with the matter that imprisons us as embodied beings" (*EGL,* p. 33).

7. On the contrast between biblical and dualistic views, see Langdon Gilkey, *Maker of Heaven and Earth* (New York: Doubleday, 1959), pp. 48–51. See also his chapter "Creation and Evil," pp. 178–205.

8. Plantinga, *God, Freedom and Evil*, p. 18.

9. Anderson, *Creation versus Chaos* (New York: Association Press, 1967), p. 161.

10. Waltke, *Creation and Chaos* (Portland, Oreg.: Western Conservative Baptist Seminary, 1974), p. 5. See, for example, Job 26:12–13 and Ps. 74:13 ff. For other discussion of the association of Chaos and the monster, see Evans, *PLGT*, p. 12.

11. Anderson, *Creation versus Chaos*, p. 164. Anderson concludes that "the 'dualism' which the myth of Satan portrays is not a metaphysical or ontological dualism (as in . . . Gnosticism, Manichaeanism [*sic*], etc.) but a historical dualism: a conflict which occurs between the beginning and the consummation of the historical drama" (p. 165). These comments, of course, apply to Chaos only if it is not primordial and if "historical" is taken in its most comprehensive sense.

12. Irenaeus, *Against Heresies*, 2.1.1 (see bk. 2 passim for both an account and a rebuttal of Gnosticism), in Roberts and Donaldson, *The Ante-Nicene Fathers*, Vol. I.

13. Augustine, *De Natura Boni Contra Manichaeos*, chap. 10, in *A Select Library of the Nicene and Post-Nicene Fathers of the Christian Church*, ed. Philip Schaff (rpt. Grand Rapids: Eerdmans, 1974), Vol. IV.

14. *Ibid.*, chap. 18.

15. Augustine, *De Duabus Animabus contra Manichaeos*, chap. 8, in Schaff, *Nicene and Post-Nicene Fathers*, Vol. IV.

16. Augustine, *Confessions*, 7.3, 16. Cf. *De Duabus Animabus*, chaps. 10–12; and *De Natura Boni*, chap. 7.

17. Berdjaev, *The Destiny of Man*, trans. Natalie Duddington (1955; rpt. New York: Harper & Row, 1960), pp. 23–4. "Calvin's horrible doctrine [of predestination]," says Berdjaev, "has the great merit of being a *reductio ad absurdum.*" I shall consider this aspect of Calvinist theology in Chapter 3.

18. *Ibid.*, p. 24. I shall return to this version of freedom and its relation to theodicy in Chapter 5.

19. *Ibid.*, p. 25. Cf. Berdjaev, *Freedom and the Spirit*, trans. O. F. Clarke, 4th ed. (London: Geoffrey Bles, 1948), p. 160:

There is in the very origin of the world an irrational freedom which is grounded in the void, in that abyss from which the dark stream of life issues forth and in which every sort of possibility is latent

. . . Freedom is not created because it is not a part of nature . . .
God is All-powerful in relation to being but not in relation to nothingness and freedom; and that is why evil exists.

See also Berdjaev's chapter entitled "Evil" in *The Divine and the
Human*, trans. R. M. French (London: Geoffrey Bles, 1949), pp. 86–
97. Another very evocative modern discussion of creation, evil,
and "nothingness" – or, as he calls it, *das Nichtige* – can be found
in Barth's Vol. III, pt. 3, of the *Church Dogmatics*, especially pp.
289–352.

20. Berdjaev, *Destiny of Man*, pp. 28–9, 33.
21. Casaubon, *The Originall Cause of Temporall Evils* (London, 1645),
    the fifth page of the preface (n.p.).
22. Charleton, *The Darknes of Atheism Dispelled by the Light of Nature*
    (London, 1652), pp. 40–1.
23. See for example Merritt Hughes's edition, *John Milton: Complete
    Poems and Major Prose* (New York: Bobbs-Merrill, 1957), pp. 179–80
    and notes to *Paradise Lost;* he cites, among others, Hesiod, Empe-
    docles, Plato, Aristotle, Ovid, and Christian redactors thereof, such
    as Boccaccio, DuBartas, and Spenser. The latter is particularly
    interesting as regards Chaos; see *Faerie Queene*, 3.6.36–8. On Mil-
    ton's Chaos generally, see two very learned articles: one by A. S. P.
    Woodhouse, "Notes on Milton's Views on the Creation: The Initial
    Phases," *Philological Quarterly*, 28 (1949), 211–36; the other by
    A. B. Chambers, Jr., "Chaos in *Paradise Lost*," *Journal of the His-
    tory of Ideas*, 24 (1963), 55–84. On Chaos primarily as it concerns
    the theme of regeneration, see Michael Lieb, *The Dialectics
    of Creation* (Amherst: Univ. of Massachusetts Press, 1970),
    16–34.
24. Hobbes, *Questions*, p. 47.
25. T. Goodwin, *Of the Creatures, and the Condition of Their State by
    Creation* (1682), p. 112, in T. Goodwin, *The Works*, Vol. II (London,
    1683).
26. Barth, *Church Dogmatics*, vol. III, pt. 3, p. 293; Berdjaev, *Destiny of
    Man*, p. 24.
27. Milton, *Christian Doctrine*, ed. Maurice Kelley, trans. John Carey,
    p. 146 (cited hereafter as *CD*), in *Complete Prose Works*, Vol. VI.
    Milton reiterates the point on p. 148 and in *PL*, 10.799–801, quoted
    earlier.
28. Hammond, *A Pacifick Discourse of Gods Grace and Decrees* (London,
    1660), rpt. in Hammond, *The Works* (London, 1674), I, 584.
29. Spenser, *Faerie Queene*, 3.2.36, in *Spenser: Poetical Works*, ed. E.

DeSelincourt and J. C. Smith (1912; rpt. London: Oxford Univ. Press, 1969). Text references are to this edition.

30. Rutherford, *Disputatio Scholastica de Divinia Providentia . . . adversus Jesuitas, Arminianos, Socinianos . . .* (Edinburgh, 1650), p. 538: "Non est quaestio, an Deus causa sit, quod idem simul posset esse et non esse, vel quod contradictoria sint simul vera, Deus enim talia efficere non potest."

31. Ibid., p. 539: "Neque res ad extra aut eorum etiam essentiae possibiles sunt origo, causae, et fontes Omnipotentiae Divinae, quasi vero rivuli essent causae fontis."

32. *CD*, p. 159. I shall discuss this matter in greater detail in Chapter 5, in the section entitled "Divine freedom and divine justice."

33. Sterry, *The Freedom of the Will* (1675), quoted in Richard Baxter, *Catholick Theologie* (London, 1675), p. 110.

34. T. Goodwin, *Of the Creatures*, pp. 32, 112, 25.

35. Harris, *A Brief Discourse of Mans Estate in the First and Second Adam* (London, 1653), pp. 9, 14.

36. See Sidney's 1587 translation of Phillip DuPlessis-Mornay's *The Trewnesse of the Christian Religion*: "S. *Austine* sayth, that the *Latins* terme an evill man *Nequam*, and an evillnesse *Nequitiam*, that is to say, *Naughtie* and *Naughtinesse*" (in *The Prose Works of Sir Philip Sidney*, ed. Albert Feuillerat [1912; rpt. Cambridge: Cambridge Univ. Press, 1962], III, 231).

37. *CD*, pp. 305–6. See George Newton Conklin, *Biblical Criticism and Heresy in Milton* (New York: King's Crown Press, 1949), p. 67; and Kelley's introduction to Milton's doctrine of creation, *CD*, pp. 87–90.

38. On parallels between Milton's version of *creatio ex deo* and that of Origen, see Harry F. Robins, *If This Be Heresy* (Urbana: Univ. of Illinois Press, 1963), pp. 75 ff.

39. See my discussion of Augustine in Chapter 1, in the section entitled "The problem of evil."

40. Milton, "Nativity Ode," line 14.

41. *CD*, pp. 145–6. Kelley's footnotes to these passages are helpful in illustrating uses of the term "Actus Purus."

42. Rutherford, *Disputatio Scholastica,* p. 557: All things, including "vera, bona, pulchra . . . [sunt] à Deo volita, . . . per liberam creationem, . . . [non] per coaeternam et naturalem emanationem."

43. Ibid.: "Possibile non est aliquid reale."

44. *CD*, pp. 130–1, which occur early in bk. 1, chap. 2, "Of God." On the term "fate," cf. Augustine, *The City of God*, ed. Vernon J.

Bourke, trans. G. G. Walsh et al. (New York: Image Books, 1958), 5.8.

45. I by no means pretend to have exhausted the topic. On the debate over the meaning of *PL,* 7.168–73, see *Milton: Man and Thinker* (New York: Dial Press, 1925), pp. 123–5, for Denis Saurat's "retraction theory"; and see Maurice Kelley's attempt to refute Saurat's theory in *This Great Argument,* pp. 209–11. However, if God is material; if all that is, originated from him; and if, at a particular time, absolutely all there was, was God and matter external to him, then the question whether God retired himself from that matter or that matter came from him seems to me to be purely relative.

46. In Pemble, *Works* (Oxford, 1659). Text references to the *Treatise* are to this edition. The *Treatise* also appeared in other editions of the *Works* in 1627, 1629, and 1635, and separately in Latin editions in 1631 and 1669. It was furthermore extensively relied on – in fact downright plagiarized – by Edward Leigh in his *Treatise of Divinity* (London, 1646), chap. 2, "The Execution of Gods Decree."

47. Patrides, *Milton and the Christian Tradition* (Oxford: Oxford University Press, Clarendon Press, 1966), p. 29.

48. Ibid., pp. 30–1. In the second parenthesis, Patrides is quoting Samuel Gott, *The Divine History* (1670).

49. Pemble contends that "no probable reason can be given for creating this confused *Chaos,* out of which afterward all things should come forth distinct: . . . it was easie for God, and certainly much more glorious, first to create the kinds of all things distinct and perfect, [than] afterward to frame them of Matter created beforehand" (*Treatise,* p. 267). See the various options discussed by Augustine, *Confessions,* bk. 12.

50. Patrides, *Milton and the Christian Tradition,* p. 31.

51. Of course heaven and hell have already been created; but we can simply assume that *their* second and third stages occurred before the second and third stages of the earth's creation.

52. In the Vulgate, Gen. 1:2 begins, "Terra autem erat inania et vacua, et tenebrae erant super faciem abyssi."

53. This is a distinction that Woodhouse ("Milton's Views," p. 224) and Chambers ("Chaos in *Paradise Lost,*" pp. 79–80), for example, fail to make. In Chambers's case, the failure to distinguish "the formless mass" Uriel speaks of in 3.708 – which in fact is "the deep" of Gen. 1:2 (cf. *PL,* 7.233) – from Chaos proper leads him to ascribe inconsistency to Milton himself.

54. Of course, the previous creation of hell and heaven, as noted in

2.977–8, implies that other territory has been won from Chaos; hence the latter is "bounded," but not in the sense of being finite or circumscribed.

55. Milton's originality in this regard is attested to by Chambers, "Chaos in *Paradise Lost*," p. 83, and by Robert M. Adams, "A Little Look into Chaos," in *Illustrious Evidence*, ed. Earl Miner (Berkeley and Los Angeles: Univ. of California Press, 1975), pp. 75–6.

56. Woodhouse, referring as he does to "Milton's hesitant and embarrassed treatment of the problem of evil at its metaphysical level" ("Milton's Views," p. 229), seems to imply that in *Paradise Lost* Chaos is theodically dysfunctional. I am arguing just the opposite.

57. Aristotle, *Metaphysics*, trans. John Warrington (London: J. M. Dent, 1961), bk. 9 (Θ), chap. 8 (p. 239).

58. This is a claim that will be discussed at greater length in Chapter 4.

59. Curry, *Milton's Ontology, Cosmogony, and Physics* (Lexington: Univ. of Kentucky Press, 1957), p. 80. Cf. Milton's *Artis Logicae*, in *The Works of John Milton*, ed. Frank Allen Patterson et al. (New York: Columbia Univ. Press, 1931–8), XI, 51, 53, 166 (cited hereafter as CM). See also Peter F. Fisher, "Milton's Theodicy," *Journal of the History of Ideas*, 17 (1956), 41 ff.

60. Daniells, *Milton, Mannerism and Baroque* (Toronto: Univ. of Toronto Press, 1963), p. 92.

61. See the abundance of navigational imagery in the account of Satan's journey, *PL*, 1.1010–44.

62. See Evans's account of how Sin and Death materialize en route to Eden (in Milton, *Paradise Lost: Books IX–X*, ed. J. Martin Evans [Cambridge: Cambridge Univ. Press, 1973], p. 41). See also n. 75 to Chapter 6 of this book.

63. See, for example, Hunter, "Milton's Arianism Reconsidered," in Hunter, Patrides, and Adamson, *Bright Essence*, pp. 29–51.

64. Berdjaev, *The Destiny of Man*, p. 32.

65. Ibid., p. 33.

66. *PL*, 12.469–73. This passage will be one of the focuses of attention in Chapter 7.

67. On these parallel journeys, see William H. Boyd, "The Secrets of Chaos," *Milton Quarterly*, 10, No. 3 (1976), 83–7.

Chapter 3. Assertion and justification

1. Coleridge, "Milton," in *The Complete Works*, IV, 303.
2. Johnson, *Lives of the English Poets*, ed. George B. Hill (Oxford: Oxford Univ. Press, Clarendon Press, 1905), I, 154.
3. *CD*, pp. 74–86. On Milton and Arminianism, see Kelley, *This Great Argument*, pp. 14–20; James Holly Hanford, *Milton Handbook*, 3rd ed. (New York: Crofts, 1939), pp. 228–31; and two articles by William B. Hunter, "The Theological Context of Milton's *Christian Doctrine*," in *Achievements of the Left Hand*, ed. Michael Lieb and John T. Shawcross (Amherst: Univ. of Massachusetts Press, 1974), pp. 269–87, and "John Milton: Autobiographer," *Milton Quarterly*, 8, No. 4 (1974), 100–4. See also Balachandra Rajan's discussion, in *The Prison and the Pinnacle* (London: Routledge and Kegan Paul, 1973), pp. 88–91; and that of John Spencer Hill, in *John Milton, Poet, Priest and Prophet* (London: Macmillan, 1979), pp. 7–13.
4. See C. Hill, *Milton and the English Revolution*, pp. 271 ff. The two branches of Arminianism were described in the following way by the Presbyterian Robert Baillie, in his *Antidote against Arminianisme* (London, 1641), pp. 18–20:

> the Arminian spirit in *Holland* leads men to hell another way then here in Britaine; . . . a *Netherlandish Arminian* will scorn the superstitions, the Idolatries, the Tyrannies of the *Romish* Church, but is much inclined after *Vorstius* and *Socinus* . . . : On the contrary, a *British Arminian* . . . will abhor the Extravagancies of *Vorstius* and *Socinus,* yet their heart is hot and inflamed after the abominations of *Rome.*

5. Milton, *An Apology against a Pamphlet,* in CM, III, 330.
6. Milton, *Of True Religion,* in CM, VI, 169.
7. McDill, "Milton and the Pattern of Calvinism," Diss. Vanderbilt 1938, p. 368.
8. Empson, *Milton's God* (London: Chatto and Windus, 1961), p. 190. The genealogy of this view is traced by Evans, *PLGT,* pp. 187–90.
9. Greene, *The Descent from Heaven* (New Haven: Yale Univ. Press, 1963), p. 407. He quotes *PL*, 11.90–3.
10. Patrides, *Milton and the Christian Tradition*, pp. 194–5, 201–2, 211.
11. Peter, *A Critique of "Paradise Lost"* (New York: Columbia Univ. Press, 1960), pp. 126–7.
12. Augustine, *Confessions,* 7.16.
13. Augustine, *City of God,* 14.27.
14. Ibid.
15. The story is told, for example, by Xenophon, in *Memorabilia,*

2.2.21 ff.; and by Cicero, in *De Officiis,* 1.32(118); 3.5(25). See Hallett Smith, *Elizabethan Poetry* (Cambridge, Mass.: Harvard Univ. Press, 1952), pp. 293 ff. and chap. 6 ("Heroic Poetry") passim; and Erwin Panofsky, *Hercules am Scheidewege* (Leipzig and Berlin: Teubner, 1930), esp. pp. 42 ff.

16. See Theodor E. Mommsen, "Petrarch and the Story of the Choice of Hercules," *Journal of the Warburg and Courtauld Institutes,* 16 (1953), 183 ff.

17. For discussion of Milton's acquaintance with Lactantius, see Chapter 6.

18. Lactantius, *Divine Institutes,* 6.3, in Roberts and Donaldson, *The Ante-Nicene Fathers,* VII, 164–5. It is clear from the examples shown by Panofsky that Renaissance depictions of the choice of Hercules tried to accommodate the kind of eternal perspective Lactantius insists on: Vice's way leads downward, and in some cases one can see the flames at the end of the road. See Panofsky, figs. 52, 57, 61, 63, 64.

19. Augustine, *A Treatise against Two Letters of the Pelagians,* 1.5 (II), Schaff, in *Nicene and Post-Nicene Fathers,* Vol. V.

20. Augustine, *On Grace and Free Will,* chap. 43 (XXI), in Schaff, *Nicene and Post-Nicene Fathers,* Vol. V.

21. Even if one grants that it is *post*lapsarian freedom that Augustine depreciates, theodical problems remain.

22. N. P. Williams, *The Ideas of the Fall and of Original Sin* (London: Longmans, 1927), pp. 369–70.

23. Erasmus, *The Free Will,* trans. Ernst F. Winter, in *Erasmus–Luther: Discourse on Free Will* (New York: Frederick Ungar, 1961), p. 84. Text references are to this edition.

24. Luther, *The Bondage of the Will,* trans. Ernst F. Winter, in *Erasmus–Luther: Discourse on Free Will,* p. 132. Text references are to this edition.

25. Calvin, *Institutes,* 3.21.5. Text references (by book, chapter, and section numbers) are to the Beveridge translation.

26. I quote the 1656 edition of Hoard, *Gods Love to Man-kinde, Manifested, By Dis-proving That Doctrine Which Telleth Us of an Absolute Decree for Their Damnation* (London), p. 49.

27. Walker, *The Decline of Hell* (Chicago: Univ. of Chicago Press, 1964), p. 55.

28. See Calvin, *Institutes,* 3.23.2, and *Concerning the Eternal Predestination of God,* trans. J. K. S. Reid (London: James Clarke, 1961), p. 179: "I detest the doctrine of the Sorbonne . . . that invents for God an absolute power. For it is easier to dissever the light of the sun

from its heat . . . than to separate God's power from His righteousness . . . The faithful . . . understand His power . . . to be tempered with righteousness and equity." Contrast with this the much more extreme, voluntarist position of William Twisse, prolocutor of the Westminster Assembly, who declares "the Will of God" to be "the very Essence of God" (in *The Riches of Gods Love . . . Consistent with His Absolute . . . Reprobation* [Oxford, 1653], p. 6).

29. I follow the account of Carl Bangs, *Arminius: A Study in the Dutch Reformation* (Nashville: Abingdon Press, 1971), pp. 138 ff. and passim. See also *The Writings of James Arminius,* trans. James Nichols and W. R. Bagnall (1853; rpt. Grand Rapids: Baker Book House, 1956), I, 9–15.

30. The latter conclusion is favored by Bangs, *Arminius,* p. 141.

31. See Louis Praamsma, "The Background of the Arminian Controversy (1586–1618)," in *Crisis in the Reformed Churches,* ed. Peter Y. DeJong (Grand Rapids: Reformed Fellowship, 1968), pp. 22–38.

32. Arminius, *Writings,* II, 472.

33. Ibid., p. 498.

34. Ibid., I, 366.

35. All five articles are in *The Creeds of Christendom,* ed. Philip Schaff (London: Hodder and Stoughton, 1877), III, 545–9.

36. For the suggestion that it was Beza and Calvin's *soi-disant* followers, rather than Calvin himself, who were responsible for this doctrine, see Brian G. Armstrong, *Calvinism and the Amyraut Heresy* (Madison: Univ. of Wisconsin Press, 1969), pp. 38–42. See also R. T. Kendall, *Calvin and English Calvinism to 1649* (Oxford: Oxford Univ. Press, 1979), pp. 145–6, 149: "What Arminius is refuting . . . is really Bezan theology"; "Arminius and Calvin have in common the belief that Christ died for all."

37. Fred H. Klooster, "The Doctrinal Deliverances of Dort," in DeJong, *Crisis,* pp. 52–3.

38. *The Ivdgement of the Synode Holden at Dort, Concerning the Fiue Articles* (London, 1619), p. 37. Again, on this point Calvin himself would seem to be less extreme than his followers. His teaching on total depravity was clearly motivated by a desire to show that not only some but "all the parts of the soul" (including intellect and will) were affected by the Fall. Accordingly, man's depravity is total in the sense of being comprehensive, though not necessarily in the sense of being utter. See the *Institutes,* 2.2.8–10.

39. For the Remonstrants' (I think convincing) defense of themselves against the charge of Pelagianism, see "Articulus Tertius et Quartus de Gratia Dei in Conversione Hominis," in *Acta et Scripta Syn-*

odalia Dordracena Ministrorum Remonstrantium in Foederato Belgio (Herder-wiici, 1620), pp. 22–4.

40. The distinction between Arminian and Pelagian is something that Christopher Hill, for one, utterly fails to take account of.

41. As Kelley points out, in discussing the perseverance of the saints and related issues, Milton explicitly cites the Remonstrants (*CD*, p. 512).

42. See n. 4 to this chapter.

43. Nicholas R. N. Tyacke, "Puritanism, Arminianism and Counter-Revolution," in *The Origins of the English Civil War*, ed. Conrad Russell (London: Macmillan, 1973), p. 130. Cf. A. W. Harrison, *Arminianism* (London: Duckworth, 1937), p. 128.

44. Prynne, *The Chvrch of Englands Old Antithesis to New Arminianisme* (London, 1629; the 1630 edition also bore the title *Anti-Arminianisme*), the first page of "The Epistle Dedicatory."

45. In Milton, *Complete Prose Works*, II, 293.

46. Ibid., II, 519–20.

47. See the notes in Carey and Fowler's edition of the poems, pp. 296–7.

48. See n. 28 to this chapter. For Milton's scurrilous comments on the Westminster Assembly, see his *History of Britain* (1670), in CM, X, 321 ff.

49. I quote John Stafford's translation, *A Dissertation on Divine Justice* (London, 1792), pp. 23, 26.

50. See Amyraldus, *Doctrinae Ioannis Calvini de Absoluto Reprobationis Decreto Defensio adversus Scriptorum Anonymum* [*i.e.*, Hoard] (Salmurii, 1641); and his *De Iure Dei in Creaturas Dissertatio*, in *Dissertationes Theologicae Quatuor* (Salmurii, 1645). On this dispute generally, see Armstrong, *Calvinism and the Amyraut Heresy*, passim.

51. DuMoulin, *Petri Molinaei de Amyraldi adversus Fridericum Spanhemium Libro Iudicum. Seu Pro Dei Misericordia, et Sapientia, et Justitia Apologia* (Rotterdam, 1649).

52. See Jacobus Arminius and Stephanus Curcellaeus, *Examen Thesium F. Gomare de Praedestinat. cum St. Curcellaei Vindiciis, Quibus Suam et Arminii Sententiam de Jure Dei Increaturas, Adversus Mosis Amyraldi Criminationes, Defendit* (Amsterdam, 1645). The only copy of this work that I know of is in the Bibliothèque nationale in Paris, catalogued under "Arminius." It is republished in Curcellaeus's *Opera Theologica* (Amsterdam, 1675).

53. See the letters exchanged between them in 1640 regarding a tract entitled *De absoluto reprobationis decreto*, in Grotius's *Operum Theologicorum* (Amsterdam, 1679), Vol. II, pt. 2, p. 1239.

54. Pierce, *The New Discoverer Discover'd* (London, 1659), p. 97.

55. More, *Calvinus* (Geneva, 1653). The work was intended as a refutation of Grotius.

56. In Milton, *Complete Prose Works, IV*, 752.

57. Westminster Confession, 7.4, 11.4, in Schaff, *Creeds of Christendom,* Vol. III.

58. Westminster Confession, 5.4. Cf. Calvin, *Institutes,* 3.23.8: "Man therefore falls, divine providence so ordering, but he falls by his own fault."

59. Arthur Sewell explores this hypothesis in *A Study in Milton's Christian Doctrine* (1939; rpt. Hamden, Conn.: Archon Books, 1967), p. 62.

60. C. Hill, *The World Turned Upside Down* (London: Temple Smith, 1972), pp. 326, 325.

61. Kelley, "The Theological Dogma of *Paradise Lost, III,* 173–202," *PMLA,* 52 (1937), 75–9.

62. Ibid., p. 78.

63. A similar hypothesis is suggested by Eila Siren Perlmutter, "Milton's Three Degrees of Grace," Diss. State University of New York, Albany, 1972. Cf. Baxter, *God's Goodness, Vindicated,* in Baxter, *The Practical Works* (London, 1707), II, 929.

64. Peter, *Critique,* p. 11.

65. Of course, as Evans rightly points out, prelapsarian virtue does, in the cultural area, have its commissive aspect, in that Adam and Eve must "dress the garden and . . . keep it." See his discussion in *PLGT,* pp. 246 ff.

66. *PL,* 11.22–30. Cf. Calvin's indirect reference (based on Matt. 15:13) to the elect as those whom God has "been pleased to plant as sacred trees in his garden" (*Institutes,* 3.23.1). See also Thomas Savile, *Adams Garden: A Meditation of Thankfulnesse and Praises vnto the Lord, for the Returne and Restore of Adam and His Posteritie, Planted as Flowers in a Garden* (London, 1611).

67. For Leon Howard's analysis of what he says is Milton's "habitual dichotomization of the efficient cause," see " 'The Invention' of Milton's 'Great Argument': A Study of the Logic of 'God's Ways to Men,' " *Huntington Library Quarterly,* 9 (1945), 149–73.

68. Harris, *A Treatise of the New Covenant* (London, 1653), pp. 62, 60.

69. On resisting God, see also *CD,* p. 295. Pierce puts the Arminian view as follows: "*Grace makes able to choose good,* but not *unable to refuse it*" (*A Correct Copy of Some Notes concerning Gods Decrees* [London, 1657], p. 57). In this general connection, note the "Pelagian" view of Satan and Beelzebub, who glory "to have scaped the

Stygian flood / As gods, . . . by their own recovered strength"
(1.239–40).

70. For a different, though not necessarily incompatible, reading of *PL*,
11.3, 19, see Fish, *Surprised by Sin*, pp. 19–20.

71. Patrides, *Milton and the Christian Tradition*, p. 204.

72. Rajan (*The Prison and the Pinnacle*, pp. 88–91) acutely demonstrates
how, in this matter of grace, the poetic dramatization of *Paradise
Lost* takes Milton beyond the prose dogma of *Christian Doctrine*.
However, Rajan's claim that "a strong sense of the importance of
man's fallen nature, before grace makes its entry, must be combined with an even stronger, affirmative sense of man's responsibility in remaking himself" (p. 89) simply goes too far. Milton is
not, by a literary sleight-of-hand, reconciling irreconcilables, but
rather giving literary shape and substance to a subtle but not
inconsistent relationship between God's agency and man's. And
in this relationship man is certainly responsible; but he does not
remake himself.

A view very similar to the one I am suggesting Milton presents,
including reference to prevenient grace and use of the seed metaphor (*PL*, 11.3, 26 ff.), was expressed by Henry Hammond: Obedience to the call of grace

> may reasonably be imputed to the humble, malleable, melting
> temper . . . owing to the preventing Graces of God, and not to the
> naturall probity, or free will of man . . . [This opinion] attributes
> nothing to free will, considered by it self, but the power of resist-
> ing . . . , yielding the glory of all the work of conversion . . . to his
> sole Grace, by which the will is first set free, then fitted and culti-
> vated, and then the seed of eternal life successfully sowed in it.
> [*Pacifick Discourse* (1660 ed.), pp. 58–9]

Although, as we shall see in Chapter 6, the Calvinists accused
the Arminians of implying that grace thus wholly cancels out the
effects of the Fall, the charge is largely unjustified, because the category of prevenient grace applies to an individual's acceptance or
rejection of salvation, and not necessarily to other areas of choice
or to the matter of so-called structural evil.

73. See *PL*, 12.561 ff.

Chapter 4. Milton and the Free Will Defense

1. Tayler, *The Faith of the Chvrch of England concerning Gods Work on
Mans Will* (London, 1641), "To the Reader," n.p.

2. Rutherford, *Disputatio Scholastica,* p. 587: "Illi [*Jesuitae* et *Arminiani*] pro creaturarum, Nos pro *Creatoris* dominio contendimus."

3. Owen, *A Display of Arminianisme* (London, 1643), pp. 2, 7.

4. Mackie, "Evil and Omnipotence," in *God and Evil,* ed. Nelson Pike (Englewood Cliffs, N.J.: Prentice-Hall, 1964), pp. 55–7.

5. Plantinga, *The Nature of Necessity* (Oxford: Oxford Univ. Press, Clarendon Press, 1974), pp. 170–1, 184.

6. Hoard, *Gods Love to Man-kinde* (1656 ed.), p. 30.

7. Rutherford, *Disputatio Scholastica,* p. 541: "Inde est quod *Philosophi, Theologi* unanimiter fateantur omne ens et non ens esse objectum Omnipotentiae, excepto eo quod involvit contradictionem, quod est simpliciter impossibile, verius incompossibile." For other discussions of possibility, impossibility, and actuality as they concern divine power, see Charleton, *The Darknes of Atheism,* pp. 242–3; and Hammond, *Pacifick Discourse,* in *Works,* pp. 585, 590–2.

8. Owen, *Dissertation on Divine Justice,* p. 138.

9. I paraphrase Mackie, "Evil and Omnipotence," p. 47.

10. Plantinga, *God, Freedom and Evil,* p. 20.

11. For further modern discussion of what might be called "quantitative theodicy," see Keith E. Yandell, "The Greater Good Defense," *Sophia,* 13, No. 3 (1974), 1–16.

12. Burgess, *Vindiciae Legis* (London, 1646), p. 105.

13. Baxter, *Gods Goodness, Vindicated,* in *Practical Works,* II, 926.

14. Baxter, *Catholick Theologie,* pp. 114–15.

15. Harris, *A Brief Discourse,* pp. 2, 4. The relationship between Christ and *un*fallen as well as fallen man is something I shall discuss in Chapter 7.

16. Pierce, *Gods Decrees,* p. 57.

17. The objections are treated in Tertullian, *Adversus Marcionem,* trans. Ernest Evans (Oxford: Oxford Univ. Press, Clarendon Press, 1972), 2.5 and 2.6, respectively. Text references (by book and chapter numbers) are to this edition.

18. Augustine, *De Libero Arbitrio,* 2.1(3), in Augustine, *The Teacher, The Free Choice of the Will, Grace and Free Will,* trans. Robert P. Russell (Washington, D.C.: Catholic Univ. of America Press, 1968). Text references are to this edition.

19. Davies, *Nosce Teipsum,* in *Silver Poets of the Sixteenth Century,* ed. Gerald Bullett (1947; rpt. London: Dent, 1975), pp. 369, 370.

20. See Raphael's speech in *PL,* 5.469–90.

21. See *CD,* bk. 1, chap. 13.

22. Pope, *An Essay on Man*, ed. Maynard Mack (London: Methuen, 1950), 1.48; italics added.
23. In Milton, *Complete Prose Works*, II, 293–4.
24. Ibid.
25. Ibid., p. 527.
26. The question whether the meaningfulness of God's love presupposes the same sort of freedom as does man's love is one I shall touch on in Chapter 5, in the section entitled "Divine freedom and divine justice."
27. See the *First Defence*, in CM, VII, 151.
28. Plantinga, *The Nature of Necessity*, p. 171.
29. The question is not merely rhetorical. See the first section of Chapter 5.
30. Lovejoy, *The Great Chain of Being* (Cambridge, Mass.: Harvard Univ. Press, 1936), p. 212. Lovejoy proffers no grounds for his opinion.
31. See n. 14 to Chapter 1.
32. Pierce, *Gods Decrees*, p. 65.
33. J. Goodwin, *Redemption Redeemed* (London, 1651), pp. 494–5.
34. Harris, *A Brief Discourse*, p. 5.
35. Baxter, *God's Goodness, Vindicated*, p. 928.
36. Cf. Northrop Frye's comments on this sort of situation as it occurs in *Paradise Lost* (*The Anatomy of Criticism* [Princeton: Princeton Univ. Press, 1957], p. 211).
37. Homes, *The Resurrection Revealed* (1653; new ed., London, 1661), p. 103.
38. Hick, *EGL*, p. 315. Milton's presentation of the prelapsarian conditions for this creative freedom will be discussed at greater length in Chapter 6. But it is worth noting here that Hick's point would have been accepted as a commonplace in certain circles within traditional Christianity. See T. Goodwin's Sermon 11 on Ephesians:

    The school-men do rightly say that the utmost beatifical vision of God doth captivate, doth swallow up the mind. When we see God to the full, we shall be so in love with him that the heart shall never turn off from him . . . Now you see the angels did fall, and therefore certainly that fulness of the sight of God they had not." [In *The Works* (Edinburgh: James Nichols, 1861–), I, 181]

39. *PL*, 8.276–9. Cf. the very beginnings of Calvin's *Institutes:* "Our wisdom . . . consists almost entirely of two parts: the knowledge of God and of ourselves . . . In the first place, no man can survey himself without forthwith turning his thoughts towards the God

in whom he lives and moves; because it is perfectly obvious, that the endowments which we possess cannot possibly be from ourselves" (1.1.1).

40. We notice too, of course, that prelapsarian choice is more active and less passive than is the postlapsarian exercise of choice discussed in Chapter 3.

41. Davies, *Nosce Teipsum*, p. 370.

42. See the section of this chapter entitled "Free Will Defense: the model and its uses."

43. T. Goodwin, *Of the Creatures*, in *Works* (1683), p. 28.

44. Geisler, *Philosophy of Religion*, p. 366. Cf. the opinion recorded in St. Anselm, *Cur Deus Homo*, in *Saint Anselm: Basic Writings*, 2nd ed. (LaSalle, Ill.: Open Court, 1962), p. 253, that the good angels "deserved [their] present inability to sin from the fact that when they could sin they refused to do so."

45. Hick, *EGL*, pp. 315 ff.

46. This point is ably argued by Anthony Low, who draws the analogy with Samson's claim in *Samson Agonistes* that "Commands are no constraints" (line 1372) ("The Parting in the Garden in *Paradise Lost*," *Philological Quarterly*, 47, No. 1 [1968], p. 34). Among those who fail to make the distinction are Fredson Bowers, "Adam, Eve, and the Fall in *Paradise Lost*," *PMLA*, 84, No. 2 (1969), 271; Elaine B. Safer, " 'Sufficient to Have Stood': Eve's Responsibility in Book IX," *Milton Quarterly*, 6, No. 3 (1972), 12; and Stella P. Revard, "Eve and the Doctrine of Responsibility in *Paradise Lost*," *PMLA*, 88, No. 1 (1973), p. 73.

47. Evans, for example, says that Adam "echoes, and validates, God's argument in III 103 ff." (in Milton, *Paradise Lost: Books IX–X*, p. 105). Cf. Fowler's note to *PL*, 9.1158.

48. In Milton, *Complete Prose Works*, II, 527.

Chapter 5. Theodicy, free will, and determinism

1. Quoted in Baxter, *Catholick Theologie*, p. 108.

2. See, for example, Plantinga's *God, Freedom and Evil*, pp. 31–2, as well as his very technical article entitled "The Incompatibility of Freedom with Determinism," *Philosophical Forum* (Boston), 1970, pp. 141–8; and *The Presumption of Atheism*, by Plantinga's compatibilist opponent Antony Flew (London: Elek/Pemberton, 1976), pp. 81–99. See also Robert Young, *Freedom, Responsibility and God* (London: Macmillan, 1975), pp. 213 ff.; the same author's "Omnipotence and Compatibilism," *Philosophia*, 6, No. 1 (1976), 49–67; and,

for a preliminary Christian critique of the traditional dichotomy, Miriam Sampson and Philip Sampson, "Necessity and Freedom," *Faith and Thought*, 106, Nos. 2/3 (1979), 151–68.

3. Baxter, *Catholick Theologie*, p. 118.

4. See n. 20 to Chapter 3.

5. Whitfield, *A Treatise Tending to Shew That the Just and Holy God, May Have a Hand in the Unjust Actions of Sinfull Men* (London, 1653), p. 39. Pierce, having quoted a similar statement of Whitfield's, indicates that the assertion "God did *absolutely decree* that men should *voluntarily sin* . . . implies a contradiction" (*Self-Condemnation* [London, 1658], p. 127). Cf. Milton's discussion of such "contradicentia," *CD*, p. 174; *CM*, XIV, 100 – part of which will be considered later in this chapter.

6. Pemble, *Treatise*, in *Works*, p. 277.

7. Twisse, *Vindiciae Gratiae* (Amsterdam, 1632), p. 27: "Neque enim tantum dicimus, Deum efficaciter ita rem totam administrasse, ut caderet homo, sed et ut libere caderet."

8. See n. 58 to Chapter 3.

9. For further discussion, see Young, *Freedom*, pp. 39–55, 116–68.

10. Owen, *Display of Arminianisme*, pp. 127, 126. Cf. Arminius, *Writings*, II, 487.

11. Charleton, *The Darknes of Atheism*, pp. 263, 271. I will not explore here the possible similarities between the balance model and that presented by the Choice of Hercules, discussed in Chapter 3, in the section entitled "Grace and free will: Augustinian roots."

12. In a sermon entitled *Gods Providence* (London, 1642), which was preached before the House of Commons on December 28, 1642, Edward Corbett affirms that "the hearts and wills of Man . . . do whatsoever liketh them, But yet they can do no more and in no other manner than God hath Decreed, He guideth them to his own Ends yet guideth according to that Nature he hath put into them" (p. 11).

13. Hoard, *Gods Love to Man-kinde* (1656 ed.), p. 32.

14. Hobbes, *Questions*, pp. 1–2. The work presents both Hobbes's and Bramhall's alternating statements and replies.

15. For a fuller account of this whole debate than I can attempt here, see Samuel I. Mintz, *The Hunting of Leviathan* (Cambridge: Cambridge Univ. Press, 1962), pp. 119, 110–23 passim.

16. Bramhall, in Hobbes, *Questions*, pp. 84–5. Cf. Hoard, *Gods Love to Man-kinde* (1656 ed.), p. 55, where he gives the Latin version of this: "Causa causae est causa causati"; and Homes, *Resurrection*

Revealed, pp. 108, 110, where he refers to this maxim as "a main Principle of Truth."

17. Flew, *The Presumption of Atheism,* p. 95.

18. Mintz, *The Hunting of Leviathan,* p. 118.

19. Nicolson, "Milton and Hobbes," *Studies in Philology,* 23, No. 4 (1926), 411, 414.

20. *CD,* p. 155. "Nihil itaque Deus decrevisse absolute consendus est, quod in potestate libere agentium reliquit" (CM, XIV, 64). Where appropriate, I shall cite the original Latin from CM in the text.

21. Fire burning was the commonplace example of natural necessity. Cf. Bramhall, in Hobbes, *Questions,* p. 222; Pemble, *Treatise,* pp. 271, 274; Whitfield, *Treatise,* p. 41; Homes, *Resurrection Revealed,* p. 118. On *necessitas naturae,* see also Milton, *Artis Logicae,* in CM, XI, 40; cf. Arminius, *Writings,* II, 487: "Internal necessity is as repugnant to liberty as external necessity."

22. See, for example, Thomas Pierce, *The Divine Purity Defended* (London, 1657), p. 78.

23. CM, XI, 39; Milton refers to this as a "common saying." See n. 16 to this chapter.

24. *PL,* 10.44–7. Cf. Henry Hammond, who uses the same model in his discussion of divine prescience: "If you say, God sees before, what in after time shall hang in the balance of humane indetermination, i.e. what [a man] . . . is free to do, or not to do, but hath not yet done, I demand, why may he not also foresee which end of the balance doth at length overpoise?" (*Works,* p. 585).

25. See Milton's opponent Alexander More, *Victoria Gratiae* (Medioburgi, 1652), I, xxxvii–xxxix, the last of these sections being headed "Non pugnat libertas cum necessitate." Cf. Rutherford, *Disputatio Scholastica,* p. 588.

26. Pierce, *The Divine Philanthropie Defended* (London, 1657), p. 22 (2nd ser.).

27. *PL,* 5.549; italics added. Raphael's earlier claim that God requires "Our voluntary service . . . / Not our necessitated" (5.529–30) likewise denies the main thesis of compatibilism.

28. Charles R. Sumner's translation of *De Doctrina Christiana* appears, of course, in CM, Vols. XIV–XVII, in parallel with Milton's original Latin.

29. Milton does mention natural causes a few pages earlier, but there his implication is that man is *not* "peccatorum suorum . . . causa naturalis" (CM, XIV, 76).

30. Burden, *The Logical Epic* (London: Routledge and Kegan Paul, 1967), p. 1.

31. What I am arguing is that in *this* circumstance, Adam and Eve ought to have stayed together. This claim does not imply, as Eve insinuates, that she should *never* have parted from Adam's side but "grown there . . . a lifeless rib" (9.1153–4). Eve's need of Adam, given the apprehended danger (9.1157), no more entails her "lifelessness" than the necessity of grace for salvation entails postlapsarian man's "total depravity" in the orthodox Calvinist sense. For a rather different view of the scene, see Revard, "Eve and the Doctrine of Responsibility," pp. 69–78.

32. Boruch A. Brody, "Logical Terms, Glossary of," in *Encyclopedia of Philosophy*, ed. Paul Edwards (New York: Macmillan, 1967). Cf. Pierce, *Divine Philanthropie*, p. 63: "I must *Teach* to distinguish betwixt the *Cause* [*proper quam rest est*] *for which a thing is*, and the *necessary condition* [*sine qua non est*] *without which it is not*."

33. Augustine, *De Correptione et Gratia*, chap. 34, in Schaff, *Nicene and Post-Nicene Fathers*, V, 485.

34. I shall argue in greater detail in the next chapter that Eve's supposed narcissism, for example, is a necessary but not a sufficient cause of the Fall.

35. Clark, "The Mechanics of Creation," *English Literary Renaissance*, 7, No. 2 (1977), 208.

36. Savage, "Freedom and Necessity," *ELH*, 44, No. 2 (1977), 288, 290.

37. Ibid., p. 297. Savage bases himself on *PL*, 12.83–4: "Since thy original lapse, true liberty / Is lost, which always with right reason dwells." Without pretending to unperplex the matter entirely, I would suggest (1) that liberty might not be the same thing as free will, and (2) that the notion of a free man's, as it were, locking himself in prison, and hence as a result of a free act becoming unfree, does not present the sort of logical problems Savage thinks it does. On "that slavish subjection to sin," see *CD*, p. 395.

38. *CD*, p. 159. "In Deo immutabilis quaedam et interna necessitas bene agendi, aliunde non pendens, cum libertate summa potest consistere" (CM, XIV, 72).

39. Lactantius, *A Treatise on the Anger of God*, chap. 5, in Roberts and Donaldson, *Ante-Nicene Fathers*, VII, 261–2.

40. Homes, *Resurrection Revealed*, p. 114.

41. Arminius, *Writings*, II, 480.

42. Ibid., I, 344–5.

43. Owen, *Dissertation on Divine Justice*, pp. 25–7. A similar charge is laid against Twisse on pp. 200–1. Owen's argument in many ways parallels that of St. Anselm in *Cur Deus Homo*, 1.12: "If sin be passed by unpunished" then it follows "that with God there will

be no difference between the guilty and the not guilty; and this is unbecoming to God" (in *Basic Writings*, p. 203).

44. *PL*, 3.203–12; italics added. Cf. 12.395–401, ending "So only can high justice rest apaid"; and *CD*, p. 443.

45. Charleton, *The Darknes of Atheism*, p. 241.

46. Patrides, *Milton and the Christian Tradition*, p. 196.

47. *CD*, p. 166. Cf. Pierce, *Gods Decrees*, p. 21: "If death is that *monster*, of which sin is the *Dam*, that *brings it forth*, how *foul* a thing must be the *Sire*? and can there be any greater *blasphemy*, than to bring God's *Providence* unto the *pedigree* of *Death*?" See also, of course, *PL*, 2.745 ff.

48. See Hammond's account and critique, *Works*, pp. 583 ff. A modern version of the Socinian position is presented by John R. Lucas in *Freedom and Grace* (London: SPCK, 1976), pp. 35 ff.

49. See, for example, Owen, *Display of Arminianisme*, p. 14, where he claims, on the basis of this close identification of foreknowledge with the decrees, that the Arminians, in denying the absolute decrees, overthrow foreknowledge "by consequence."

50. Hammond, *Pacifick Discourse* (1660 ed.), para. 8 of the preface (n. p.).

51. Augustine, *City of God*, 5.10; Hammond, *Works*, p. 587, where Augustine is quoted in the original Latin.

52. Charleton, *The Darknes of Atheism*, pp. 247, 254.

53. *CD*, pp. 164–5. In the original, the order is actually reversed, but the point is the same: "Tenendum est, Deum praescire quidem futura omnia, non autem omnia absolute decrivisse, ne peccata omnia Deo imputentur . . ." (CM, XIV, 84). The repetition of *omnia* conveys just the kind of doctrinal balance that is being sought: foreknowledge, yes; absolute decrees, no; theodicy, yes.

54. Pierce, *Gods Decrees*, p. 60. Milton, in *CD*, was not forgetful of the distinction; see p. 165.

55. Pierce, *Self-Condemnation*, p. 128. Cf. p. 133, where the position is typically linked with the need to avoid making God the author of sin.

56. Charleton, *The Darknes of Atheism*, p. 247.

57. Pierce, *Self-Condemnation*, p. 124.

58. Hammond, *Works*, p. 586.

59. I argue this point in greater detail in "Timelessness, Foreknowledge, and Free Will," *Mind*, 86, No. 343 (1977), 430–2.

60. For Plantinga's "possible worlds" discussion of this issue, see *God, Freedom and Evil*, pp. 66–73.

61. Hammond, *Works*, p. 600. Cf. Milton, *Artis Logicae*, in CM, XI, 48–

50: "Ex hypothesi divinae praescientiae certa quidem esse omnia, non necessaria"; and J. Goodwin, *Redemption Redeemed*, p. 27: "Notwithstanding the certainty of the knowledge of God concerning things, . . . yet there is no more, no other necessity of their coming to passe, in respect of such his foreknowledge, then there would, or should, have been, in case no such knowledge were, or had been, in him. For certaine it is, that no knowledge, as such, hath any influence at all upon the object, or the thing known."

62. Origen, *Opera Omnia*, 7 vols., in *Patrologia Graeca*, ed. J.-P. Migne (Paris, 1857–), IV, 1123: "Si enim quos praescivit, hos et praedestinavit conformes esse imaginis Filii sui, nullus autem malus conformis potest imaginis esse Filii Dei, manifestum est quia de bonis tantum dicit: 'Praesciit quos et praedestinavit . . .' "

63. Ibid., p. 1125: "Ad consuetudinem Scripturae redeundum puto, quae vernacula quadam appellatione in hoc sermone, id est in cognoscendo uti solet: velut cum dicit: 'Et cognovit Adam Evam uxorem suam.' "

64. *CD*, p. 182; *CM*, XIV, 120–2. The term Milton uses, "notitia approbationis," already had a long history. Aquinas notes that "God's knowledge as the cause of things has come to be called the 'knowledge of approbation' [*scientia approbationis*]," as distinct from "knowledge of vision [*scientia visionis*]" (*Summa Theologiae*, 60 vols. [London: Blackfriars, 1964–6], IV, 30–3 [1a.14, 8–9]). Bramhall says that Hobbes "confounds that speculative knowledge, which is called the *knowledge of vision*, which does not produce the intellective objects, . . . with that other knowledge of God, which is called the *knowledge of approbation*, . . . that is, knowledge joyned with an act of the Will" (in Hobbes, *Questions*, p. 81). John Goodwin asserts that in many places in Scripture, Rom. 8:29 among them, "πρόγνωσις, or foreknowledge . . . rather imports a Pre-approbation, then a simple Prescience" (*Redemption Redeemed*, p. 28). Cf. *Paradise Regained*, 3.60–2: "This is true glory and renown, when God, / Looking on the earth, with approbation marks / The just man."

65. Origen, *Opera Omnia*, IV, 1126: "Non propterea erit aliquid, quia id scit Deus futurum: sed quia futurum est, scitur a Deo antequam fiat." This passage is quoted by Aquinas in his discussion of foreknowledge in *Summa Theologiae*, IV, 28–9 [1a.14, 8].

66. Pierce, *Self-Condemnation*, p. 48.

67. Boethius, *The Consolation of Philosophy*, trans. Richard Green (Indianapolis: Bobbs-Merrill, 1962), p. 116. Cf. Aquinas, *Summa Theologiae*, IV, 50–1 [1a.14, 13]:

Future contingents cannot be certain to us, because we know them *as* future contingents; they can be certain only to God, whose act of knowledge is in eternity, above time. In the same way a man going along a road does not see those who come behind him; but the man who sees the whole road from a height sees all those who are passing along the road.

68. Evans, in Milton, *Paradise Lost: Books IX–X*, p. 178. Evans's whole review of foreknowledge and free will (pp. 176–8) is useful in the present context.
69. Hammond, *Works*, pp. 600, 602.

Chapter 6. Eden and the "soul-making" theodicy

1. Milton, *Areopagitica*, in *Complete Prose Works*, II, 516. Text references are to this edition.
2. Owen, *Display of Arminianisme*, p. 85. In the course of attacking a Jesuit opponent, Alexander More makes a similar charge: "Adeone sibi blanditur haec aetas, ut hominem, qualis nunc nascitur, eodem quo Adamus fuit loco statuat?" (*Victoria Gratiae*, p. 64).
3. N. P. Williams, *Ideas*, p. 360.
4. Bangs, " 'All the Best Bishoprics and Deaneries,' " *Church History*, 42, No. 1 (1973), 16. Cf. Walker, *The Decline of Hell*, p. 11.
5. Augustine, *City of God*, 14.26.
6. Ibid.; italics added.
7. Plotinus, *Enneads*, 3.2, 11. On the aesthetic theme in Augustine, see Hick, *EGL*, pp. 88–91.
8. Hick, "Evil, the Problem of," in *Encyclopedia of Philosophy*, III, 138. On the distinction between "image" and "likeness," see Irenaeus, *Against Heresies*, 5.6.1, in Roberts and Donaldson, *The Ante-Nicene Fathers*, Vol. 1. Text references are to this edition. See also Hick's comments, *EGL*, pp. 217, 290.
9. *The Letters of John Keats*, ed. M. B. Forman (Oxford: Oxford Univ. Press, 1952), pp. 334–5. Keats makes the point in the course of rejecting the notion that this world is a "vale of tears."
10. William King, for example, an eighteenth-century "Augustinian" theodicist, teaches in effect that God was not free to create man anything but free. For without a free creature such as man, "a monstrous Defect and *Hiatus* would have been left in Nature" (*An Essay on the Origin of Evil*, trans. Edmund Law [London, 1731], p. 229). Cf. Pope, who implies ironically that, given the Chain of Being and the principle of plenitude, "There *must be*, somewhere, such a rank

as Man" (*Essay on Man,* 1.48). See also Augustine, *De Libero Arbitrio,* 3.9 (26).

11. Tatian, *Address to the Greeks,* chap. 7, in Roberts and Donaldson, *Ante-Nicene Fathers,* II, 67.

12. Theophilus, *To Autolycus,* 2.24, 25, quoted in N. P. Williams, *Ideas,* p. 176.

13. Origen, *Contra Celsum,* quoted in Robins, *If This Be Heresy,* p. 128.

14. Origen, *Homily on Numbers,* 14.2, quoted in Benjamin Drewery, *Origen and the Doctrine of Grace* (London: Epworth Press, 1960), p. 94. As we shall see, the soul-making theodicy need not insist on the presence of *actual* evil as a necessary condition for the contrast with good, as Origen seems to do here.

15. Hick, "Evil, the Problem of," p. 139. Cf. Richard Swinburne, *The Existence of God* (Oxford: Oxford Univ. Press, Clarendon Press, 1979), p. 201: "A perfectly good God might well allow the occurrence of biologically useful pain – to encourage free agents to make right choices, without forcing them to do so."

16. Hick, *EGL,* p. 291.

17. Evans, *PLGT,* p. 94. See pp. 85–94 passim.

18. Hick, *EGL,* p. 225.

19. Grant, *The Transformation of Sin* (Amherst: Univ. of Massachusetts Press, 1974), p. 186; see also pp. 170–97 passim.

20. Evans, *PLGT,* p. 78. See, too, Evans's account of the Hebrew textual basis for the Irenaean view, pp. 18 ff.

21. Roberts, *Mysterium et Medulla Bibliorum* (London, 1657), p. 31.

22. Burgess, *Vindiciae Legis,* p. 102. See Faustus Socinus, *De Statu Primi Hominis ante Lapsum Disputatio,* in Socinus, *Opera* (Irenopoli, 1656), II, 257–64.

23. Hick, *EGL,* pp. 285–6.

24. See *PL,* 3.129–32.

25. Browne, *Religio Medici,* 2.4, in *The Prose of Sir Thomas Browne,* ed. Norman Endicott (1967; rpt. New York: Norton, 1972), p. 73. Cf. William of Shoreham's rather extreme application of the principle, discussed by Evans in *PLGT,* pp. 186–7.

26. Seneca, *Moral Essays,* trans. John W. Basore (London: Heinemann, 1928), pp. 33, 9. Interestingly, the essay here quoted was published by itself in 1648: *Seneca's Answer to Lucilius His Quaere. Why Good Men Suffer Misfortune Seeing There Is a Divine Providence?* trans. Edward Sherburne (London). John Ward, in *The Good Will of Him That Dwelt in the Bush* (London, 1645), a sermon preached before the House of Lords on July 22, 1645, cites Seneca to the effect that "the excellent things of adversity are and ought to be admired" (p.

14; cf. p. 35). Cf. Francis Woodcock, *Joseph Paralleled by the Present Parliament, in His Sufferings and Advancement* (London, 1646), p. 5: "The blessing of adversity is better then the blessing of prosperity." See also John Klause's discussion in "The Unfortunate Fall: An Essay toward a Spiritual Biography of Andrew Marvell," Diss. Stanford 1976, p. 37: "The ethical good is defined by process." Klause's whole chapter "The Metaphysics of Violence," pp. 27–64, is relevant to the history of theodicy in this context.

27. Milton, *Complete Prose Works*, I, 363; CM, XVIII, 128.

28. Hartwell, *Lactantius and Milton* (Cambridge, Mass.: Harvard Univ. Press, 1929), pp. 18–32; Mohl, *John Milton and His Commonplace Book* (New York: Frederick Ungar, 1969), pp. 44–50.

29. N. P. Williams, *Ideas*, p. 297.

30. Lactantius, *A Treatise on the Anger of God*, chap. 13, in Roberts and Donaldson, *Ante-Nicene Fathers*, VII, 271.

31. Lactantius, *Divine Institutes*, 5.7, in Roberts and Donaldson, *Ante-Nicene Fathers*, VII, 142.

32. Perhaps something like "however, even these are not sufficient" would convey what appears to be Milton's approval of the reasons *as far as they go.*

33. Lactantius, *Divine Institutes*, 5.7, in *Ante-Nicene Fathers*, VII, 142.

34. Mohl (*Milton and His Commonplace Book*, p. 49) points to the following examples: "If there were no opposition where were the triall of an unfained goodnesse and magnanimity?" (*The Reason of Church Government*, in CM, III, 223); "Doth [Christ] not illustrate best things by things most evill?" (*An Apology*, in CM, III, 311); "It is by evil that virtue is chiefly exercised, and shines with greater brightness" (*Christian Doctrine*, in CM, XV, 115).

35. Lewis, *A Preface to "Paradise Lost"* (London: Oxford Univ. Press, 1942), pp. 65, 66, 67.

36. Waldock, *"Paradise Lost" and Its Critics*, pp. 27, 28.

37. See Hick, *EGL*, pp. 181, 285.

38. Ibid., p. 264. Cf. Clement Dore, "An Examination of the 'Soul-Making' Theodicy," *American Philosophical Quarterly*, 7, No. 2 (1970), p. 119.

39. Hick, "Evil, the Problem of," p. 139.

40. On the question of natural evil, which I am not pursuing in detail in this book, it is worth noting what appears to be a tension in *Paradise Lost* between the traditional notion that natural evil is decreed as punishment for sin (10.651–706; cf. *CD*, p. 330) and the more subtle, though not necessarily antithetical, idea that natural evil occurs as a natural, almost organic consequence of the going

wrong of man himself. Even though applying it incorrectly, Adam acknowledges the latter principle when he refers to God's "works, which in our fall, / For us created, needs must fail, / Dependent made" (9.941–3). In this view, "earth's feeling the wound" of sin (9.782) was not something specially decreed; the potentiality for natural as for moral evil already existed, and in some sense these possibilities were actualized simultaneously, as the juxtaposition of 9.781 and 782 seems to suggest.

41. In Milton, *Complete Prose Works,* I, 751, 752.

42. Tillyard, *Milton* (1930), p. 282, quoted in Evans, *PLGT,* p. 244.

43. Evans, *PLGT,* pp. 245, 246, 248. See *PL,* 4.135–7, 624–32; 5.212–15, 294–7.

44. Twisse, *The Riches of Gods Love,* p. 234.

45. Evans, *PLGT,* p. 249. Evans's entire chapter entitled "Native Innocence," pp. 242–71, is relevant to the question of Milton's use of a soul-making theodicy. Also relevant to the matter of "process" in Eden is Milo Kaufmann's chapter "Paradise and Miltonic Theodicy," in *Paradise in the Age of Milton, English Literary Studies* Monograph Series, No. 11 (Victoria, B.C.: Univ. of Victoria, 1978), pp. 34–50. Dr. Kaufmann was kind enough to read and comment on an earlier draft of this present chapter in July 1976.

I should perhaps admit here that this chapter was in penultimate draft before I consulted Barbara K. Lewalski's exceptional article "Innocence and Experience in Milton's Eden," in *New Essays on "Paradise Lost,"* ed. Thomas Kranidas (Berkeley and Los Angeles: Univ. of California Press, 1971), pp. 86–117. I have therefore refrained from studding my notes with references to her article, because this book has not, except *im zeitgeistlichen Sinn,* been influenced by it. However, I openly acknowledge both its excellence and its importance for the whole issue of Milton's prelapsarian vision.

46. Irenaeus, *Against Heresies,* 5.29.1.

47. E. M. W. Tillyard, *Milton,* rev. ed. (London: Chatto and Windus, 1966), p. 239.

48. T. Goodwin, *Of the Creatures,* in *Works* (1683), p. 42.

49. Lewis, *Preface,* pp. 42, 120.

50. Ibid., p. 118.

51. Augustine, *De Nuptiis et Concupiscentia,* 2.59, in Schaff, *Nicene and Post-Nicene Fathers,* Vol. V.

52. Augustine, *De Gratia Christi, et de Peccato Originali, contra Pelagium,* 2.43, in Schaff, *Nicene and Post-Nicene Fathers,* Vol. V.

53. Augustine, *De Nuptiis,* 2.59.

54. Ricks, *Keats and Embarrassment* (Oxford: Oxford Univ. Press, Clarendon Press, 1974), p. 21.

55. Blushing can, alternatively, imply joy. In 1548 the Renaissance physiologist Thomas Vicary wrote in his *Anatomie of the Bodie of Man:* "As the Philosophers say, the cheefe beautie in man is in the cheekes; and there the complexion of man is most knowen . . . And as Auicen sayth, the Cheekes doo not only shewe the diuersities of complexions, but also the affection and will of the hart: for by the affection of the hart, by sodaine ioy or dreede, he waxeth eyther pale or redde" (Early English Text Society Extra Series, No. 53 [London: N. Trübner and Co., 1888], p. 41).

56. Ricks, *Milton's Grand Style* (Oxford: Oxford Univ. Press, Clarendon Press, 1963), p. 110.

57. Fish, *Surprised by Sin*, p. 142.

58. See Lewis, *Preface*, p. 120.

59. What *was* occasioned by the Fall is lust; see *PL*, 9.1027–45.

60. T. Goodwin, *Of the Creatures*, p. 38.

61. Blackburn, " 'Uncloister'd Virtue': Adam and Eve in Milton's Paradise," *Milton Studies*, 3 (1971), 124, 127.

62. *PL*, 5.117–19, italics added. See n. 64 to Chapter 5.

63. See Chapter 4, the subsection entitled "Theodical paradigm: Abdiel and Satan."

64. *CD*, p. 332. For further discussion of how Satan's wickedness provides its own punishment, see my short article "On Toads and the Justice of God," *Milton Quarterly*, 13, No. 1 (1979), 12–14.

65. Quoted by Evans in Milton, *Paradise Lost: Books IX–X*, p. 187.

66. Milton, *Areopagitica*, p. 527.

67. Sirluck, "Milton Revises *The Faerie Queene*," *Modern Philology*, 48 (1950), 90–6.

68. Waldock, *"Paradise Lost" and Its Critics*, p. 61.

69. Bell, "The Fallacy of the Fall in *Paradise Lost*," *PMLA*, 70 (1953), p. 863. The debate occasioned by Bell's article is summarized by John S. Diekhoff, "Eve's Dream and the Paradox of Fallible Perfection," *Milton Quarterly*, 4, No. 1 (1970), 5–7. Cf. Joseph H. Summers, *The Muse's Method* (Cambridge, Mass.: Harvard Univ. Press, 1962), pp. 148 ff.

70. Tillyard, *Studies in Milton* (London: Chatto and Windus, 1951), p. 10.

71. See H. V. S. Ogden's cogent reply to critics such as Bell and Tillyard, "The Crisis of *Paradise Lost* Reconsidered," *Philological Quarterly* 36, No. 1 (1957), 1–19. See also Irene Samuel's section entitled "Theodicy or *Paideia*" in her article *"Paradise Lost,"* in *Critical*

Approaches to Six Major English Works, ed. R. M. Luminiansky and Herschel Baker (Philadelphia: Univ. of Pennsylvania Press, 1968), pp. 225–32. As Samuel says later in her chapter, "In addition to beauty, spontaneity, fertility, variety, intellectual and artistic activity, [Milton's Eden] can contain a nightmare, an understanding of evil, mistaken notions that need correction; nothing that can be the stuff of growth is alien to Eden" (pp. 237–8). My own argument, of course, is that unfallen *paideia* is a component of, not an alternative to, theodicy. As Lewalski says ("Innocence and Experience," p. 116), "The Edenic portion of *Paradise Lost* displays the process whereby Adam and Eve grow in knowledge and acquire experience within the State of Innocence, and thereby become steadily more complex, more conscious of manifold challenges and difficulties, more aware of large responsibilities, and by this very process, more complete and more perfect." Such *increasing* perfection, clearly, justifies God in allowing the existence of that which provides the challenges, difficulties, and so on. Cf. Diane McColley, "Eve's Dream," *Milton Studies*, 12 (1978), 28; and J. S. Hill, *Poet, Priest and Prophet*, pp. 126–40.

72. Owen, *Display of Arminianisme*, p. 86. See pp. 85–89 passim.

73. CD, p. 383. The original is "a natura ipsa hominis non immutabili profectum." Sumner's translation of this as "in the liability to fall with which man was created" is interesting but most unfortunately ambiguous (CM, XIV, 180–1).

74. Pierce, *Divine Philanthropie*, p. 24 (2nd ser.). I am not suggesting that Pierce's and Milton's positions are perfectly equivalent. Pierce seems to equivocate on "inclination": Does it imply mere fallibility (which is all his argument requires), or a real *propensity*? Milton's phrase "natura ipsa hominis non immutabili" implies the former but not the latter. However, contrast Roberts, *Mysterium*, p. 41: "Never meer man since *Adam*, had such perfection of mind, Conscience, will, . . . being habitually prone to no evil, but propense to all good . . . But for *Adam* to sin, who had no sinful inclination in him, how strange is it and inexcusable!"

75. Cf. Pierce, *Divine Philanthropie*, p. 25 (2nd ser.):

The power to *sin* is very *innocent* whil'st not *reduced* into *act*. For *Adam* and the *angels* were very *innocent* before they *sinn'd*; and they had *power* to *sinne* before they *sinn'd*; how else *could* they *sinne*? had they been *able* without the *power*? and was not God the *Author* of *all*, with which they were indued before they sinn'd? So that if the very *power* to sin is *sinful* (as Mr. *B*. [Pierce's opponent] saith)

Mr. *B.* makes *God* to be the *Author of sin.* Unlesse he can prove (by way of *subterfuge*) that a man can *sin* without the *power* to *sin,* or that he hath not the *power* to *sin* before he *sins.* That *Potentia* is not *Prior actu.*

See *PL,* 10.586–7: "Sin there in power before, / Once actual, now in body . . ."; and also Chapter 2 of this book, the section entitled "Creation, new creation, and the theodicy of *Paradise Lost.*"

76. Milton, *Areopagitica,* p. 527.
77. I am indebted in this paragraph to points presented by J. M. Evans in a forthcoming article, " 'Mortals' Chiefest Enemy': Security in *Paradise Lost.*"
78. In *Poems of John Milton,* p. 812.
79. See n. 27 to this chapter.

Chapter 7. *Paradise Lost* and the Unfortunate Fall

1. Lovejoy, *The Great Chain of Being,* p. 212.
2. Lovejoy, "Milton and the Paradox of the Fortunate Fall," *ELH,* 4, No. 3 (1937), rpt. in *Critical Essays on Milton from ELH* (Baltimore: John Hopkins Univ. Press, 1969), p. 164 (cited hereafter, from the reprint, as Lovejoy, "MPFF").
3. Empson, *Milton's God,* pp. 189, 190, 192.
4. See in particular Virginia R. Mollenkott, "Milton's Rejection of the Fortunate Fall," *Milton Quarterly,* 6, No. 1 (1972), 1–5; John C. Ulreich, Jr., "A Paradise Within: The Fortunate Fall in *Paradise Lost,*" *Journal of the History of Ideas,* 32 (1971), 351–66; and Dick Taylor, Jr., "Milton and the Paradox of the Fortunate Fall Once More," *Tulane Studies in English,* 9 (1959), 35–51.
5. Burgess, *Vindiciae Legis,* p. 105.
6. The Latin is quoted in Lovejoy, "MPFF," pp. 171–2; the English translation is my own.
7. Grandsen, "Milton, Dryden, and the Comedy of the Fall," *Essays in Criticism,* 26, No. 2 (1976), 123. In this article Milton is lumped together with Pope (an avowed optimist), as well as with Dryden. Grandsen's essay is ably criticized by R. D. Bedford, "Milton's Logic," *Essays in Criticism,* 27, No. 1 (1977), 84–6.
8. *The Reason of Church Government,* CM, III, 276.
9. As Frank L. Huntley says, "Milton knew well the difference between violently opposed points of view and those which, by being complementary rather than contradictory, can allow a reconciliation" ("Before and after the Fall: Some Miltonic Patterns of

Systasis," in *Approaches to Paradise Lost,* ed. C. A. Patrides [Toronto: Univ. of Toronto Press, 1968], p. 8).

10. Marshall, *"Paradise Lost: Felix Culpa* and the Problem of Structure," *Modern Language Notes,* 76 (Jan. 1961), 19.

11. Grandsen, "Milton, Dryden, and the Comedy of the Fall," pp. 116, 119. Cf. Lovejoy, "MPFF," p. 165: The paradox of the Fortunate Fall "served . . . to give to . . . history as a whole the character, not of tragedy, but of a divine comedy." See n. 34 to this chapter.

12. Twisse, *The Riches of Gods Love,* pp. 85, 86.

13. Hoard, *Gods Love to Man-kinde* (1656 ed.), p. 30.

14. J. Goodwin, *Redemption Redeemed,* p. 40.

15. Pierce, *Divine Philanthropie,* pp. 132, 137. Here Pierce is quoting (or paraphrasing) Johannes Piscator.

16. Ball, *A Treatise of the Covenant of Grace* (London, 1645), p. 7.

17. Whitfield, *Treatise,* pp. 31, 38, 46; italics added.

18. T. Goodwin, *Of the Creatures,* in *Works* (1683), p. 39.

19. More, *Victoria Gratiae,* p. 64: "Non esse autem potiora multo Christi dona donis Adami quis nisi valde ingratus dixerit? Unde igitur illa vox, *O Felix culpa . . .*"

20. Roberts, *Mysterium,* p. 60. Even though this exclamation was probably not written by Augustine, it is significant that Roberts thinks it was. He quotes the original – accurately – in the margin: "O felix culpa mea, ad quam diluendam dum ille charitate trahitur, ipsa quoque ejus charitas mihi eam desideranti et eam totis praecordiis concupiscenti aperitur! Nunquam tam bene dilectionem ejus agnoscerem, nisi in tantis periculis expertus eam fuissem. O quam feliciter cecedi, qui post lapsum felicius resurrexi!" Roberts cites the passage as being from "August. in meditat. lib. cap. 6. Tom. 9." In J.-P. Migne's edition of Augustine's *Opera Omnia* (Paris, 1841), Vol. VI, the passage in fact appears in *De Diligendo Deo,* chap. 6, which together with the work mentioned by Roberts is printed in an appendix headed "Subdititia Quaedam Opuscula." Migne at least considers the work to be probably contemporary with Augustine's own writings. Given the importance of Augustinian authority, the quotation, I think, is noteworthy. It is not cited by Lovejoy in "MPFF."

21. Twisse, *The Riches of Gods Love,* p. 86.

22. Hughes, in Milton, *Complete Poems and Major Prose,* p. 197. Hick claims that the words of the Exultet (*"O felix culpa . . ."*) "are at the heart of Christian theodicy" and are "common to both [Augustinian and Irenaean] types" (*EGL,* pp. 400, 265).

23. Lovejoy, "MPFF," p. 165.

24. Ibid., p. 164.
25. Mollenkott, "Milton's Rejection of the Fortunate Fall," p. 3. Cf. Mary Ann Radzinowicz, " 'Man as a Probationer of Immortality': *Paradise Lost* XI–XII," in Patrides, *Approaches to Paradise Lost*, p. 36: "The most [Milton] says is that the fall cannot thwart God's power and glory. He does not hint that Adam and Eve receive a better reward for the struggle to repair what they needlessly defaced." Contrast Allan Gilbert, "The Problem of Evil in *Paradise Lost*," *Journal of English and Germanic Philology*, 22 (1923), 186–7: "The Adam who has sinned and through effort risen again is 'happier far' than the sinless Adam of the garden. The nature of man was, it is true, originally good and pure, but the wisdom of human experience and the excellence gained through suffering are still better."
26. Lovejoy, "MPFF," p. 164. Even Augustine, in some of his writings, can be counted among the supporters of this view. See, for example, *City of God*, 14.10, where he suggests that man might have been promoted to angelic status had he persevered in obedience. See also *Enchiridion*, chaps. 8 and 28; and Evans's discussion in *PLGT*, pp. 93–4. Cf. Anselm, *Cur Deus Homo*, in *Basic Writings*, p. 241: "Man, had he not sinned, was to have been transferred with the same body to an immortal state."
27. Arminius, *Writings*, II, 73. Cf. John Donne's similar though more "Augustinian" view in *Death's Duel*: "If we had not sinned in Adam, *mortality had not put on immortality* (as the apostle speaks), *nor corruption had not put on incorruption*, but we had had our transmigration from this to the other world without any mortality, any corruption at all" (in Donne, *Devotions* [Ann Arbor: Univ. of Michigan Press, 1959], p. 173).
28. J. Goodwin, *Redemption Redeemed*, p. 486.
29. Burgess, *Vindiciae Legis*, pp. 102, 107.
30. Baxter, *Aphorismes of Justification* (London, 1649), p. 31. Cf. Milton, CD, p. 614: "Before the law the type of this [complete] glorification was Enoch, who was taken up into heaven, Gen. v. 24, and Elijah, II Kings ii. 11."
31. Baxter, *The Divine Life* (London, 1664), rpt. in Baxter, *Practical Works*, III, 730.
32. Baxter, *Catholick Theologie*, p. 31.
33. Baxter, *An End of Doctrinal Controversies* (London, 1691), p. 116.
34. Burden, *The Logical Epic*, p. 37. Barbara Lewalski approaches the matter less grudgingly, and from a somewhat different angle: Milton's dynamic "imagination of the State of Innocence sets the Fall in the proper tragic perspective in the poem, as the event which

blasted man's opportunity to develop – without suffering, violence, despair and death, though not in the least without tension and trial – the rich resources and large potentialities of the human spirit" ("Innocence and Experience in Milton's Eden," in *New Essays on "Paradise Lost,"* ed. Thomas Kranidas [Berkeley and Los Angeles: Univ. of California Press, 1971], p. 116).

35. Ball, *Treatise*, p. 10.

36. T. Goodwin, *Of the Creatures*, p. 48.

37. Lovejoy, "MPFF," p. 164.

38. Ibid. Herbert Weisinger makes the same assumption in *Tragedy and the Paradox of the Fortunate Fall* (East Lansing: Michigan State College Press, 1953), p. 19. Cf. Richard Sheldon, *The First Sermon . . . after His Conversion from the Romish Church* (London, 1612), p. 20: "O Christ . . . if sinne had not been permitted, thou haddest not beene sent . . . Therefore, I dare boldly pronounce . . . *O Felix Adae peccatum*, &c."

39. It is true, of course, that in *CD* Milton defines man's *restoration* as "the act by which man, freed from sin and death by God the Father through Jesus Christ, is raised to a far more excellent state of grace and glory than that from which he fell" (p. 415; CM, XV, 250). Nevertheless, Milton describes the *Redemption* as merely a part of this restoration, and in fact his reference to man's being "freed from sin" suggests that he has in mind the view that one's being raised to a full and willing realization of Christ's headship coincides with one's entering the state of *non posse peccare* – obviously a more excellent one than that from which Adam fell, that of *posse non peccare*. Goodwin on Eph. 1:10, for example, sees the good angels' "impeccability" as resulting from their being "united, . . . headed in Christ" (*Works* [1683], I, 141). The saints, of course, achieve the state of *non posse peccare* only beyond this earthly life.

The main thing to be emphasized here, however, is that Milton in his prose emphatically does *not* say that either restoration or Redemption involves man's being raised to a state more excellent than that which man ultimately *could have achieved* without the Fall.

40. Wolter, "Duns Scotus and the Predestination of Christ," *The Cord*, 5, No. 12 (1955), 366. I am grateful to Fr. Wolter for his kindness in providing me with a copy of this article.

41. Fiore, " 'Account Mee Man': The Incarnation in *Paradise Lost*," *Huntington Library Quarterly*, 39, No. 1 (1975), 51. See Fiore's first footnote for a useful list of this view's adherents, most of them medieval.

42. I translate from the *Reportata Parisiensia*, bk. 3, dist. 7, question 4,

in Scotus's *Opera* (Lugduni, 1639), Vol. XI, pt. 1, p. 451:

Tertio declarandum est, quis sit ordo huius praedestinationis ad alias praedestinationes? Dicitur quod lapsus hominis est ratio necessaria huius praedestinationis. Ex hoc quod Deus vidit Adam casurum, vidit Christum per hanc viam redempturum, & ideo praevidit naturam humanam assumendam, & tanta gloria glorificandam.

Dico tamen quod lapsus non fuit causa praedestinationis Christi, imo si nec fuisset Angelus lapsus, nec homo, adhuc fuisset Christus sic praedestinatus.

43. Scotus, *Ordinatio*, bk. 3, dist. 7, question 3, which Wolter translates in "Duns Scotus," p. 371. The *Ordinatio* and the *Reportata* (see n. 42) are separate versions of Scotus's lectures on the *Sentences of Peter Lombard*, the latter given at Paris, the former at Oxford.

44. Pierce, *Self-Condemnation*, p. 193. Cf. Pierce, *Gods Decrees*, pp. 69–70.

45. Although I have already discussed his ideas elsewhere, it is worth noting here that this Goodwin (no relation to John Goodwin, the Arminian) attended Christ's College, Cambridge, from 1613 to 1616, was a member of the Westminster Assembly, and in August 1650 was appointed to a commission – on which Milton also served – whose job it was to make an inventory of the records of the Westminster Assembly. His works were published posthumously. See W. R. Parker, *Milton: A Biography* (Oxford: Oxford Univ. Press, Clarendon Press, 1968), p. 1094.

46. T. Goodwin, *A Discourse of Election* (London, 1682), p. 89, in *Works* (1683), Vol. II. Subsequent references are to the *Works*. Cf. Harris, *A Brief Discourse*, p. 2, where he mentions the "opinion of *Zanchy's* and others, who conceive that Christ assumed mans nature for a pattern whereby *Adam* should be made." See also Goodwin, *Of the Knowledge of God the Father, and His Son Jesus Christ*, p. 141, in *Works* (1683), Vol. II, where he refers to "the Original Pattern of Human Nature, first set up in Christ's Ordination to be Man."

47. T. Goodwin, *Of Election*, pp. 91, 306, 307 (cf. 93), 308. I will not discuss the relationship between Goodwin's position here and what elsewhere appears to be his acceptance of the Fortunate Fall, except to say that I do not think there is any necessary connection between the two positions.

48. J. Goodwin, *Redemption Redeemed*, p. 436.

49. T. Goodwin, *An Exposition on . . . Ephesians*, pt. 1, pp. 133–4, in *Works* (1683), Vol. I.

50. *CD*, pp. 334–5; *CM*, XV, 98–101. The Latin of Eph. 1:10 as Milton

quotes it makes both the notion of headship and that of *recapitu-lation* clearer than do most English translations: "Ut sub unum caput recolligere omnia in Christo, tum quae in coelis sunt" (CM, XV, 98; cf. XIV, 88).

51. T. Goodwin, *An Exposition on . . . Ephesians,* pt. 1, p. 158.

52. Gilbert, *On the Composition of "Paradise Lost": A Study of the Order-ing and Insertion of Material* (Chapel Hill: Univ. of North Carolina Press, 1947), p. 114.

53. Hunter, "The War in Heaven: The Exaltation of the Son," in Hunter, Patrides, and Adamson, *Bright Essence,* p. 117.

54. J. Goodwin, *Redemption Redeemed,* p. 438.

55. It is in fact used ten times: 5.664, 691, 765, 883; 6.43, 68, 718, 775, 796, 881. "Messiah," of course, is a synonym of "Christ," both meaning "anointed." In *CD*, Milton says "that God begot the Son in the sense of making him a king, Psal. ii. 6, 7: *anointing my king, I have set him upon my holy hill of Sion.* Then, in the next verse, having anointed his king, from which process the name 'Christ' is derived, he says: *I have begotten you today"* (p. 207).

56. Cf. J. Goodwin, *Redemption Redeemed,* p. 438: "Neither Men, nor Angels, are necessitated or compelled by God, to accept of *Christ* for their *Head, . . .* though they be necessitated and compelled, with all other Creatures, to subject to his will and pleasure in the exercise of his Power."

57. Carey and Fowler, in *Poems of John Milton,* p. 727.

58. This point does not seem to me to be affected by Milton's alleged antitrinitarianism. Eventually, "God shall be all in all" (*PL,* 3.341), but in this regard Milton goes no farther than his scriptural source (1 Cor. 15:28). Moreover, as he says in *CD,* "[Christ's] kingdom will not *pass away,* like something ineffectual, nor will it be *destroyed.* Its end will not be one of dissolution but of perfection and consummation" (p. 627).

59. Relevant to this suggestion is the fact – pointed out by Hunter in his chapter "Milton on the Incarnation," in Hunter, Patrides, and Adamson, *Bright Essence,* p. 140 – that Milton uses the same word, *coalescere,* in describing both "the union of Christians in the mys-tical body of Christ" and the union that obtains in the Incarnation (see CM, XVI, 2, XIV, 228, 312, XV, 272). Hunter adds in a note: In *PL,* 5.609–11, "perhaps the angels are similarly united with the Son."

60. Aquinas, *Summa Theologiae,* IX, 138 [Ia.57, 5]: "Inter omnia mys-teria excellentius est mysterium Incarnationis Christi. Sed hoc angeli cognoverunt a principio."

61. *A Commentarie of John Caluine, vpon the First Booke of Moses Called Genesis,* trans. Thomas Tymme (London, 1578), p. 87.
62. *CD,* p. 420: "The incarnation is frequently spoken of as a mystery: . . . Eph. i. 9, 10: *he has made known to us the mystery of his will, which . . . to collect together all things in Christ."*
63. Here and in the rest of this paragraph I echo Lovejoy's premises, "MPFF," pp. 164–5. See Fiore, " 'Account Mee Man,' " pp. 54–6; focusing only on bk. 3, he concludes that Milton upholds the more usual view that the Fall was indeed the occasion for the Incarnation, and that it was likewise therefore a *felix culpa.*
64. See n. 14 to this chapter.
65. Lovejoy, "MPFF," p. 168.
66. Mollenkott, "Milton's Rejection of the Fortunate Fall," p. 2.
67. I adapt this term from Lancelot Andrewes, who in Sermon 14 of the Resurrection, Easter 1620, refers to Mary Magdalene as "this . . . *faelix peccatrix,* (as the Fathers terme her)" (*Sermons,* ed. G. M. Story [Oxford: Oxford Univ. Press, Clarendon Press, 1967], p. 196).
68. Barbour, *Myths,* p. 69.

Epilogue

1. Homes, *Resurrection Revealed* (1661 ed.), p. 114.
2. *Poems of John Milton,* p. 7.

Appendix: The unfortunate fall of Satan

1. A similar question, of course, could be asked about the fall of Samson: Is it not, in the final analysis, for the *best?* (*Samson Agonistes,* line 1745). Does not the "optimism" of this conclusion render Samson's sin fortunate, and does it not in an even broader sense vitiate Milton's overall theodicy? I shall forbear discussing these questions here, simply because they have been admirably treated in two very impressive articles in recent volumes of *Milton Studies.* In the first, "Liberty under the Law: The Chorus and the Meaning of *Samson Agonistes"* (*Milton Studies,* 12 [1978], 141–63), Joan S. Bennett challenges explicitly the assumption that "the Chorus's *felix culpa* resolution . . . [is] Milton's as well" (p. 161). And in the second, "Samson's God: 'Beastly Hebraism' and 'Asinine Bigotry' " (*Milton Studies,* 13 [1979], 109–28), Robert West brilliantly argues his more generally theodical claims: "first, that Samson is not a protagonist so morally unsympathetic . . . that his testimony about God must

impress us unfavorably; second, that his testimony does not include a persisting doubt on his part of God's goodness; and third, that the divine mystery concerning which Samson settles into confidence can still be literarily acceptable and imposing" (p. 126).

2. St. Anselm, *Cur Deus Homo* (1.18), in *Basic Writings*, p. 210.

3. Ibid., p. 211. Text references are to the pagination of the *Basic Writings*. Cf. Milton, *CD*, pp. 312–14.

4. *PL*, 7.146–7, 150–6. See Fowler's notes on these lines in *Poems of John Milton*.

5. Augustine, *City of God*, 22.1: "Ac sic illa dilecta et superna ciuitas non fraundetur suorum numero ciuium, quin etiam fortassis et uberiore laetetur." Unaccountably, this passage is cited by at least one editor who nevertheless affirms that, for Milton, "the creation of man was a consequence of the revolt of the angels." See *Paradise Lost*, ed. Scott Elledge (New York: Norton, 1975), pp. 24, 154.

Selected bibliography

Seventeenth-century and earlier primary works

Acta et Scripta Synodalia Dordracena Ministrorum Remonstrantium in Foederato Belgio. Herder-wiici, 1620.

Allen, Richard. *An Antidote against Heresy; or, A Preservation for Protestants against the Poyson of Papists, Anabaptists, Arrians, Arminians, etc. and Their Pestilent Errours.* London, [1648].

Amyraldus, Moses. *Dissertationes Theologicae Quatuor.* Salmurii, 1645.

Doctrinae Ioannis Calvini de Absoluto Reprobationis Decreto Defensio Adversus Scriptorum Anonymum. Salmurii, 1641.

Fidei Mosis Amyraldi Circa Errores Arminianorum Declaratio. Salmurii, 1646.

Andrewes, Lancelot. *Sermons.* Ed. G. M. Story. Oxford: Oxford Univ. Press, Clarendon Press, 1967.

Anselm, St. *Cur Deus Homo.* In *Saint Anselm: Basic Writings.* 2nd ed. LaSalle, Ill.: Open Court, 1962. Pp. 171–288.

Aquinas, St. Thomas. *An Aquinas Reader.* Ed. Mary T. Clark. New York: Image Books, 1972.

Summa Theologiae. 60 vols. London: Blackfriars, 1964–6.

Aristotle. *Metaphysics.* Trans. John Warrington. London: J. M. Dent, 1961.

Arminius, Jacobus. *The Just Mans Defence; or, The Declaration of the Judgment of James Arminius . . . before the States of Holland, and Westfriezland.* Trans. Tobias Conyers. London, 1657.

The Writings of James Arminius. 3 vols. Trans. James Nichols and W. R. Bagnall. 1853; rpt. Grand Rapids: Baker Book House, 1956.

Arminius, Jacobus, and Stephanus Curcellaeus. *Examen Thesium F. Gomare de Praedestinat. cum St. Curcellaei Vindiciis, Quibus Suam et Arminii Sententiam de Jure Dei Increaturas, Adversus Mosis Amyraldi Criminationes, Defendit.* Amsterdam, 1645.

Augustine, Aurelius. *Anti-Pelagian Works.* Trans. Peter Holmes and Robert E. Wallis. Vol. V of *A Select Library of the Nicene and Post-*

Nicene Fathers of the Christian Church. Ed. Philip Schaff. Rpt. Grand Rapids: Eerdmans, 1975.

The City of God. Ed. Vernon J. Bourke. Trans. G. G. Walsh et al. New York: Image Books, 1958.

The Confessions of St. Augustine. Trans. Rex Warner. New York: New American Library, 1963.

The Essential Augustine. Ed. Vernon J. Bourke. Toronto: New American Library, 1964.

Opera Omnia. Ed. J.-P. Migne. Paris, 1841.

The Teacher, The Free Choice of the Will, Grace and Free Will. Trans. Robert P. Russell. Washington, D.C.: Catholic Univ. of America Press, 1968.

The Works of Aurelius Augustine. Ed. Marcus Dods. Edinburgh: T. and T. Clark, 1871–.

Writings in Connection with the Manichaean Controversy. Trans. Richard Stothert and Albert H. Newman. In Vol. IV of *A Select Library of the Nicene and Post-Nicene Fathers of the Christian Church.* Ed. Philip Schaff. Rpt. Grand Rapids: Eerdmans, 1974.

[Baillie, Robert]. *An Antidote against Arminianisme; or, A Plain and Brief Discourse Wherein the State of the Question in All the Five Infamous Articles of Arminius Is Set Downe, and the Orthodox Tenets Confirmed by Cleere Scriptural Grounds. Framed of Purpose for the Capacity of the More Simple Sort of People.* London, 1641; rpt. 1652.

Baker, Thomas. *Gods Providence Asserted.* [London?], 1656.

Ball, John. *A Treatise of the Covenant of Grace: Wherein . . . Divers Errours of Arminians and Others are Confuted.* London, 1645.

Baxter, Richard. *Aphorismes of Justification.* London, 1649.

Catholick Theologie: The First Book. Pacifying Principles . . . for the Reconciling of the Church-Dividing and Destroying Controversies, Especially about Predestination, Providence, Grace and Free-Will, . . . London, 1675.

The Divine Life. London, 1664. Rpt. in Baxter, *The Practical Works.* London, 1707. III, 665–764.

An End of Doctrinal Controversies Which Have Lately Troubled the Churches by Reconciling Explication, without Much Disputing. London, 1691.

Gods Goodness, Vindicated for the Help of Such . . . as Are Tempted to Deny It, and Think Him Cruel, Because of the . . . Misery of Mankind . . . London, 1671. Rpt. in Baxter, *The Practical Works.* London, 1707. II, 923–30.

The Grotian Religion Discovered, at the Invitation of Mr. Thomas Pierce. London, 1658.

The Reasons of the Christian Religion. Rpt. in Baxter, *The Practical Works*. London, 1707. II, 1–224.

Boehme, Jacob. *Concerning the Election of Grace*. Trans. John Sparrow. London, 1655.

Boethius. *The Consolation of Philosophy*. Trans. Richard Green. Indianapolis: Bobbs-Merrill, 1962.

Bramhall, John. See Hobbes.

Browne, Sir Thomas. *The Prose of Sir Thomas Browne*. Ed. Norman Endicott. 1967; rpt. New York: Norton, 1972.

Bullett, Gerald, ed. *Silver Poets of the Sixteenth Century*. 1947; rpt. London: Dent, 1975.

Burgess, Anthony. *Vindiciae Legis; or, A Vindication of the Morall Law and the Covenants, from the Errours of the* Papists, Arminians, Socinians, *and more especially,* Antinomians. London, 1646.

Calvin, John. *A Commentarie of John Caluine, vpon the First Booke of Moses Called Genesis*. Trans. Thomas Tymme. London, 1578.

    Concerning the Eternal Predestination of God. Trans. J. K. S. Reid. London: James Clarke, 1961.

    Institutes of the Christian Religion. Trans. Henry Beveridge. 2 vols. Rpt. Grand Rapids: Eerdmans, 1975.

Carleton, George. *An Examination of Those Things Wherein the Author of the Late Appeale Holdeth the Doctrines of the Pelagians and Arminians, to be the Doctrines of the Church of England*. London, 1626.

Carpenter, Richard. *Experience, Historie, and Divinitie*. London, 1642.

Casaubon, Meric. *The Originall Cause of Temporall Evils*. London, 1645.

Charleton, Walter. *The Darknes of Atheism Dispelled by the Light of Nature*. London, 1652.

Corbett, Edward. *Gods Providence: A Sermon Preached before the Honourable House of Commons . . . Decemb. 28. Anno 1642*. London, 1642.

Cudworth, Ralph. *The True Intellectual System of the Universe*. 3 vols. Trans. John Harrison. London, 1845.

Curcellaeus, Stephanus. *Opera Theologica*. Amsterdam, 1675.

Davenant, John. *Animadversions . . . upon a Treatise Intitled Gods Love to Mankind*. Cambridge, 1641.

Donne, John. *Devotions*. Ann Arbor: Univ. of Michigan Press, 1959.

Dort, Synod of. *The Ivdgement of the Synode Holden at Dort, Concerning the Fiue Articles*. London, 1619.

DuMoulin, Pierre. *The Anatomy of Arminianisme*. London, 1626.

    Petri Molinaei de Amyraldi adversus Fridericum Spanhemium Libro Iudicum. Seu Pro Dei Misericordia, et Sapientia, et Justitia Apologia. Rotterdam, 1649.

Duns Scotus, Johannes. *Opera.* Lugduni, 1639.

Edwards, Thomas. *Gangraena; or, A Catalogue and Discovery of Many of the Errours, Heresies, Blasphemies and Pernicious Practices of the Sectaries of This Time . . .* London, 1646.

Erasmus, Desiderus. *The Free Will.* Trans. Ernst F. Winter. In *Erasmus–Luther: Discourse on Free Will.* New York: Frederick Ungar, 1961.

Goodwin, John. *Cretensis; Or, A Briefe Answer to an Ulcerous Treatise, Lately Published by Mr. Thomas Edwards, Intituled, Gangraena.* London, 1646.

Redemption Redeemed. London, 1651.

Goodwin, Thomas. *The Works.* London, 1683–.

The Works. Edinburgh: James Nichol, 1861–.

Grotius, Hugo. *His Discourses: i. Of God, and His Providence. ii. Of Christ, His Miracles and Doctrine.* Trans. Clement Barksdale. London, 1652.

On the Truth of Christianity. Trans. Spencer Madan. London, 1782.

Operum Theologicorum. 3 vols. Amsterdam, 1679.

Haggar, Henry. *The Order of Causes of Gods Fore-knowledge, Election, and Predestination . . . Laid Down So Clearly . . . That Even the Meanest Capacity amongst Rational Men May Understand It, to Their Great Satisfaction.* London, 1654.

Hakewill, George. *An Apologie or Declaration of the Power and Providence of God in the Government of the World.* Oxford, 1635.

Hammond, Henry. *A Pacifick Discourse of Gods Grace and Decrees.* London, 1660. Rpt. in Hammond, *The Works.* London, 1674.

H[arington], J[ames]. *A Holy Oyl; and, a Sweet Perfume: Taken out of the Sanctuary of the Most Sacred Scriptures.* [London], 1669.

Harris, Robert. *A Brief Discourse of Mans Estate in the First and Second Adam.* London, 1653.

Gods Goodnes and Mercie. Laid Open in a Sermon, Preached at Pauls-Crosse, on the Last of June, 1622. 4th ed. London, 1631.

A Treatise of the New Covenant. London, 1653.

Hoard, Samuel. *Gods Love to Man-kinde, Manifested, by Dis-proving That Doctrine Which Telleth Us of an Absolute Decree for Their Damnation.* 1633; new ed., London, 1656.

Hobbes, Thomas. *The Questions concerning Liberty, Necessity, and Chance, Clearly Stated and Debated between Dr. Bramhall Bishop of Derry, and Thomas Hobbes of Malmesbury.* London, 1656.

Homes, Nathaniel. *The Resurrection Revealed.* 1653; new ed., London, 1661.

Irenaeus. *Against Heresies.* In Vol. I of *The Ante-Nicene Fathers.* Ed.

Alexander Roberts and James Donaldson. Rpt. Grand Rapids: Eerdmans, 1975.

Lactantius. *The Divine Institutes* and *A Treatise on the Anger of God* [*De Ira Dei*]. Trans. William Fletcher. In Vol. VII of *The Ante-Nicene Fathers*. Ed. Alexander Roberts and James Donaldson. Rpt. Grand Rapids: Eerdmans, 1975.

L[ane], S[amuel]. *A Vindication of Free Grace: In Opposition to This Arminian Position*. London, 1645.

Leigh, Edward. *A Treatise of Divinity Consisting of Three Bookes . . . The Third Handleth the Three Principall Workes of God, Decree, Creation, and Providence*. London, 1646.

Luther, Martin. *The Bondage of the Will*. Trans. Ernst F. Winter. In *Erasmus–Luther: Discourse on Free Will*. New York: Frederick Ungar, 1961.

Milton, John. *Complete Prose Works of John Milton*. Ed. Don M. Wolfe et al. New Haven: Yale Univ. Press, 1953–.

John Milton: Complete Poems and Major Prose. Ed. Merritt Y. Hughes. New York: Bobbs-Merrill, 1957.

Paradise Lost: Books IX–X. Ed. J. Martin Evans. Cambridge: Cambridge Univ. Press, 1973.

The Poems of John Milton. Ed. John Carey and Alastair Fowler. London: Longmans, 1968.

The Works of John Milton. Ed. Frank Allen Patterson et al. 18 vols. New York: Columbia Univ. Press, 1931–8.

More, Alexander. *Calvinus: Oratio Genevae Habita pro More Academicae ac Rectoris Munere, in qua Vir Amplissimus H. GROTIVS Refellitur*. Geneva, 1653.

Victoria Gratiae: De Gratia et Libero Arbitrio. Medioburgi, 1652.

Newport, William. *The Fall of Man by Sinne*. London, 1644.

Origen, Adamantius. *Opera Omnia*. 7 vols. In *Patrologia Graeca*. Ed. J.-P. Migne. Paris, 1857–.

Owen, John. *Diatriba de Justitia Divina*. Oxford, 1653.

A Display of Arminianisme: Being a Discovery of the Old Pelagian Idol Free-Will. London, 1643.

A Dissertation on Divine Justice. Trans. John Stafford. London, [1792].

Pemble, William. *A Treatise of the Providence of God*. Oxford, 1658. In Pemble, *Works*. Oxford, 1659.

Vindiciae Gratiae: A Plea for Grace . . . Wherein . . . the Maine Sinewes of Arminivs Doctrine Are Cut Asunder. Oxford, 1627, 1629, 1635, 1659. In Pemble, *Works*. Oxford, 1659.

Pierce, Thomas. *A Correct Copy of Some Notes concerning Gods Decrees*. London, 1657.

The Divine Philanthropie Defended. London, 1657.

The Divine Purity Defended. London, 1657.

The New Discoverer Discover'd. By way of Answer to Mr. Baxter His Pretended Discovery of the Grotian Religion. London, 1659.

Self-Condemnation. London, 1658.

Plato, *Timaeus.* Trans. Desmond Lee. Harmondsworth: Penguin, 1965.

Plotinus. *The Enneads.* Trans. Stephen MacKenna. 2nd ed. London: Faber, 1956.

Prynne, William. *The Chvrch of Englands Old Anti-thesis to New Arminianisme. Wherein 7 . . . Arminian (Once Popish and Pelagian) Errors Are Manifestly Disproued.* London, 1629; new ed. with *Anti-Arminianism* added as the main title, 1630.

   God, No Imposter nor Deluder; or, An Answer to a Popish and Arminian Cauill, in the Defence of Free-Will, and Vniversal Grace London, 1629; new ed., 1630.

Roberts, Francis. *Mysterium et Medulla Bibliorum. The Mysterie and Marrow of the Bible: viz. God's Covenants with Man, In the First Adam, before the Fall: and In the Last Adam IESVS CHRIST, After the Fall.* London, 1657.

Rutherford, Samuel. *Disputatio Scholastica de Divina Providentia . . . adversus Jesuitas, Arminianos, Socinianos . . .* Edinburgh, 1650.

   A Free Disputation against Pretended Liberty of Conscience Tending to Resolve Doubts Moved by Mr. John Goodwin, John Baptist, Dr. Jer. Taylor, *the* Belgick Arminians, Socinians, *and other Authors.* London, 1649.

Savile, Thomas. *Adams Garden: A Meditation of Thankfulnesse and Praises vnto the Lord, for the Returne and Restore of* Adam *and His Posteritie, Planted as Flowers in a Garden.* London, 1611.

Schaff, Philip, ed. *The Creeds of Christendom.* London: Hodder and Stoughton, 1877.

Sedgwick, Obadiah. *The Shepherd of Israel, . . . Together with the Doctrine of Providence Practically Handled.* London, 1658.

Seneca. *Moral Essays.* Trans. John W. Basore. London: Heinemann, 1928.

   Seneca's Answer to Lucilius His Quaere. Why Good Men Suffer Misfortune Seeing There Is a Divine Providence? Trans. Edward Sherburne. London, 1648.

Sheldon, Richard. *The First Sermon . . . after His Conversion from the Romish Church.* London, 1612.

Sidney, Philip. *The Prose Works of Sir Philip Sidney.* Ed. Albert Feuillerat. 4 vols. 1912; rpt. Cambridge: Cambridge Univ. Press, 1962.

S[nawsell], R. *A Looking Glasse.* London, 1610.

Socinus, Faustus. *De Statu Primi Hominis ante Lapsum Disputatio.* In Socinus, *Opera.* Irenopoli, 1656.

Spenser, Edmund. *Spenser: Poetical Works.* Ed. E. DeSelincourt and J. C. Smith. 1912; rpt. London: Oxford Univ. Press, 1969.

Strong, William. *A Treatise Shewing the Subordination of the Will of Man unto the Will of God.* London, 1657.

Tatian. *Address to the Greeks.* In Vol. II, of *The Ante-Nicene Fathers.* Ed. Alexander Roberts and James Donaldson. Rpt. Grand Rapids: Eerdmans, 1975.

Tayler, Francis. *The Faith of the Chvrch of England concerning Gods Work on Mans Will.* London, 1641.

Taylor, Jeremy. *Deus Justificatus; or, A Vindication of the Glory of the Divine Attributes in the Question of Original Sin. Against the Presbyterian Way of Understanding it.* London, 1656.

Tertullian. *Adversus Marcionem.* Trans. Ernest Evans. Oxford: Oxford Univ. Press, Clarendon Press, 1972.

Twisse, William. *The Riches of Gods Love unto the Vessells of Mercy, Consistent with His Absolute Hatred or Reprobation of the Vessells of Wrath; or, An Answer unto a Book Entituled Gods Love unto Mankind.* Oxford, 1653.

Vindiciae Gratiae, Potestatis, ac Providentiae Dei Hoc Est, ad Examen Libelli Perkinsiani de Praedestinationis Modo et Ordine, Institutum a Iacobo Arminio, Responsio Scholastica. Amsterdam, 1632.

Vicary, Thomas. *The Anatomie of the Bodie of Man: The Edition of 1548, as Re-issued . . . in 1577.* Early English Text Society Extra Series, No. 53. London: N. Trübner and Co., 1888.

Ward, John. *The Good Will of Him That Dwelt in the Bush; or, The Extraordinary Happiness of Living under an Extraordinary Providence. A Sermon Preached before . . . the House of Lords . . . July 22, 1645. At Their Publicke Thanksgiving for the Good Successe Given to the Parliaments Forces, under the Command of Sir Thomas Fairfax.* London, 1645.

[Ward, Seth]. *A Philosophicall Essay towards an Eviction of the Being and Attributes of God.* Oxford, 1652.

Whitfield, Thomas. *Doctrines of the Arminians and Pelagians Truly Stated and Clearly Answered.* London, 1652.

A Treatise Tending to Shew That the Just and Holy God, May Have a Hand in the Unjust Actions of Sinfull Men: And That in Such a Way As Shall Be without Any Impeachment of His Justnesse and Holinesse, or Diminution of His Power and Providence. London, 1653.

Wilkins, John. *A Discourse concerning the Beauty of Providence in All the Rugged Passages of It. Very Seasonable to Quiet and Support the Heart in These Times of Publicke Confusion.* London, 1649.

Wilson, Thomas. *Aenigmata Sacra: Misticall Cases and Secrets of Diuinitie, with Their Resolutions.* London, 1615.

Woodcock, Francis. *Joseph Paralleled by the Present Parliament, in His Sufferings and Advancement.* London, 1646.

Literary studies and works on Milton

Adams, Robert M. "A Little Look into Chaos." In *Illustrious Evidence: Approaches to English Literature of the Early Seventeenth Century.* Ed. Earl Miner. Berkeley: Univ. of California Press, 1975. Pp. 71–89.

Arnold, Matthew. *The Complete Prose Works.* 11 vols. Ann Arbor: Univ. of Michigan Press, 1960–.

Auerbach, Erich. *Mimesis: The Representation of Reality in Western Literature.* Trans. Willard R. Trask. 1953; rpt. Princeton: Princeton Univ. Press, 1973.

Bedford, R. D. "Milton's Logic." *Essays in Criticism,* 27, No. 1 (1977), 84–6.

Bell, Millicent, and Wayne Shumaker. "The Fallacy of the Fall in *Paradise Lost.*" *PMLA,* 68 (1953), 863–83; 70 (1955), 1185–1203.

Bennett, Joan S. "Liberty under the Law: The Chorus and the Meaning of *Samson Agonistes.*" *Milton Studies,* 12 (1978), 141–63.

Blackburn, Thomas H. " 'Uncloister'd Virtue': Adam and Eve in Milton's Paradise." *Milton Studies,* 3 (1971), 119–37.

Bowers, Fredson. "Adam, Eve, and the Fall in *Paradise Lost.*" *PMLA,* 84, No. 2 (1969), 264–73.

Boyd, William H. "The Secrets of Chaos." *Milton Quarterly,* 10, No. 3 (1976), 83–7.

Burden, Dennis H. *The Logical Epic: A Study of the Argument of "Paradise Lost."* London: Routledge and Kegan Paul. 1967.

Campbell, Gordon. "The Intellect and the Imagination: A Study of the Relationship between Milton's *De Doctrina Christiana* and *Paradise Lost.*" D. Phil. thesis, York University (England), 1973.

Chambers, A. B., Jr. "Chaos in *Paradise Lost.*" *Journal of the History of Ideas,* 24 (1963), 55–84.

Clark, Mili N. "The Mechanics of Creation: Non-Contradiction and Natural Necessity in *Paradise Lost.*" *English Literary Renaissance,* 7, No. 2 (1977), 207–42.

Coleridge, Samuel Taylor. *The Complete Works*. Ed. W. G. T. Shedd. New York: Harper, 1853–. Vol. IV.

Conklin, George Newton. *Biblical Criticism and Heresy in Milton*. New York: King's Crown Press, 1949.

Curry, Walter Clyde. *Milton's Ontology, Cosmogony, and Physics*. Lexington: Univ. of Kentucky Press, 1957.

Daniells, Roy. *Milton, Mannerism and Baroque*. Toronto: Univ. of Toronto Press, 1963.

Danielson, Dennis R. "Milton's Arminianism and *Paradise Lost*." *Milton Studies*, 12 (1978), 47–73.

"On Toads and the Justice of God." *Milton Quarterly*, 13, No. 1 (1979), 12–14.

Diekhoff, John S. "Eve, the Devil, and *Areopagitica*." *Modern Language Quarterly*, 5 (1944), 429–34.

"Eve's Dream and the Paradox of Fallible Perfection." *Milton Quarterly*, 4, No. 1 (1970), 5–7.

Milton's "Paradise Lost": A Commentary on the Argument. New York: Columbia Univ. Press, 1946.

Drummond, C. Q. "An Anti-Miltonist Reprise: I. The Milton Controversy" and "II. Antagonistic Styles and Contradictory Demands." *The Compass: A Provincial Review* (Edmonton, Alberta), No. 2 (Dec. 1977), pp. 28–45, No. 3 (Apr. 1978), pp. 39–59.

Empson, William. *Milton's God*. London: Chatto and Windus, 1961.

Evans, J. Martin. *"Paradise Lost" and the Genesis Tradition*. Oxford: Oxford Univ. Press, Clarendon Press, 1968.

Fiore, Peter A., O.F.M. " 'Account Mee Man': The Incarnation in *Paradise Lost*." *Huntington Library Quarterly*, 39, No. 1 (1975), 51–6.

Fish, Stanley Eugene. *Surprised by Sin: The Reader in Paradise Lost*. Berkeley and Los Angeles: Univ. of California Press, 1971.

Fisher, Peter F. "Milton's Theodicy." *Journal of the History of Ideas*, 17 (1956), 28–53.

Frye, Northrop. *The Anatomy of Criticism*. Princeton: Princeton Univ. Press, 1957.

Gardner, Helen. *A Reading of "Paradise Lost."* Oxford: Oxford Univ. Press, Clarendon Press, 1965.

Giamatti, A. Bartlett. *The Earthly Paradise and the Renaissance Epic*. Princeton: Princeton Univ. Press, 1966.

Gilbert, Allan H. *On the Composition of "Paradise Lost": A Study of the Ordering and Insertion of Material*. Chapel Hill: Univ. of North Carolina Press, 1947.

"The Problem of Evil in *Paradise Lost*." *Journal of English and Germanic Philosophy*, 22 (1923), 175–94.

Grandsen, K. W. "Milton, Dryden, and the Comedy of the Fall." *Essays in Criticism*, 26, No. 2 (1976), 116–33.

Grant, Patrick. *The Transformation of Sin: Studies in Donne, Herbert, Vaughan, and Traherne.* Amherst: Univ. of Massachusetts Press, 1974.

Green, Clarence C. "The Paradox of the Fall in *Paradise Lost.*" *Modern Language Notes*, 53, No. 8 (1938), 557–71.

Greene, Thomas. *The Descent from Heaven: A Study in Epic Continuity.* New Haven: Yale Univ. Press, 1963.

Hamilton, Gary David. "Milton and Arminianism." Diss. Univ. of Wisconsin, 1968.

Hanford, James Holly. *Milton Handbook.* 3rd ed. New York: Crofts, 1939.

Hartwell, Kathleen Ellen. *Lactantius and Milton.* Cambridge, Mass.: Harvard Univ. Press, 1929.

Hill, John Spencer. *John Milton, Poet, Priest and Prophet: A Study of Divine Vocation in Milton's Poetry and Prose.* London: Macmillan, 1979.

Howard, Leon, " 'The Invention' of Milton's 'Great Argument': A Study of the Logic of 'God's Ways to Men.' " *Huntington Library Quarterly*, 9 (1945), 149–73.

Hunter, W. B. "John Milton: Autobiographer." *Milton Quarterly*, 8, No. 4 (1974), 100–4.

"Some Problems in John Milton's Theological Vocabulary." *Harvard Theological Review*, 57 (1964), 353–65.

Hunter, W. B., C. A. Patrides, and J. H. Adamson. *Bright Essence: Studies in Milton's Theology.* Salt Lake City: Univ. of Utah Press, 1971.

Huntley, Frank L. "Before and after the Fall: Some Miltonic Patterns of Systasis." In *Approaches to "Paradise Lost": The York Tercentenary Lectures.* Ed. C. A. Patrides. Toronto: Univ. of Toronto Press, 1968. Pp. 1–14.

Johnson, Samuel. *Lives of the English Poets.* Ed. George B. Hill. Oxford: Oxford Univ. Press, Clarendon Press, 1905. Vol. I.

Kaufmann, U. Milo. *Paradise in the Age of Milton. English Literary Studies* Monograph Series, No. 11. Victoria, B.C.: Univ. of Victoria, 1978.

Kelley, Maurice. "Milton and the 'Nameless Discourse Written at Delft.' " *Modern Language Notes*, 76 (1961), 214–16.

"Milton's Debt to Wolleb's *Compendium Theologiae Christianae.*" *PMLA*, 50 (1935), 156–65.

"The Theological Dogma of *Paradise Lost*, III, 173–202." *PMLA*, 52 (1937), 75–9.

This Great Argument: A Study of Milton's "De Doctrina Christiana" as a Gloss upon "Paradise Lost." Princeton: Princeton Univ. Press, 1941.

Kermode, Frank, ed. *The Living Milton*. London: Routledge and Kegan Paul, 1960.

Klause, John Louis. "The Unfortunate Fall: An Essay toward a Spiritual Biography of Andrew Marvell." Diss. Stanford, 1976.

Kranidas, Thomas, ed. *New Essays on Paradise Lost*. Berkeley: Univ. of California Press, 1969.

Leavis, F. R. *Revaluation: Tradition and Development in English Poetry*. London: Chatto and Windus, 1956.

Lewis, C. S. *The Discarded Image: An Introduction to Medieval and Renaissance Literature*. Cambridge: Cambridge Univ. Press, 1964.

A Preface to "Paradise Lost." London: Oxford Univ. Press, 1942.

Lieb, Michael. *The Dialectics of Creation: Patterns of Birth and Regeneration in "Paradise Lost."* Amherst: Univ. of Massachusetts Press, 1970.

Lieb, Michael, and John T. Shawcross, eds. *Achievements of the Left Hand: Essays on the Prose of John Milton*. Amherst: Univ. of Massachusetts Press, 1974.

Lovejoy, Arthur O. "Milton and the Paradox of the Fortunate Fall." *ELH*, 4, No. 3 (1937), 161–79. Rpt. in *Critical Essays on Milton from ELH*. Baltimore: Johns Hopkins Univ. Press, 1969. Pp. 163–81.

Low, Anthony. "Angels and Food in *Paradise Lost*." *Milton Studies*, I (1969), 135–45.

"The Parting in the Garden in *Paradise Lost*." *Philological Quarterly*, 47, No. 1 (1968), 30–5.

Lumpkin, Ben Gray. "Fate in *Paradise Lost*." *Studies in Philology*, 44 (1947), 56–68.

McColley, Diane Kelsey. "Eve's Dream." *Milton Studies*, 12 (1978), 25–45.

"Free Will and Obedience in the Separation Scene in *Paradise Lost*." *Studies in English Literature, 1500–1900*, 12, No. 1 (1972), 103–20.

McDill, Joseph M. "Milton and the Pattern of Calvinism." Diss. Vanderbilt, 1938.

Madsen, William G. "The Fortunate Fall in *Paradise Lost*." *Modern Language Notes*, 74 (1959), 103–5.

Marshall, William H. "*Paradise Lost: Felix Culpa* and the Problem of Structure." *Modern Language Notes*, 76 (Jan. 1961), 15–20.

Miner, Earl. "*Felix Culpa* in the Redemptive Order of *Paradise Lost.*" *Philological Quarterly*, 47 (1968), 43–54.

Mohl, Ruth. *John Milton and His Commonplace Book.* New York: Frederick Ungar, 1969.

Mollenkott, Virginia R. "Milton's Rejection of the Fortunate Fall." *Milton Quarterly*, 6, No. 1 (1972), 1–5.

Nicolson, Marjorie H. "Milton and Hobbes." *Studies in Philology*, 23, No. 4 (1926), 405–33.

Ogden, H. V. S. "The Crisis of *Paradise Lost* Reconsidered." *Philological Quarterly*, 36, No. 1 (1957), 1–19.

Parker, William R. *Milton: A Biography.* 2 vols. Oxford: Oxford Univ. Press, Clarendon Press, 1968.

Patrides, C. A. *Milton and the Christian Tradition.* Oxford: Oxford Univ. Press, Clarendon Press, 1966.

Patrides, C. A., ed. *Approaches to "Paradise Lost": The York Tercentenary Lectures.* Toronto: Univ. of Toronto Press, 1968.

Milton's Epic Poetry: Essays on "Paradise Lost" and "Paradise Regained." Harmondsworth: Penguin, 1967.

Perlmutter, Eila Siren. "Milton's Three Degrees of Grace: A Study of Predestination in *Paradise Lost* and the *De Doctrina Christiana.*" Diss. State University of New York, Albany, 1972.

Peter, John. *A Critique of "Paradise Lost."* New York: Columbia Univ. Press, 1960.

Radzinowicz, Mary Ann. " 'Man as a Probationer of Immortality': *Paradise Lost* XI–XII." In *Approaches to "Paradise Lost": The York Tercentenary Lectures.* Ed. C. A. Patrides (Toronto: Univ. of Toronto Press, 1968). Pp. 31–51.

Rajan, Balachandra. *The Lofty Rhyme: A Study of Milton's Major Poetry.* London: Routledge and Kegan Paul, 1970.

"Paradise Lost" and the Seventeenth Century Reader. London: Chatto and Windus, 1947.

Rajan, Balachandra, ed. *The Prison and the Pinnacle: Papers to Commemorate the Tercentenary of "Paradise Regained" and "Samson Agonistes."* London: Routledge and Kegan Paul, 1973.

Revard, Stella P. "Eve and the Doctrine of Responsibility in *Paradise Lost.*" *PMLA*, 88, No. 1 (1973), 69–78.

Richmond, Hugh M. *The Christian Revolutionary: John Milton.* Berkeley and Los Angeles: Univ. of California Press, 1974.

Ricks, Christopher. *Keats and Embarrassment.* Oxford: Oxford Univ. Press, Clarendon Press, 1974.

Milton's Grand Style. Oxford: Oxford Univ. Press, Clarendon Press, 1963.

Robins, Harry F. *If This Be Heresy: A Study of Milton and Origen.* Illinois Studies in Language and Literature, 51. Urbana: Univ. of Illinois Press, 1963.

Rudrum, Alan, ed. *Milton: Modern Judgements.* London: Macmillan, 1968.

Safer, Elaine B. " 'Sufficient to Have Stood': Eve's Responsibility in Book IX." *Milton Quarterly,* 6, No. 3 (1972), 10–14.

Samuel, Irene. *"Paradise Lost."* In *Critical Approaches to Six Major English Works: "Beowulf" through "Paradise Lost."* Ed. R. M. Luminiansky and Herschel Baker. Philadelphia: Univ. of Pennsylvania Press, 1968. Pp. 209–53.

Saurat, Denis. *Milton: Man and Thinker.* New York: Dial Press, 1925.

Savage, J. B. "Freedom and Necessity in *Paradise Lost.*" *ELH,* 44, No. 2 (1977), 286–311.

Schoen, Raymond George. "Cosmology, Angelic Eating, and Free Will in *Paradise Lost:* A Study in Milton's Poetic Technique." Diss. Univ. of Wisconsin, 1971.

Scott-Craig, Thomas S. K. "The Craftsmanship and Theological Significance of Milton's *Art of Logic.*" *Huntington Library Quarterly,* 17, No. 1 (1953), 1–16.

"Milton's Use of Wolleb and Ames." *Modern Language Notes,* 55 (1940), 403–7.

Shumaker, Wayne. See Bell.

Sirluck, Ernest. "Milton Revises *The Faerie Queene.*" *Modern Philology,* 48 (1950), 90–6.

Smith, Hallett. *Elizabethan Poetry: A Study of Conventions, Meaning, and Expression.* Cambridge, Mass.: Harvard Univ. Press, 1952.

Stapleton, Laurence. "Milton's Conception of Time in *Christian Doctrine.*" *Harvard Theological Review,* 57 (1964), 9–21.

Steadman, John M. *Milton and the Renaissance Hero.* Oxford: Oxford Univ. Press, Clarendon Press, 1967.

Summers, Joseph H. *The Muse's Method: An Introduction to "Paradise Lost."* Cambridge, Mass.: Harvard Univ. Press, 1962.

Taylor, Dick, Jr. "Milton and the Paradox of the Fortunate Fall Once More." *Tulane Studies in English,* 9 (1959), 35–51.

Ulreich, John C., Jr. "A Paradise Within: The Fortunate Fall in *Paradise Lost.*" *Journal of the History of Ideas,* 32 (1971), 351–66.

Waldock, A. J. A. *"Paradise Lost" and Its Critics.* Cambridge: Cambridge Univ. Press, 1947.

Weisinger, Herbert. *Tragedy and the Paradox of the Fortunate Fall.* East Lansing: Michigan State College Press, 1953.

West, Robert H. "Samson's God: 'Beastly Hebraism' and 'Asinine Bigotry.' " *Milton Studies*, 13 (1979), 109–28.

Woodhouse, A. S. P. "Notes on Milton's Views on the Creation: The Initial Phases." *Philological Quarterly*, 28 (1949), 211–36.

Post-seventeenth-century works on philosophy, theology, and intellectual history

Anderson, Bernhard W. *Creation versus Chaos: The Reinterpretation of Mythical Symbolism in the Bible*. New York: Association Press, 1967.

Armstrong, Brian G. *Calvinism and the Amyraut Heresy: Protestant Scholasticism and Humanism in Seventeenth-Century France*. Madison: Univ. of Wisconsin Press, 1969.

Bangs, Carl. " 'All the Best Bishoprics and Deaneries': The Enigma of Arminian Politics." *Church History*, 42, No. 1 (1973), 5–16.

"Arminius and the Reformation." *Church History*, 30 (1961), 155–70.

Arminius: A Study in the Dutch Reformation. Nashville: Abingdon Press, 1971.

Barbour, Ian G. *Myths, Models and Paradigms*. London: SCM Press, 1974.

Barfield, Owen. *Saving the Appearances: A Study in Idolatry*. New York: Harcourt Brace Jovanovich, 1965.

Barth, Karl. *Church Dogmatics*. Edinburgh: T. and T. Clark, 1956–69.

Berdjaev, Nicolas. *The Destiny of Man*. Trans. Natalie Duddington. 1955; rpt. New York: Harper & Row, 1960.

Freedom and the Spirit. Trans. O. F. Clarke. 4th ed. London: Geoffrey Bles, 1948.

Bube, Richard H. *The Human Quest: A New Look at Science and the Christian Faith*. Waco: Word Books, 1971.

Camus, Albert. *The Rebel: An Essay on Man in Revolt*. Trans. Anthony Bower. New York: Random House, Vintage Books, 1956.

Copinger, W. A. *A Treatise on Predestination, Election, and Grace*. London: James Nisbet, 1889.

Danielson, Dennis R. "Timelessness, Foreknowledge, and Free Will." *Mind*, 86, No. 343 (1977), 430–2.

Davies, Godfrey. "Arminian versus Puritan in England, ca. 1620–1640." *Huntington Library Bulletin*, 5 (1934), 157–79.

DeJong, Peter Y., ed. *Crisis in the Reformed Churches: Essays in Commemoration of the Great Synod of Dort, 1618–1619*. Grand Rapids: Reformed Fellowship, 1968.

Dore, Clement. "An Examination of the 'Soul-Making' Theodicy." *American Philosophical Quarterly,* 7, No. 2 (1970), 119–30.

Drewery, Benjamin. *Origen and the Doctrine of Grace.* London: Epworth Press, 1960.

Ehrhardt, Arnold. *The Framework of the New Testament Stories.* Manchester: Manchester Univ. Press, 1964.

Encyclopedia of Philosophy. Ed. Paul Edwards. New York: Macmillan, 1967.

Flew, Antony. *The Presumption of Atheism and Other Philosophical Essays on God, Freedom and Immortality.* London: Elek / Pemberton, 1976.

Geisler, Norman L. *Philosophy of Religion.* Grand Rapids: Zondervan, 1974.

The Roots of Evil. Grand Rapids: Zondervan, 1978.

Gilkey, Langdon. *Maker of Heaven and Earth: A Study of the Christian Doctrine of Creation.* New York: Doubleday, 1959.

Harrison, A. W. *Arminianism.* London: Duckworth, 1937.

Hebblethwaite, Brian. *Evil, Suffering and Religion.* London: Sheldon Press, 1976.

Henry, Paul. "Augustine and Plotinus." *Journal of Theological Studies,* 38 (1937), 1–23.

Hick, John. *Evil and the God of Love.* London: Macmillan, 1966.

Hill, Christopher. *Milton and the English Revolution.* New York: Viking Press, 1977.

The World Turned Upside Down: Radical Ideas during the English Revolution. London: Temple Smith, 1972.

Kalsbeek, L. *Contours of a Christian Philosophy: An Introduction to Herman Dooyeweerd's Thought.* Toronto: Wedge Publishing, 1975.

Keats, John. *The Letters of John Keats.* Ed. M. B. Forman. Oxford: Oxford Univ. Press, 1952.

Kendall, R. T. *Calvin and English Calvinism to 1649.* Oxford: Oxford Univ. Press, 1979.

Kenny, Anthony, ed. *Aquinas: A Collection of Critical Essays.* London: Macmillan, 1970.

King, William. *An Essay on the Origin of Evil.* Trans. Edmund Law. London, 1731.

Leibniz, G. W. *Theodicy: Essays on the Goodness of God, the Freedom of Man, and the Origin of Evil.* Ed. Austin Farrer. Trans. E. M. Huggard. London: Routledge and Kegan Paul, 1951.

Lewis, C. S. *The Problem of Pain.* London: Fontana Books, 1957.

Lovejoy, Arthur O. *The Great Chain of Being: A Study of the History of an Idea.* Cambridge, Mass.: Harvard Univ. Press, 1936.

Lucas, John R. *Freedom and Grace: Essays*. London: SPCK, 1976.

The Freedom of the Will. Oxford: Oxford Univ. Press, 1970.

McCullough, H. B. "Theodicy and Mary Baker Eddy." *Sophia: A Journal for Discussion in Philosophical Theology*, 14, No. 1 (1975), 12–18.

Mintz, Samuel I. *The Hunting of Leviathan: Seventeenth-Century Reactions to the Materialism and Moral Philosophy of Thomas Hobbes*. Cambridge: Cambridge Univ. Press, 1962.

Mitchell, Basil, ed. *The Philosophy of Religion*. Oxford: Oxford Univ. Press, 1971.

Mommsen, Theodor E. "Petrarch and the Story of the Choice of Hercules." *Journal of the Warburg and Courtauld Institutes*, 16 (1953), 178–92.

Packer, James I. "The Redemption and Restoration of Man in the Thought of Richard Baxter." D. Phil. Thesis Oxford, 1954.

Panofsky, Erwin. *Hercules am Scheidewege und Andre Antike Bildstoffe in der Neueren Kunst*. Leipzig and Berlin: Teubner, 1930.

Patrides, C. A. "Adam's 'Happy Fault' and XVIIth-Century Apologetics." *Franciscan Studies*, 23 (1963), 238–43.

Pike, Nelson, ed. *God and Evil: Readings on the Theological Problem of Evil*. Englewood Cliffs, N.J.: Prentice-Hall, 1964.

Plantinga, Alvin. *God and Other Minds: A Study in the Rational Justification of Belief in God*. Ithaca: Cornell Univ. Press, 1967.

God, Freedom and Evil. London: George Allen and Unwin, 1975.

"The Incompatibility of Freedom with Determinism." *Philosophical Forum* (Boston), 1970, pp. 141–8.

The Nature of Necessity. Oxford: Oxford Univ. Press, Clarendon Press, 1974.

Pope, Alexander. *An Essay on Man*. Ed. Maynard Mack. London: Methuen, 1950.

Ricoeur, Paul. *The Symbolism of Evil*. Trans. Emerson Buchanan. New York: Harper & Row, 1967.

Sampson, Miriam and Philip Sampson. "Necessity and Freedom." *Faith and Thought*, 106, Nos. 2 / 3 (1979), 151–68.

Sartre, Jean-Paul. *Being and Nothingness: An Essay on Phenomenological Ontology*. Trans. Hazel E. Barnes. London: Methuen, 1957.

Schaeffer, Francis A. *Genesis in Space and Time*. London: Hodder and Stoughton, 1973.

Silvester, Hugh. *Arguing With God: A Christian Examination of the Problem of Evil*. London: Inter-Varsity Press, 1971.

Swinburne, Richard. *The Existence of God*. Oxford: Oxford Univ. Press, Clarendon Press, 1979.

Tyacke, Nicholas R. N. "Arminianism in England, in Religion and Politics, 1604 to 1640." D. Phil. Thesis Oxford, 1968.

"Puritanism, Arminianism and Counter-Revolution." In *The Origins of the English Civil War*. Ed. Conrad Russell. London: Macmillan, 1973. Pp. 119–43.

Voltaire. *Candide; or, Optimism*. Harmondsworth: Penguin, 1947.

Walker, D. P. *The Decline of Hell: Seventeenth-Century Discussions of Eternal Torment*. Chicago: Univ. of Chicago Press, 1964.

Waltke, Bruce K. *Creation and Chaos: An Exegetical and Theological Study of Biblical Cosmogony*. Portland, Oreg.: Western Conservative Baptist Seminary, 1974.

Wenham, John W. *The Goodness of God*. London: Inter-Varsity Press, 1974.

Williams, Arnold. *The Common Expositor: An Account of the Commentaries on Genesis, 1527–1633*. Chapel Hill: Univ. of North Carolina Press, 1948.

Williams, Norman P. *The Ideas of the Fall and of Original Sin*. London: Longmans, 1927.

Wolter, Allan B., O.F.M. "Duns Scotus and the Predestination of Christ." *The Cord: A Franciscan Spiritual Review*, 5, No. 12 (1955), 366–72.

Yandell, Keith E. "The Greater Good Defense." *Sophia: A Journal for Discussion in Philosophical Theology*, 13, No. 3 (1974), 1–16.

Young, Robert. *Freedom, Responsibility and God*. London: Macmillan, 1975.

"Omnipotence and Compatibilism." *Philosophia*, 6, No. 1 (1976), 49–67.

Index

Law, Edmund, 257n10
Leavis, F. R., 16, 236n19
Leibniz, Gottfried W., 94, 142, 234n2, 255n4
Leigh, Edward, 241n46
Lewalski, Barbara K., 260n45, 261n71, 265n34
Lewis, C. S., 20, 177, 184–8
Lieb, Michael, 239n23
Lombard, Peter, 267n43
Lovejoy, Arthur O., 108, 202, 264n20; and his theory of the Fortunate Fall, 15, 202–4, 207, 210–11, 212, 214–15, 224–5, 269n63
Low, Anthony, 251n46
Lucas, John R., 255n48
Lucretius, 33
Luther, Martin, 66–8

MacCaffrey, Isabel, 21–2
McColley, Diane, 261n71
McDill, Joseph M., 60
MacIntyre, Alasdair, 22
Mackie, J. L., 93–5, 104
Mammon, Cave of, 189, 194
Manichaeism, 28–30, 38
Marcion, 98
Marshall, W. H., 206
Marvell, Andrew, 258n26
Messiah, 113, 225; Satan's response to, 117, 223; see also Son of God
Michael, 56, 89–90, 163, 204, 222, 225–6
Migne, J.-P., 264n20
Miner, Earl, 242n55
Mintz, Samuel I., 138, 252n15
models: Copernican and Ptolemaic, 20; the notion of, 20–3, 226–7
Mohl, Ruth, 175
Molinaeus, Petrus, see DuMoulin, Pierre
Mollenkott, Virginia R., 211, 225, 263n4
Mommsen, Theodore E., 244n16
More, Alexander, 80, 209, 253n25, 257n2
Moses, 24, 45
Muir, Edwin, 192

Neoplatonism, 5–6, 29, 40–1, 101, 167
Nicolson, Marjorie, 138, 142, 144

Ogden, H. V. S., 261n71
Olevian, Gaspar, 237n4
optimism, 31, 57, 205, 208–9, 269n1; definition of, 8–9
Origen, 160, 169, 240n38
Ovid, 239n23
Owen, John, 78–9, 92, 95, 134, 152–3, 165, 196, 255n49

Panofsky, Erwin, 243n15, 244n18
paradise, 125, 181, 182, 209, 211, 213,
226; geography of, 51–3; see also Eden, garden of; heaven
Patrides, C. A., 237n26; his view of Milton as theologico-poetic schizoid, 19, 236n23, 236n25; on Milton's account of the creation, 45; on Milton's presentation of grace and free will, 61, 62, 90; on Milton's treatment of foreknowledge, 155
Pelagianism, 59, 73, 74, 134, 145, 247n69; Augustine and, 65, 67, 132, 186; Milton's avoidance of, 76, 86
Pelagius, 67, 71; see also Pelagianism
Pemble, William, 43–5, 78, 79, 133, 253n21
Perkins, William, 78
Perlmutter, Eila Siren, 247n63
Peter, John, 62, 84
Petrarch, 244n16
Pierce, Thomas, 79–80, 208, 217, 247n69, 252n5, 253n22, 255n47; on divine freedom, 152; on fallibility and the Fall, 196–7, 262n75; on foreknowledge, 158–9, 161; on the Free Will Defense, 101, 105; as an incompatibilist, 141; on prelapsarian grace, 109–10
Piscator, Johannes, 264n15
Plantinga, Alvin, 26, 94–5, 103, 106, 251n2, 255n60
Plato, 25–7, 33, 36, 45, 239n23
Platonism, 48; see also Neoplatonism
Plotinus, 5–7, 167–8
Pope, Alexander, 101–2, 257n10, 263n7
Praamsma, Louis, 245n31
predestination, see Calvin; Calvinism, orthodox
Presbyterians, 59
Protestantism, 207
Prynne, William, 76–8
Puritans, 59, 76

Radzinowicz, Mary Ann, 265n25
Rajan, Balachandra, 243n3, 248n72
Ramist logic, 180
Ranters, 75, 81–2
Raphael, 39–40, 183, 253n27; his dialogue with Adam, 111–13, 120–2, 183–4, 195, 197, 198, 199, 212–13; and Milton's models, 20–2
redemption, 61; creation, Fall, and, 24; as new creation, 55–7, 58; and the satisfaction of Christ, 152–4; see also Incarnation, Son of God
Reformed theology, 25, 58, 66–75
Remonstrance of 1610, 70–1
Remonstrants, 70–5, 85; see also Arminianism
Restoration (1660), 13, 81
Revard, Stella P., 251n46, 254n31

292